DEGREES OF EXCELLENCE

The Institute of Ismaili Studies

Ismaili Texts and Translations Series, 8

Previously published titles:

1. Ibn al-Haytham. *The Advent of the Fatimids: A Contemporary Shiʿi Witness*. An edition and English translation of Ibn al-Haytham's *Kitāb al-munāẓarāt*, by Wilferd Madelung and Paul E. Walker (2000).
2. Muḥammad b. ʿAbd al-Karīm al-Shahrastānī. *Struggling with the Philosopher: A Refutation of Avicenna's Metaphysics*. A new Arabic edition and English translation of al-Shahrastānī's *Kitāb al-muṣāraʿa*, by Wilferd Madelung and Toby Mayer (2001).
3. Jaʿfar b. Manṣūr al-Yaman. *The Master and the Disciple: An Early Islamic Spiritual Dialogue*. Arabic edition and English translation of Jaʿfar b. Manṣūr al-Yaman's *Kitāb al-ʿālim waʾl-ghulām*, by James W. Morris (2001).
4. Idrīs ʿImād al-Dīn. *The Fatimids and their Successors in Yaman: The History of an Islamic Community*. Arabic edition and English summary of Idrīs ʿImād al-Dīn's *ʿUyūn al-akhbār*, vol. 7, by Ayman F. Sayyid, in collaboration with Paul E. Walker and Maurice A. Pomerantz (2002).
5. Naṣīr al-Dīn Ṭūsī. *Paradise of Submission: A Medieval Treatise on Ismaili Thought*. A new Persian edition and English translation of Naṣīr al-Dīn Ṭūsī's *Rawḍa-yi taslīm*, by S.J. Badakhchani with an introduction by Hermann Landolt and a philosophical commentary by Christian Jambet (2005).
6. al-Qāḍī al-Nuʿmān. *Founding the Fatimid State: The Rise of an Early Islamic Empire*. An annotated English translation of al-Qāḍī al-Nuʿmān's *Iftitāḥ al-daʿ*wa, by Hamid Haji (2006).
7. Idrīs ʿImād al-Dīn. *ʿUyūn al-akhbār wa-funūn al-āthār*. Arabic critical edition in 7 volumes by Ahmad Chleilat, Mahmoud Fakhoury, Yousef S. Fattoum, Muhammad Kamal, Maʾmoun al-Sagherji and Ayman F. Sayyid (2007–2009).

9. Ḥamīd al-Dīn Aḥmad b. ʿAbd Allāh al-Kirmānī. *Master of the Age: An Islamic Treatise on the Necessity of the Imamate.* A critical edition of the Arabic text and English translation of Ḥamīd al-Dīn al-Kirmānī's *al-Maṣābīḥ fī ithbāt al-imāma,* by Paul E. Walker (2007).
10. *Orations of the Fatimid Caliphs: Festival Sermons of the Ismaili Imams.* An edition of the Arabic texts and English translation of Fatimid *khuṭbas*, by Paul E. Walker (2009).
11. Taqī al-Dīn Aḥmad b. ʿAlī al-Maqrīzī. *Towards a Shiʿi Mediterranean Empire: Fatimid Egypt and the Founding of Cairo.* The reign of the Imam-Caliph al-Muʿizz, from al-Maqrīzī's *Ittiʿāẓ al-ḥunafāʾ bi-akhbār al-aʾimma al-Fāṭimiyyīn al-khulafāʾ*, translated by Shainool Jiwa (2009).

Degrees of Excellence:

A Fatimid Treatise on Leadership in Islam

A new Arabic edition and English translation of
Aḥmad b. Ibrāhīm al-Naysābūrī's
Kitāb ithbāt al-imāma
by

Arzina R. Lalani

I.B.Tauris *Publishers*
LONDON • NEW YORK
in association with
The Institute of Ismaili Studies
LONDON

Published in 2010 by I.B.Tauris & Co Ltd
6 Salem Rd, London W2 4BU
175 Fifth Avenue, New York NY 10010
www.ibtauris.com

in association with The Institute of Ismaili Studies
210 Euston Road, London NW1 2DA
www.iis.ac.uk

In the United States of America and in Canada distributed by
St Martin's Press, 175 Fifth Avenue, New York NY 10010

ISBN 978 1 84511 145 8

A full CIP record for this book is available from the British Library
A full CIP record for this book is available from the Library of Congress

Library of Congress catalog card: available

Typeset in Minion Tra for The Institute of Ismaili Studies
Printed and bound in Great Britain by TJ International Ltd, Padstow, Cornwall

The Institute of Ismaili Studies

The Institute of Ismaili Studies was established in 1977 with the object of promoting scholarship and learning on Islam, in the historical as well as contemporary contexts, and a better understanding of its relationship with other societies and faiths.

The Institute's programmes encourage a perspective which is not confined to the theological and religious heritage of Islam, but seeks to explore the relationship of religious ideas to broader dimensions of society and culture. The programmes thus encourage an interdisciplinary approach to the materials of Islamic history and thought. Particular attention is also given to issues of modernity that arise as Muslims seek to relate their heritage to the contemporary situation.

Within the Islamic tradition, the Institute's programmes promote research on those areas which have, to date, received relatively little attention from scholars. These include the intellectual and literary expressions of Shiʿism in general, and Ismailism in particular.

In the context of Islamic societies, the Institute's programmes are informed by the full range and diversity of cultures in which Islam is practised today, from the Middle East, South and Central Asia, and Africa to the industrialized societies of the West, thus taking into consideration the variety of contexts which shape the ideals, beliefs and practices of the faith.

These objectives are realized through concrete programmes and activities organized and implemented by various departments of the Institute. The Institute also collaborates periodically, on a programme-specific basis, with other institutions of learning in the United Kingdom and abroad.

The Institute's academic publications fall into a number of interrelated categories:

1. Occasional papers or essays addressing broad themes of the relationship between religion and society, with special reference to Islam.
2. Monographs exploring specific aspects of Islamic faith and culture, or the contributions of individual Muslim thinkers or writers.
3. Editions or translations of significant primary or secondary texts.
4. Translations of poetic or literary texts which illustrate the rich heritage of spiritual, devotional and symbolic expressions in Muslim history.
5. Works on Ismaili history and thought, and the relationship of the Ismailis to other traditions, communities and schools of thought in Islam.
6. Proceedings of conferences and seminars sponsored by the Institute.
7. Bibliographical works and catalogues which document manuscripts, printed texts and other source materials.

This book falls into category three listed above.

In facilitating these and other publications, the Institute's sole aim is to encourage original research and analysis of relevant issues. While every effort is made to ensure that the publications are of a high academic standard, there is naturally bound to be a diversity of views, ideas and interpretations. As such, the opinions expressed in these publications must be understood as belonging to their authors alone.

This work is dedicated in devotion to
The Guiding Intellect
that both transcends and informs
the human intellect

Table of Contents

Preface and Acknowledgements

The question of the imamate or leadership in Islam has historically aroused heated discussions alongside a range of responses from intellectuals within the Muslim community. Amongst those who grappled with this challenging subject is Aḥmad b. Ibrāhīm al-Naysābūrī, a distinguished scholar from the Fatimid period. Al-Naysābūrī came from Nīshāpūr, an eclectic and vibrant city in Khurāsān, noted particularly for its erudition and the use of rationalistic philosophy by its scholars. He has several works to his credit, but it is the *Kitāb ithbāt al-imāma* that is of decisive importance to the philosophical curriculum of medieval Muslim thought. It is here that he applies rational tools to explain and expound his theology, allowing us to capture and understand not only the significance of his own thought, but also the beliefs of his age.

Beginning with the premise that supreme leadership, the imamate, is the pole and foundation of religion, al-Naysābūrī establishes his thesis by using several approaches, foremost amongst which is the theory of 'degrees of excellence'. Accordingly, God created each genera and species with a unique capacity and distinct advantage not existing in the other. Citing examples from the so-called ten Aristotelian categories and other natural metaphors from mineral, plant and animal kingdoms, he acknowledges the disparities within each genus and species and provides paradigms of perfect examples in each variety, demonstrating in a parallel manner that the imam is at the apex of humanity.

The *Kitāb ithbāt al-imāma* provides an unparalleled insight into the intricacies of the Imam-Caliph al-Ḥākim's rule (386–411/996–1021), adding considerably to our understanding of that period.

Editing and translating a manuscript presents a host of unique textual and interpretive problems. Thankfully, I was mentored by Professor Wilferd Madelung, a distinguished expert in the field, who ably directed me through the various stages of this work. The project itself was initiated by Dr Farhad Daftary, Head of the Department of Academic Research and Publications at the The Institute of Ismaili Studies who invited me as a Visiting Research Fellow and placed before me several manuscript titles to choose from as my research project. To both of them, I convey my immense gratitude and deep appreciation for engendering a steep learning curve, resulting in this publication.

It goes without saying that I bear the primary responsibility for this edition and translation of the *Kitab ithbāt al-imāma* of Aḥmad b. Ibrahim al-Naysābūrī, but would like to add that Professor Madelung read several drafts, giving numerous suggestions which I subsequently incorporated. Sadruddin Fattoum was very helpful with his indigenous knowledge of Arabic, and helped unravel many complex passages whilst I was exploring the text. Professors Hermann Landolt, Heinz Halm and Paul E. Walker read the text and translation, offering many valuable suggestions.

This work could not have been realized without the help of several other institutions and individuals. Some of these institutions invited me for lectures as well as present at conferences where many of my thoughts were crystallized. These include the Department of Theology and Religious Studies, University of Bristol (April 2002), BRISMES (Edinburgh) and MESA (California) Conferences in 2001, the Institute's Department of Community Relations and our Forum at the Department of Academic Research and Publications (DARP) and, more recently, at the Seventeenth Colloquium on the History of Egypt and Syria in the Fatimid, Ayyubid and Mamluk Eras (10th–15th centuries), at the Department of the Cultures and Languages of Near East and North Africa in University of Ghent, Belgium. In this context, I appreciate the written comments from Professor Michael Brett of the University of London's School of Oriental and African Studies.

Many individuals and colleagues have provided personal support, references, offprints, comments, criticisms and suggestions. Soraiya Khan Mohamed, recommended by Zinat Merali, very generously typed my handwritten Arabic manuscript and Haitham Sharba helped me plough through the onerous task of proofreading the Arabic text. I thank them all, including Rita Bishop, Karim Valimohamed, Wendy Robinson and Julia Kolb for their moral support, encouragement and friendship. Maha Sharba was of considerable help in the final stages with several aspects, including locating several sources in the library and in checking the Arabic text.

Numerous others have helped me and although I cannot name them all, I would like to acknowledge some individuals at the Institute and beyond who have assisted me in different capacities over a period of time: Drs Josef W. Meri, Reza Shah-Kazemi, Leonard Lewisohn, Shainool Jiwa, Nader El-Bizri, Delia Cortese, Toby Mayer, Verena Klemm, Jalal Badakhchani, Shin Nomoto, Abdeali Qutbuddin and Faquir M. Hunzai. Fayaz S. Alibhai helped me while my translations were in their initial stages, Dr Shafique N. Virani and Alnoor Merchant read my entire English text, giving many suggestions, and Asif Alidina assisted in incorporating some revisions electronically. Many thanks are due to Dr Neil Frearson and his team of the Institute's IT department for their technical assistance. A special note of acknowledgement is due to Muhammad Jozi who helped me locate a number of traditions.

Finally, it remains for me to thank Dr Farhad Daftary, Kutub Kassam and Fayaz Alibhai for the time and effort they have spent over the years on this project, sometimes beyond the call of duty. Fayaz has had the thankless task of not only taking over the editorial work in the later stages but also of liaising with a number of individuals, coordinating the several versions and incorporating revisions as we have progressed to this stage. In this connection, I would like to highlight the contribution of Hamid Haji, who has managed to select an appropriate font that would not only format the Arabic text to specification but also present the Qur'anic verses elegantly. I appreciate his diligence in this matter as well his help over the years in many instances including insertion of corrections and in preparing the Arabic indices.

The Institute's library has reason to be proud of its extensive collection of manuscripts where I managed to locate not one, two or three, but ten variants of the *Kitāb ithbāt al-imāma*. I acknowledge and admire the efforts of the Chairman and the Board of Governors, the former Director Professor Azim Nanji, the library's former Heads Professor Eric Ormsby, the late Dr Duncan Haldane and the Acting Head Alnoor Merchant, as well as all those responsible for maintaining this formidable process of collecting and preserving manuscripts. My sincere thanks go to all of them for making the relevant manuscripts available. Khadija Lalani has been particularly helpful in locating several sources during the course of this work as well as in photocopying the relevant documents. I appreciate the cordial services of all library staff, old and new, all of which significantly accelerated my research.

The editing process itself involved locating and exploring all existing variants of the manuscript and deciphering their content. Not long after embarking on the project, we discovered (thanks to Delia Cortese) that an edition of the *Ithbāt* already existed (Muṣṭafā Ghālib, Beirut, 1404/1984), which then involved ascertaining whether a new edition was justified and warranted. Going through all ten manuscripts plus the existing edition meticulously, it soon transpired that not only were there significant omissions in the edited text, but that it included certain additions that should never have been there.

I feel blessed and grateful for having my three wonderful children Ali, Baqir and Abida, patiently and lovingly following the progress of this work. The support from my own family, especially my parents, and my brother and sister, together with their respective families, has been exceptional. I should not, however, overlook the invisible inspiration flowing from the Guiding Intellect that both transcends and informs the human intellect.

Arzina R. Lalani
London

Introduction

The establishment of the Fatimid caliphate in Ifrīqiya (present-day Tunisia and eastern Algeria) in 297/909 exemplified an unparalleled success not only for the Ismaili Shiʿis but for the whole Shiʿa community. After the reign of ʿAlī b. Abī Ṭālib, this was the first major Shiʿi leadership of an Islamic state. The Ismaili imam-caliphs managed to transform the budding Fatimid *dawla* (state) into a flourishing empire, which found its own place among the diverse civilizations of Islam. Their reign turned out to be one of the most outstanding periods in Islamic history, not only politically but also in terms of literary, artistic, scientific and economic achievements.

The tenacity of Shiʿi efforts was rewarded from around the middle of the 3rd/9th century. The Ḥamdānids, the Būwayhids, the Zaydī states in the Yemen and the Caspian region, and the Fatimids in the Maghrib and Egypt, were all Shiʿis. The achievements of the Fatimid Ismailis, however, were clearly exceptional. First appearing openly on the scene of world history in the 260s/870s, the Ismailis founded a network of communities extending from the Maghrib in the west to Sind in the east, from the mountains of Daylam on the Caspian shores to the Yamani highlands in the south. They rose to prominence in the 4th/10th century[1] when they began to develop an exceptional and comprehensive intellectual programme to sustain their cause. Their strength lay in being able to assimilate the new sciences successfully within the Islamic tradition and to offer a comprehensive theory of the universe and humanity's place within

1. The 4th/10th century has been called by Louis Massignon the 'Ismaili century' in the history of Islam. See his 'Mutanabbi devant le siècle ismaëlien de l'Islam', in *Al Mutannabi: Recueil publié à l'occasion de son millénaire* (Beirut, 1936), p. 1.

it. This intellectual vision was expressed in the writings of many remarkable scholars, some of whom also elaborated the central Shiʿi principle of the imamate.[2] The imamate was evidently the most central doctrine of the Fatimids; it provided the very *raison d'être* for their caliphate.

Historically, the question of the imamate has stimulated and generated a range of responses from scholars within the Muslim community. Among a genre of works on the subject is an important treatise, the *Kitāb ithbāt al-imāma* of Aḥmad b. Ibrāhīm al-Naysābūrī, an Ismaili Shiʿi scholar from the Fatimid period. Although many manuscript sources on Ismaili thought are now readily accessible, there are very few critical editions available and even fewer translated into English. The primary aim of this work is to introduce the ideas of this highly significant scholar of the early 5th/11th century to specialists in the field as well as to the general reader.

As in the earlier period, Muslim society of the fourth and the fifth centuries was pluralistic, portraying elements of diverse traditions, cultures and communities of interpretation, with all groups searching for their own bearings and defending their own positions.[3] By the time al-Naysābūrī wrote his treatise on the imamate during the early decades of the 5th/11th century, the Sunni perspective of *ahl al-sunna wa'l-jamāʿa* (lit. 'people of the practice and community' or 'people of community practice') was well established. The Khārijīs, after several uprisings, had moved to the fringes, both geographically and ideologically. The Muʿtazilīs, having been quite active, had important representatives among Muslim thinkers and writers. They argued that the roots of true knowledge lay both in scriptural law or revelation and in reason. As observed by Madelung,[4] Muʿtazilī thought spread among the

2. See Wilferd Madelung, 'Das Imamat in der frühen ismailitischen Lehre', *Der Islam*, 37 (1961), pp. 43–135, and also his article 'Imāma', in *EI2*, vol. 3, pp. 1163–1169.

3. Among recent works on the subject are: Patricia Crone, *Medieval Islamic Political Thought* (Edinburgh, 2004) and Asma Afsaruddin, *Excellence and Precedence: Medieval Islamic Discourse on Legitimate Leadership* (Leiden, 2002).

4. Wilferd Madelung, 'Imamism and Muʿtazilite Theology', in his *Religious Schools and Sects in Medieval Islam* (London, 1985), article VII.

Imāmiyya who were initially associated with the Banū Nawbakht family. This spurred a strong reaction from the school of Qumm under the leadership of Ibn Bābawayh (d. 381/991), who afterwards moved to Rayy. Shaykh al-Mufīd (d. 413/1022), who led the school of Baghdad, wrote a correction later to the creed of Ibn Bābawayh, criticizing him on several issues, and maintaining especially that the imams had encouraged argumentation in the defence of religion. He maintained that reason or intellect is able to establish the basic truths of religion in conjunction with God's revelation.[5]

The Ismailis had accepted neither the Neoplatonic philosophy nor Muʿtazilī theology, as noted by Paul Walker in his work on al-Kirmānī,[6] and their scholars were at pains to show the difference between their own teachings and those of the Muʿtazila and the philosophers (*falāsifa*). Although the Ismailis acknowledged the role of reason, their theology was more revelational than rational at its core.[7] Ismaili theology categorically denied the philosophic view of God being the first cause and described God as beyond reason and being. These were among some of the issues that were being broadly discussed and debated by Muslim scholars at the time.

The 5th/11th century marked a culmination of literary activity among Ismaili scholars of the Fatimid period. When al-Naysābūrī came on the scene, Ismaili theology had already undergone a significant evolution. Heinz Halm compares this process to the development of Christian theology three hundred years later at the time of Thomas Aquinas.[8] Like other Muslim scholars, the Ismaili thinkers of the time had known and absorbed the Platonian, Aristotelian and Neoplatonic traditions from the translations of Greek works into Arabic well in advance of medieval Europe. The Ismaili scholars had managed to

5. See the discussion in Martin J. McDermott, *The Theology of al-Shaikh al-Mufīd* (Beirut, 1978), pp. 57–70.

6. Paul E. Walker, *Ḥamīd al-Dīn al-Kirmānī: Ismaili Thought in the Age of al-Ḥākim* (London, 1999), p. 52.

7. Wilferd Madelung, 'Aspects of Ismāʿīlī Theology: The Prophetic Chain and the God Beyond Being', in S.H. Nasr, ed., *Ismāʿīlī Contributions to Islamic Culture* (Tehran, 1398/1977), pp. 53–65.

8. Heinz Halm, *The Fatimids and their Traditions of Learning* (London, 1997), pp. 50ff.

articulate their tradition using the philosophical terminology of the time without in any way compromising the essence of their Shiʿi Islamic message.

The Author and his Works

An important Ismaili Shiʿi scholar and writer of the early 5th/11th century, Aḥmad b. Ibrāhīm al-Naysābūrī flourished during the reigns of the Fatimid Imam-Caliphs al-ʿAzīz (365–386/975–996) and al-Ḥākim bi-Amr Allāh (386–411/996–1021). There is very little biographical information available on al-Naysābūrī, but his talent, character and cultural background can be gleaned from several of his works that have survived and been copied through the centuries, which in itself points to his significance and popularity. His *nisba* 'Nīshāpūrī' (al-Naysābūrī in Arabic) suggests he came from Nīshāpūr, the centre of the Ismaili *daʿwa* in Khurāsān, particularly noted for its use of rationalistic philosophy.[9] It was here that Muḥammad al-Nasafī and his colleagues elaborated the metaphysics of Shiʿi theology, within a framework referred to sometimes as Neoplatonic rationalism. Muḥammad b. Aḥmad al-Nasafī (d. 332/943), who had succeeded the Amīr al-Marwāzī as head of the *daʿwa* in Khurāsān, was an important philosopher among the early Ismailis.[10] He wrote the *Kitāb al-maḥṣūl* (The Book of Outcome), perhaps the first major work employing philosophy to serve Ismaili theology. Unfortunately, this work, written around 300/913, seems lost, but its basic doctrine can be recovered

9. Khurāsān, with its capital Nīshāpūr, was a thriving region politically, socially and culturally at the time. Refer to the excellent study on the Ghaznavids by Clifford E. Bosworth, *The Ghaznavids: Their Empire in Afghanistan and Eastern Iran* 994–1040 (2nd edition, Beirut, 1973). See also Guy Le Strange, *The Lands of the Eastern Caliphate* (London, 1966), pp. 382–432. Richard W. Bulliet's work, *The Patricians of Nishapur: A Study in Medieval Islamic Social History* (Cambridge, MA, 1972), also provides a very useful background to this city and the rivalry between the Ḥanafīs and Shāfiʿīs at the time.

10. See Wilferd Madelung's article on 'Cosmogony and Cosmology: VI. in Ismaʿilism', *Encyclopaedia Iranica*, vol. 6, pp. 322–326. See also Farhad Daftary, *A Short History of the Ismailis: Traditions of a Muslim Community* (Edinburgh, 1998) pp. 84–89, as well as pp. 43ff, which relates the establishment of the Ismaili mission in Khurāsān.

from later citations, especially the *Kitāb asrār al-Bāṭiniyya*[11] and al-Kirmānī's *Kitāb al-riyāḍ*. It was subsequently exposed to a series of refutations and reviews not only among Sunni and Zaydī authors, but also by al-Nasafī's fellow Ismaili scholars, especially Abū Ḥātim al-Rāzī (d. 322/934–935) who wrote his treatise, *Kitāb al-iṣlāḥ* (The Book of Correction), to correct some of his colleague's views.[12] On the other hand, Abū Ya'qūb al-Sijistānī (d. after 361/971), wrote his *Kitāb al-nuṣra* (The Book of Support) to defend al-Nasafī's position and Ḥamīd al-Dīn al-Kirmānī (d. after 411/1020) harmonized them all in his *Kitāb al-riyāḍ* (The Book of Meadows).[13]

Al-Naysābūrī's work *Kitāb istitār al-imām wa tafarruq al-du'āt fi'l-jazā'ir li-ṭalabi-hi* (Book on the Imam's Concealment and the Dispersal of *Dā'īs* in Search of him to Different 'Islands'),[14] is a significant historical treatise that reveals the names of the three hidden Ismaili imams after Muḥammad b. Ismā'īl. The Russian scholar Wladimir Ivanow (1886–1970) rightly observed that 'in the *Istitār* we have precious crumbs of information about a period which is a lost world in history, information which cannot be found anywhere

11. 'Abu'l-Qāsim al-Bustī, *Min kashf asrār al-Bāṭiniyya wa-'iwār madhhabihim*, ed. 'Ādil Sālim al-'Abd al-Jādir, in his *al-Ismā'īliyyūn: kashf asrār wa-naqd al-afkār* (Kuwait, 2002) pp. 187–369. Samuel M. Stern has an article on this work entitled 'Abu'l-Qāsim al-Bustī and his Refutation of Ismā'īlīsm', *Journal of the Royal Asiatic Society* (1961), pp. 14–35; reprinted in his *Studies in Early Ismā'īlism* (Leiden and Jerusalem, 1983), pp. 299–320, and 307 especially for the citation.

12. Abū Ḥātim al-Rāzī, *Kitāb al-iṣlāḥ*, ed. Ḥ. Mīnūchihr and M. Muḥaqqiq (Tehran, 1377Sh./1998). See Shin Nomoto's doctoral dissertation on 'Early Ismaili Thought on Prophecy according to *Kitāb al-Iṣlāḥ* by Abū Ḥātim al-Rāzī (d. ca. 322/934–5)' (McGill University, 1999).

13. Ḥamīd al-Dīn Aḥmad al-Kirmānī, *Kitāb al-riyāḍ*, ed. 'Ārif Tāmir (Beirut, 1960), pp. 119–126. For details see Paul E. Walker, *Early Philosophical Shiism: The Ismaili Neoplatonism of Abū Ya'qūb al-Sijistānī* (Cambridge, 1993), pp. 14–16 and 55–60, and W. Ivanow, *Studies in Early Persian Ismailism* (Leiden, 1948), especially the fifth chapter on 'An Early Controversy in Ismailism', pp. 115–159.

14. Aḥmad b. Ibrāhīm al-Naysābūrī, *Kitāb istitār al-imām* (with Muḥammad al-Yamanī's *Sīrat al-ḥājib*), ed. W. Ivanow, in *Bulletin of the Faculty of Arts, Egyptian University*, vol. 4, 1936 (Cairo, 1939), pp. 89–133; English trans. W. Ivanow, *Ismaili Tradition Concerning the Rise of the Fatimids* (London, etc., 1942), pp. 157–183.

else ...'[15] This work relates important details concerning the 'hidden imams' 'Abd Allāh al-Akbar and his successors down to 'Abd Allāh al-Mahdī, the founder of the Fatimid dynasty. The narrative refers to hardships suffered by 'Abd Allāh al-Akbar and the quest for him by some *dāʿīs* who had lost contact with him. The *Istitār* also provides valuable information regarding the early Ismaili *daʿwa* as well as setbacks faced by 'Abd Allāh al-Mahdī in his journey from Salamiyya to the Maghrib. Al-Naysābūrī is particularly well versed on the *daʿwa* in the *dawr al-satr* or 'period of concealment' in early Ismaili history.

Al-Naysābūrī's other work, *Risāla al-mūjaza al-kāfiya fī adab al-duʿāt* (Brief and Concise Epistle on the Etiquette of the Summoners) belongs to a genre of literature known as *adab* (appropriate behaviour). In it he gives an excellent description of the characteristics and duties of an ideal *dāʿī*. The *dāʿī*, in al-Naysābūrī's opinion, has high educational qualifications, extraordinary moral and intellectual attributes, and strong organizational abilities. Having sufficient knowledge of the *ẓāhir* and *bāṭin*, the *sharīʿa* and its esoteric interpretation (*taʾwīl*), the *dāʿī* was often trained in jurisprudence and well versed in the Qurʾan and *ḥadīth* besides being knowledgeable in philosophy, history and religions other than Islam.[16] Ivanow's pioneering article on the organization of the Fatimid *daʿwa* was based on this treatise.[17]

---

15. Ivanow, *Ismaili Tradition*, p. 8.

16. Verena Klemm, *Memoirs of a Mission: The Ismaili Scholar, Statesman and Poet al-Muʾayyad fiʾl-Dīn al-Shīrāzī* (London, 2003), pp. 55–66. Her fourth chapter on 'The self-portrayal of a *dāʿī*' includes al-Naysābūrī's description of the qualities necessary for a *dāʿī* as well as the etiquette of the various professional groups which al-Muʾayyad followed conscientiously. See also Heinz Halm's chapter on the organization of the *daʿwa* in *The Fatimids*, pp. 62–70, and Daftary, *A Short History*, pp. 91–92.

17. See W. Ivanow, 'The Organization of the Fatimid Propaganda', *Journal of the Bombay Branch of the Royal Asiatic Society*, NS 15 (1939), pp. 1–35. The *Risāla al-mūjaza* is preserved in Ḥātim al-Ḥāmidī's *Tuḥfāt al-qulūb* and also in Ḥaṣan al-Bharūchī's *Kitāb al-aẓhar*, as cited in Ismail Poonawala's *Biobibliography of Ismāʿīlī Literature* (Malibu, CA, 1977), pp. 91–92. Verena Klemm, *Die Mission des fāṭimidischen Agenten al-Muʾayyad fī d-dīn in Šīrāz* (Frankfurt, 1989), pp. 205–277, contains a fascimile edition of the text. A summary English translation appears in her *Memoirs of a Mission*, Appendix 2, pp. 117–127.

It is evident that al-Naysābūrī's works and ideas had considerable influence on many of his contemporaries, but more especially on the chief *dāʿī*, al-Muʾayyad fiʾl-Dīn al-Shīrāzī (d. 470/1077) who, besides being a scholar and a poet, became a prominent statesman as well. Verena Klemm maintains that al-Muʾayyad actually lived by the ideals of the *dāʿī* articulated by al-Naysābūrī in his *Risāla al-mūjaza.*[18] Al-Muʾayyad not only looked up to al-Naysābūrī as his benchmark in ideals and morals, but used him confidently as a point of reference in his works.[19] Al-Muʾayyad in turn, influenced the famous philosopher-poet Nāṣir-i Khusraw, a central figure in the Central Asian Ismaili tradition.[20]

A work that is frequently ascribed to al-Naysābūrī is the *Risālā al-zāhira fī maʿrifat al-dār al-ākhīra* (The Resplendent Treatise on the Recognition of the Abode of the Hereafter), an eschatological treatise, but this ascription by Ivanow has since been questioned by Poonawala.[21] Still another work of al-Naysābūrī is the *Kitāb al-tawḥīd* (The Book of Unity),[22] which he mentions in his *Kitāb ithbāt al-imāma,* the subject of this study.

The *Kitāb ithbāt al-imāma* of al-Naysābūrī, alongside other such works, is an extremely important representation of the Fatimid vision

18. See Klemm, *Die Mission*, for details. Also, refer to the epilogue of her *Memoirs of a Mission,* pp. 107–108.

19. Al-Mu'ayyad in fact follows in al-Naysābūrī's footsteps and has a work on affirming the imamate entitled *Ithbāt al-imāma min baʿd Jaʿfar al-Ṣādiq*; see Poonawala, *Biobibliography*, p. 108, for a brief note on this work. He mentions this *Ithbāt* in his *al-Ibtidaʾ wa al-intihāʾ* [attr.], which is in The Institute of Ismaili Studies library and consists of 32 folios, copied in the 14th/20th century, with a shelf mark Ms 1250 (Ar1, ZA), folio 24a.

20. See the seventh chapter of Klemm's *Memoirs of a Mission*, pp. 97ff.

21. Ivanow mentions *al-Zāhira fī maʿrifat* in his *Ismaili Tradition* (p. 7) with an added reference in his *Ismaili Literature* (Tehran, 1963), p. 39. Poonawala makes no mention of this work in his *Biobibliography* when describing al-Naysābūrī's works. However, he states that the treatise belongs to another author, Aḥmad b. Ibrāhīm al-Yaʿbūrī al-Hamdānī; see Poonawala, *Biobibliography*, p. 207. Poonawala adds that Ivanow mistook the author as Aḥmad b. Ibrāhīm al-Naysābūrī because in the *Fihrist of al-Majdūʿ* he is simply referred to as Aḥmad b. Ibrāhīm.

22. See Delia Cortese, *Ismaili and Other Arabic Manuscripts: A Descriptive Catalogue of Manuscripts in the Library of The Institute of Ismaili Studies* (London, 2000), pp. 94 and 96.

of the imamate. These other works include the *Risāla fi'l-imāma* of Abu'l-Fawāris,[23] a contemporary of al-Naysābūrī who has been discussed below, and *al-Maṣābiḥ fī ithbāt al-imāma* of al-Kirmānī, yet another contemporary of al-Naysābūrī.[24] In addition, there is an earlier work in this category, the *Tathbīt al-imāma,* written by the Fatimid Imam-Caliph al-Manṣūr (334–341/946–953).[25] The text is in a form of questions and answers where al-Manṣūr sets out the essential need for an imam rationally. The imamate was, for him, *farḍ akbar,* that is the greatest religious duty on humanity without which it cannot function or act righteously.[26] It is this tradition of rationality that al-Naysābūrī follows and his work is, therefore, highly noteworthy in this particular genre. The unique feature of al-Naysābūrī is his use of Aristotelian logic with regard to 'degrees of excellence' as a virtue. He thus emerges as a formidable scholar of Ismaili theology, one whose significance and contribution has hitherto been largely ignored.

Traditionally, the imamate was discussed in works dealing with principles of the faith (*uṣūl al-dīn*) rather than in legal treatises (*furū'*), but later Sunni scholars, following al-Juwaynī and al-Ghazālī, generally treated the imamate within expositions of the law.[27] This was mainly in opposition to the Shi'is who earlier placed the imamate at the core of religion. Al-Naysābūrī's treatise and those of others noted earlier are, therefore, essential since they focus on a Shi'i and specifically, Ismaili view of the imamate. A pertinent aspect of al-Naysābūrī's work is his intellectual demonstration of the imamate as a rational necessity. This was timely and crucial in a milieu where there

---

23. Abu'l-Fawāris Aḥmad b. Ya'qūb, *al-Risāla fi'l-imāma*, ed. and tr. Sami N. Makarem as *The Political Doctrine of the Ismā'īlīs* (Delmar, NY, 1977).

24. See the new edition and translation of this work in Paul E. Walker, *Master of the Age: An Islamic Treatise on the Necessity of the Imamate* (London, 2007).

25. See *Kitāb tathbīt al-imāma* Ms 1120 (ArI, ZA) in the library of The Institute of Ismaili Studies. For a description and analysis of this work see Wilferd Madelung, 'A Treatise on the Imamate of the Fatimid Caliph al-Manṣūr bi-Allāh', in Chase Robinson, ed., *Texts, Documents and Artefacts: Islamic Studies in Honour of D.S. Richards* (Leiden and Boston, 2003), pp. 69–77.

26. Madelung, 'Treatise on the Imamate', p. 73.

27. Madelung, 'Imāma', pp. 1163–1169.

was an intense debate and discussion on whether the imamate was incumbent only on grounds of revelation or whether it was necessary also on the basis of intellect or reason.

The Contents of *Kitāb ithbāt al-imāma*

The *Kitāb ithbāt al-imāma* is divided into seven sections (*fuṣūl*) of varying lengths. The first section is a preliminary paragraph of prayer, salutations and an introduction in which the author lays out how his work differs from those previously written:

> Therefore, we wish to write a treatise on affirming the imamate using evidence (*istishhād*) and deduction (*istidlāl*) from the [outer] horizons (*al-āfāq*) and [our] inner selves (*anfūs*), from politics or governance (*siyāsa*) and norms (*rusūm*) by way of intellect (*ʿaql*), self-evidence (*ḍarūra*), innate constitution (*al-fiṭra*), natural disposition (*al-jibla*), and agreement (*al-ittifāq*) from all religious communities (*ahl kull milla*), as well as from philosophers (*al-falāsifa*) and mathematicians (*ahl al-ḥisāb*). We shall further deduce evidence from the structure of religious duties (*farāʾiḍ*) and practices in a way that has not been done by the elders of the *daʿwa*.[28]

Al-Naysābūrī's theme and purpose here are clear. He wants to affirm the authoritative leadership of the true imams not only through citations from the Qurʾan and the Prophet's traditions, as done by his predecessors, but is also keen to establish the imamate logically through induction and deduction using rational and philosophical arguments, including evidence from mathematicians and consensus from all communities. He substantiates his arguments, where necessary, with Qurʾanic verses and traditions from the Prophet and the imams. In his introduction, he defines the imamate as the pole (*quṭb*) and foundation of religion (*asās al-dīn*). He wants to avoid giving the impression that proof of the messengership has precedence over that of the imamate since, as he argues, the latter is contained within the former.

Al-Naysābūrī further maintains that acknowledging the imam means acknowledging the messenger, although not all who accept the

28. Paragraph [5] of the text and translation.

messengers believe in the imam. In his view, proofs for recognizing the messenger are meant for those outside the sphere of Islam, while argumentations for the imamate are for Muslims. It is thus apparent that his work was intended for a large audience, that is, the Muslim community (*umma*) as a whole rather than his own community alone, or even the Shiʿa in general.

The imam, al-Naysābūrī states categorically, is always present in the world; the world is never deprived of him, while the messenger comes forth at certain times and not at others. Thus, the imamate remains forever present in the world, in all ages and at all times. It is the imam who preserves the religious law and its esoteric truths, the revealed law (*sharīʿa*) and its inner dimension (*ḥaqīqa*). For this reason the evolution of religious cycles depends on him and it remains his prerogative to interpret and act upon the prophet's religious law; the imam alone is able to make changes or replacements.[29] It is, therefore, only through the imam that one attains the inner truth of religious law, its esoteric interpretation and its meaning.

Following this first introductory section, al-Naysābūrī presents six other sections. The second section states the necessity of the imamate innately and intellectually as well as in nature, in self-evident patterns and norms. He lays emphasis on the fact that people argue and differ over the imamate in the same way as they dispute about God's existence after having accepted Him.

The third section describes the disparity and degrees of excellence in all species, which al-Naysābūrī believes to be the firmest indication and proof for the imamate and the imams. Just as a corporeal body needs the various elements from which it is created, similarly, he says, the soul, spirit and religious noetic forms depend on the imam for their nourishment. In this, there is a testimony of the symbol (*mathal*) for the symbolized (*mamthūl*). His argument is that if people were to struggle for the needs of the soul in the same manner as they do for the requirements of the body, they would not remain in doubt, and neither drift away nor ascribe human qualities to God.

In the fourth section, al-Naysābūrī gives various examples of degrees of excellence, notably of the sun's superiority among the

29. Paragraph [4] of the text and translation.

planets,[30] relating it to the imam's position in religion. The fifth section cites further analogies of degrees of excellence from minerals, precious stones and grains, with paradigms of perfect example in each variety to demonstrate that the imam is at the apex of humanity. Similarly, in section six, al-Naysābūrī presents examples from the plant and animal kingdoms that have attained the heights of refinement. He makes a case that just as humans have command over all minerals, plants and animals in the world, so too the imam, being the quintessence of mankind, has supremacy over all humanity. Following this, al-Naysābūrī shows why humanity needs a teacher for learning and then deduces evidence for the necessity of the imam from arithmetic and geometry, as well as from the structure of religious duties (*farā'iḍ*) and practices. These include the meaning of the Ka'ba, the imam as the protector of the Muslim treasury (*bayt al-māl*), as well as the meaning of *jihād* or struggle, the pilgrimage, and the imam's role in purifying believers, executing legal punishments and in upholding the duty of 'ordering good and forbidding evil'.

The last and seventh section of the *Ithbāt* seeks to establish the imamate from the time of Adam, and shows how in Adam's designation of his son to the imamate, there is proof that the world could never be without an imam. Giving examples of the prophets Adam, Noah, Abraham, Moses and Jesus, al-Naysābūrī enquires pertinently: 'If people accepted the imamate in previous cycles, how can they [now] deny designation (*naṣṣ*) and call for choice (*ikhtiyār*) in the family of Muḥammad?' He then argues at length for 'Alī's succession and, in establishing the superiority of 'Alī, he demonstrates the weaknesses of the caliphs before him. At the same time, he enumerates the virtues of the guardian of the time (*walī al-'aṣr*) and the Commander of the Faithful, that is, the Imam-Caliph al-Ḥākim, although without naming him. He establishes that just as every genus and species have their summit, the imams, too, have their utmost limit, which is unattainable and that that position is reserved for 'Alī, as the Commander of the Faithful.

30. In Aristotelian natural science, the sun occupies the fourth and middle position among the celestial bodies: Saturn, Jupiter, Mars, Sun, Venus, Mercury and the Moon.

Themes in the Text

A notable feature of the *Ithbāt al-imāma* is that while al-Naysābūrī speaks of the dignitaries of the Ismaili *daʿwa*, he mentions none by name. The Ismaili *dāʿīs* Ḥamīd al-Dīn al-Kirmānī and Abu'l-Fawāris were both contemporaries of al-Naysābūrī, although none of them cite each other in their works. Yet, all of them wrote on the imamate at one time or another, even if from different angles. Abu'l-Fawāris was a *dāʿī* in Syria, while al-Kirmānī and al-Naysābūrī hailed from Iran before moving to Cairo. It is quite plausible that al-Naysābūrī spent some time in Syria before heading for Cairo, since in his *Istitār al-imām* he is particularly well-informed about the inner workings of the *daʿwa* in Salamiyya during the *dawr al-satr*, as well as being the only writer privy to the names of the hidden imams.[31] He was certainly in Cairo by the time of al-ʿAzīz and lived well into the time of al-Ḥākim. Consequently, it is quite likely that he would have met and known several dignitaries in the Fatimid hierarchy.

The concept of the *qā'im* and that of the *qiyāma* is a recurring theme in Fatimid literature. In early Ismaili cosmogony and cosmology, there is an emphasis on a series of seven cycles or heptads of imams who convey knowledge of the Unity of God (*tawḥīd*) to mankind in seven stages, namely those of Adam, Noah, Abraham, Moses, Jesus, Muḥammad and finally that of the *qā'im* or the 'One who arises'. Each 'proclaimer' (*nāṭiq*) sets a stage further in the evolvement of the knowledge, and is helped in the task by a legatee, also known as the 'silent one' (*ṣāmit*). The pairs in the first six eras were Adam-Seth, Noah-Shem, Abraham-Ismāʿīl, Moses-Aaron, Jesus-Simon Peter and Muḥammad-ʿAlī b. Abī Ṭālib. The final cycle, that of the *qā'im*, is when this spiritual knowledge becomes realized by man reaching his perfection through God's divine word. The position of the *qā'im* as the seventh imam of the era of Islam was accorded to Muḥammad b. Ismāʿīl by early Ismailis.[32]

---

31. The Fatimids gave their authorization to this presentation of their own early history. See Heinz Halm, *Das Reich des Mahdi Der Aufstieg der Fatimiden* (Munich, 1991), p. 22; English trans. M. Donner, *The Empire of the Mahdi: The Rise of the Fatimids* (Leiden, 1996), p. 13.

32. Wilferd Madelung, 'The Fatimids and the Qarmaṭīs of Baḥrayn', in Farhad

In early Ismaili literature, the terms *mahdī* and *qā'im* are both used for the expected messianic imam. Some predictions became realized by the Fatimid Imam-Caliph al-Mahdī, the founder of the dynasty, while others were to be fulfilled by his successors. This theory was elaborated by al-Qāḍī al-Nuʿmān (d. 363/974) in his *Sharḥ al-akhbār* where numerous traditions on the *mahdī* are quoted from varying sources and applied to the Fatimid al-Mahdī and his successors.[33] Thus, the title 'al-Mahdī' was reserved for the first Fatimid caliph, while the eschatological imam still expected in future was called the *qā'im*.[34]

For al-Naysābūrī, his ruling Commander of the Faithful (al-Ḥākim) is 'the *qā'im* in his time and age and the *qā'im* of all those who preceded him, and the perfector of them all'.[35] He notes that the imams must always remain present in the world, while the messengers arise at certain times and not at others. All messengers are imams first, that is, they initially attain the rank of imamate, and only then rise as the seventh imam of their cycle when necessary, to establish a religious law. Al-Kirmānī, writing his *Rāḥāt al-ʿaql*[36] after al-Naysābūrī's *Ithbāt*, also regards the imam as the *qā'im* in his age.

Al-Naysābūrī was evidently a high ranking official in the *daʿwa*, in view both of the various works he wrote, as well as his description in the *Risāla al-mūjaza* of the professional etiquette for those working for the imam. In it, as well as in the *Ithbāt*, he enumerates the hierarchical ranks of the *daʿwa* as 'proofs' (*ḥujaj*), 'adjuncts' (*lawāḥiq*), 'summoner' (*dāʿī*), 'wing' (*janāḥ*), and 'licensee'

Daftary, ed., *Mediaeval Ismaʿili History and Thought* (London, 1996), pp. 21–73.

33. al-Qāḍī al-Nuʿmān, *Sharḥ al-akhbār fī faḍā'īl al-a'imma al-aṭhār*, ed. S.M. Ḥusaynī al-Jalālī (2nd ed., Qumm, 1414/1993), vol. 3, pp. 355–368.

34. Ivanow, *Ismaili Tradition*, pp. 97–122, Arabic texts, pp. 1–31. See also the discussion in Farhad Daftary, *The Ismāʿīlīs: Their History and Doctrines* (2nd ed., Cambridge, 2007), pp. 96–97 and pp. 116–119 as well as his analysis on the Fatimid doctrine of the *qa'im*, pp. 164–165, 207–208.

35. Paragraph [81] of the text and translation.

36. Ḥamīd al-Dīn al-Kirmānī, *Rāḥat al-ʿaql*, ed. M. Kāmil Ḥusayn and M. Muṣṭafā Ḥilmī (Leiden and Cairo, 1953), pp. 426–427, and his *Kitāb al-riyāḍ*, ed. ʿArif Tāmir, pp. 182–184 and 199–206; also see Wilferd Madelung, 'Ismāʿīliyya', in *EI2*, vol. 4, pp. 198–206.

(*ma'dhūn*) and 'motivator' (*mukallib*), with the imam being the supreme embodiment of the *da'wa*. He is the apex of humanity whose status, rank and position no one else can attain in his age or time. In al-Naysābūrī's hierarchy therefore, there are six grades with the imam forming the seventh. During al-Naysābūrī's time, the supreme embodiment of the *da'wa* was the Imam-Caliph al-Ḥākim bi-Amr Allāh.

Al-Naysābūrī also mentions the philosophers (*al-falāsifa*) without identifying any of them. He refers to the degrees of excellence in all genera and species using Aristotelian logic in many of his arguments, including those of the ten categories.[37] When listing these categories, he extols the sages amongst the philosophers, yet declares that in reality the true sages are the imams from whom people acquired the principles of all disciplines in knowledge and wisdom.[38] It is less clear, however, whom he is referring to when citing the 'philosophers' in a critical manner. Quite likely he was referring to al-Fārābī (d. 339/950) or even al-Kindī (d. 256/870). Ibn Sīnā (d. 428/1037) was certainly a contemporary. Could al-Naysābūrī have known him? Both came from Khurāsān although from different cities. Ibn Sīnā admits, as is well known, that he did not follow the Ismaili views of his father and brother. He turned away from them and joined the Peripatetic tradition represented by al-Fārābī. He did subscribe to the views of Aristotle, but did not follow them in those aspects which Ismailis found most congenial to their thought. The rational metaphysics of Ibn Sīnā confronted the Ismaili prophetic theology with a serious challenge.[39] It is, therefore, quite possible that al-Naysābūrī was responding to him and al-Fārābī while at the same time using Aristotelian logic to prove his theology. Like his predecessors, al-Naysābūrī did not reject all philosophy but only that which did not conform to his own concept

---

37. Thomas Aquinas (1225–1274) applied these Aristotelian arguments in Christian theology, one of them being that there are degrees of value or perfection in things. However, long before him al-Naysābūrī used these philosophical arguments in Islamic theology to prove the necessity of the imamate.

38. Paragraph [52] of the text and translation.

39. Madelung, 'Aspects of Ismaili Theology', p. 58

of accurate knowledge.[40] Al-Kirmānī too, as we well know, argued his case against the philosophers in many of his works, just as he did against the Zaydīs, many of whom had adopted the Muʿtazilī doctrine. His critique was against those who believed that human intellect was able to determine basic truths of knowledge on its own without being taught and that in order to know the oneness of God one did not need a prophet.[41] By extension, for the Shiʿis, this also meant the need for an imam, which is what both al-Kirmānī and al-Naysābūrī appear to be arguing for in their respective treatises.

In his long section on governance, al-Naysābūrī relates the qualifications specified by the philosophers for a political leader. He divides authority (*siyāsa*) into three categories: the authority of the individual (*siyāsat al-khāṣṣa*), the authority of the family (*siyāsat al-ḥāmma*), and the authority of the general public (*siyāsat al-ʿāmma*).[42] In governing himself, the individual should be able to restrain himself from all vices, bad traits, bestial habits and blameworthy lusts, and to govern his own self resolutely, his own (higher) self against his (lower) self. He is thus able to discipline his soul when it errs with reproach and repentance while rewarding it when it does well by praise, happiness and by being consistent in doing that. The governance of one's own family is that the individual manages his own household and dependents by protecting their welfare, encouraging them to acquire virtues and pleasing character, disciplining those who err by reprimanding them and through other such ways whilst rewarding those who do 'good' by commendation and by other such means.[43] The governance of the general public or majority is that of governing

40. See also the section on philosophy and the philosophers in Walker's *Early Philosophical Shiism*, pp. 30–36. Walker describes similar attitudes in al-Naysābūrī's predecessors, Abū Ḥātim al-Rāzī and Abū Yaʿqūb al-Sijistānī, who complain about false philosophical ideas and the difficulty of deciphering authentic from corrupt notions.

41. Walker, *Ḥamīd al-Dīn al-Kirmānī*, pp. 53–55.

42. These qualities are also mentioned by the author in his other work, *al-Risāla al-mūjaza,* which he composed as a guide of etiquette for professionals working for the imam. See Klemm's book on al-Mu'ayyad fi'l-Dīn al-Shīrāzī, *Memoirs of a Mission.*

43. Paragraph [48–49] of the text and translation.

cities, protecting the welfare of people's livelihoods and averting them from reprehensible morals and bad deeds.

Al-Naysābūrī then concurs with the philosophers that he who is incapable of governing his own self should not be put in charge of managing his family, and he who cannot manage his own family does not deserve the privilege of managing [other] people or communities in any way. At this stage, he specifies a particular scholar without naming him, stating that 'the author of this classification aimed at encouraging obedience to the imam, for he describes the imam by an attribute of a ruler in order that they would look for a ruler with such a qualification and description.'[44] In all probability, al-Naysābūrī is referring to al-Fārābī for whom 'the meaning of the philosopher, first chief, king, legislator and imam are all one.' In his *Taḥṣīl al-saʿāda*, al-Fārābī concludes that the intellectual virtues acquired by the philosopher are to be actualized into circumstances and conditions leading to the formation of a state.[45]

This relates to al-Naysābūrī's other critique of the philosophers which is in regard to the maxim *anna al-falsafa hiya al-tashabbuh bi'l-bāri'*, meaning 'that philosophy is seeking to resemble the Creator' according to human capacity. In his view, seeking to resemble the Creator means dealing with humanity in the same way as God deals with them, and interacting with them and with his own self in a way that God acts with him and mankind and in accordance with their nature.[46] This maxim is cited in varying forms and quoted by al-Kindī, Abū Bakr al-Rāzī, al-Fārābī, Isaac Israeli, the Ikhwān al-Ṣafā', and Maimonides. The commentators of Aristotle have also included

44. Refer to paragraph [49] in the text and translation. See al-Fārābī's *Taḥṣīl al-saʿāda*, ed. Jaʿfar Āl Yāsin (Beirut, 1983), pp. 92–93, and Muhsin Mahdi's English translation, *Alfarabi's Philosophy of Plato and Aristotle* (Ithaca, NY, 1963), pp. 46–47, where al-Fārābī describes the imam, philosopher and legislator as a single idea. See also Richard Walzer, ed. and tr., *Al-Fārābī on the Perfect State: Abū Naṣr al-Fārābī's Mabādī' ārā' ahl-al-madīnah al-fāḍilah* (Oxford, 1985).

45. See Lawrence V. Berman, 'The Political Interpretation of the Maxim: The Purpose of Philosophy is the Imitation of God', *Stvdia Islamica*, 15 (1961), pp. 53–61.

46. Refer to paragraph [83] of the text and translation.

this definition of philosophy, ascribing it to Plato.[47] In al-Naysābūrī's view, the philosophers have stolen this speech from the 'people of the truth' (*ahl al-ḥaqīqa*),[48] as for him only the Commander of the Faithful (al-Ḥākim) has been able to carry out the real meaning of this phrase. In his view, the imam-caliph's treatment of humanity is similar to God's treatment of them with respect to the nature of the world, in providing sustenance and in other such matters. He follows this by describing and illustrating the circumstances that are relevant to the time of al-Ḥākim.

Degrees of Excellence

In his *Ithbāt*, al-Naysābūrī affirms the imamate using several approaches that include religious duties, tales of the prophets and arguments from philosophers and mathematicians. However, the theory of 'degrees of excellence' is one that features most prominently in the author's text, and which in his view is the firmest proof of the imamate. He argues that the imamate or supreme leadership is everywhere in the universe as well as within our inner selves, in the very essence of our being. Defining imamate as the pole and foundation of religion, the author uses a number of methods to establish his thesis ranging from the philosophers' ten categories to the natural phenomena from minerals, plants and animals as metaphors for comparison. Accepting that there are differences and disparities within each genus and species, al-Naysābūrī gives paradigms of perfect examples in each variety, and thus demonstrates, by analogy, that it is the imam who stands at the apex of humanity.

Abu'l-Fawāris, a contemporary of al-Naysābūrī, in his *Risāla fi'l-imāma* uses this theme of degrees of excellence in terms of disparity amidst humanity and alludes to it briefly in one of his chapters:

> The judgement of reason assures and testifies that the presence of disparity among mankind is devised wisdom. Had we been equal

47. Plato, *Theaetetus*, 176 B cited in Berman, 'The Political Interpretation', pp. 53–61. Berman also gives references to many Muslim philosophers including al-Kindī, al-Fārābī and the Ikhwān al-Ṣafā'.

48. The author is referring to his own community.

> in qualities, conditions and knowledge, we would have all been on a par, and no order would be accomplished. Wisdom would be corrupted; we would not have obeyed each other, and each one of us would have claimed to be perfect in every science and craft, and to be able to handle all matters whether great or little, big or small, noble or base. Disparity among us leads, therefore, to our advantage. In accordance with this divine wisdom God (glory be to Him) made the superior among us a mediator between Him and us. Hence He may guide us.[49]

In dealing with the question of the imamate, Abu'l-Fawāris usually begins with Qur'anic verses followed by Prophetic traditions to support his thesis, and then substantiates these with rational arguments. The quotation above is in response to a question asked in his fifth chapter: 'If God accords the imamate to someone in preference to another, then where was the justice of God?' Al-Naysābūrī, by contrast, usually begins with intellectual arguments at the outset and then makes use of Qur'anic verses inter-textually to substantiate a point that he elucidates rationally.

This same premise of *tafāwut* or disparity occurs also in al-Sijistānī's *Ithbāt al-nubuwwa,* especially in his opening section where he emphasizes this differential disparity as being essential to the creation and in the maintenance of the world. All things, he holds, are structured on the basis that some are inherently better than others and that it is this that determines the place of everything in the world. He also mentions briefly that celestial spheres cause the elements to mix in various ways through their motions, in order to create the species as well as individuals with differences.[50] His work reveals a frequent use of the terms *faḍl* and *tafāḍul* and his differential disparity clearly depicts a hierarchy whose zenith is the messenger-prophet.

---

49. Abu'l-Fawāris, *al-Risāla fi'l-imāma*, ed. and tr. Makarem, *Political Doctrine*, p. 34 of the English trans. and p. 18 of Arabic text. See also Hans Daiber, 'Abū Ḥātim ar-Rāzī (10th century A.D.) on the Unity and Diversity of Religions', in J. Gort et al., ed., *Dialogue and Syncretism: An Interdisciplinary Approach* (Grand Rapids, MI, 1989), p. 91, on diversity among men with regard to their intelligence, insight, and power of distinction and perception.

50. See al-Sijistānī, *Ithbāt al-nubuwwa*, ed. 'Ārif Tāmir (Beirut, 1966), pp. 24–29. Paul Walker has discussed this in his *Early Philosophical Shiism*, p. 109.

Al-Naysābūrī is clearly inspired by this approach of al-Sijistānī, which he applies to his treatise on the imamate. The question of who has the right to lead the Muslim community does not however, seem to interest al-Sijistānī and his discussion on prophecy is celestial and theoretical rather than pragmatic and political which is what al-Naysābūrī seeks to accomplish in his own work. The subject of the imamate as an institution has no place in al-Sijistānī[51] while for al-Naysābūrī, it is at the very crux of creation as well as being an inner aspect of prophecy. Although al-Naysābūrī employs the premise of *tafāwut*, he mainly pursues and builds on the theme of 'degrees of excellence' under the term *tafāḍul,* on which he systematically argues his whole thesis, making it a base for his work. He extends this concept to all genera of minerals, plants and animals, arguing his case on a number of premises beginning with the ten metaphysical categories, mentioned by the sages amongst the philosophers.[52] He compares the fact that just as the substance (*jawhar*) in these categories is at the summit of all other nine accidents—quantity (*kammiyya*), quality (*kayfiyya*), relation (*iḍāfa*), place (*makān*), time (*zamān*), possession (*jida*), posture (*nuṣba*), action (*fā'il*), and affection (*maf'ūl*)[53]—through which they are established, similarly the imam is the *jawhar* or substance in relation to all other ranks in the hierarchy of the *da'wa.*

In elaborating his hypothesis, al-Naysābūrī refers to the four basic constituents of heat, cold, dryness and humidity. Among these, he observes that heat has precedence over others, as it is through heat that they are all established. In the same manner, the imam has precedence over all ranks in hierarchy as it is he who illumines the souls, giving them intellectual light, motion and sublimity. He states:

---

51. His brief chapter on the imamate in *Kitāb al-iftikhār,* ed. Muṣṭafā Ghālib (Beirut, 1980); ed. I.K. Poonawala (Beirut, 2000), is an exception.

52. Aristotle maintained that these categories were applicable to all phenomena. Everything has a natural function and thus strives to fulfil that function which is its best natural state.

53. See J.N. Mattock, 'Maḳūlāt', *EI2*, vol. 6, pp. 203–205. Affection or *maf'ūl* is also rendered 'passion' in many translations, but what it actually means here is the thing acted upon. In rephrasing the Aristotelian categories, al-Naysābūrī uses the form *fā'il/maf'ūl* rather than the more common *fi'l/infi'āl*. I would like to thank Professor Hermann Landolt for pointing this out to me.

> We also say that among the four basic constituents (*al-ʿanāṣir)* from which the first composites (*tarākib*) were composed; two are active and two passive. The two active ones are heat and cold while the two passive ones are dryness and humidity. The ultimate and the noblest among them is heat, from which arises luminosity, light, motion, movement and elevation while the other three are established through it. Heat thus has precedence in origin and in existence. No foundation or realm of nature would be complete without it. Likewise, the imam illumines the souls[54] and from him comes intellectual light (*al-nūr al-ʿaqlī*), motion (*al-ḥaraka*) and elevation (*al-ʿulūw*). No principle or religious realm is complete without him.[55]

In discussing the celestial spheres, al-Naysābūrī cites the outermost sphere (*falak al-aflāk)*, within which all other spheres orbit, as being the supreme one and corresponds it to the imam in relation to other dignitaries in the *daʿwa:*

> All heavenly bodies and religious signs of the zodiac function under his command. If someone were to claim that this is rather a symbol for the *qāʾim* (resurrector), given that the highest principle in the world points to the intellect in respect to the four principles, then we would answer that the imam is the *qāʾim* in his time, he is the proclaimer (*nāṭiq*) in his age and time and he is the one who assumes the position of the *qāʾim*. The imam's position in his realm is that of the Universal Intellect (*ʿaql al-kullī*).[56]

This concept is further elucidated when al-Naysābūrī discusses the disparities (*tafāwut*) and degrees of excellence (*tafāḍul*) in the physique. He argues that the foremost organ is the head as the face, by which an individual is recognized, is placed in it. He then considers the internal organs, asserting that the brain is the best, being the source of the intellect. In a like manner, he argues for the position of the imam in the world, around whom all affairs of creation revolve just as all actions pertaining to the body are controlled by the brain. As intellect happens to be the most pre-eminent faculty

54. Literally, 'the imam is the light of the souls'.
55. Refer to paragraph [16] in the text and translation.
56. End of paragraph [16] in the text and translation.

in man, so too, the imam is the universal intellect (*ʿaql al-kullī*), being the source of all human intellect in whom one and all become united.[57]

On the differences and degrees of excellence among planets, al-Naysābūrī cites the sun as the summit, without whose light human eyes can not function and without which no growth transpires in plants, animals or newborns. In a parallel manner, the imam is the sun of religion (*shams al-dīn*) through whom human insight is enlightened, souls are illumined and hearts shine, becoming blissful.[58] Using gold as a metaphor, al-Naysābūrī describes the imam as the most excellent religious and intellectual substance, just as gold has supremacy amongst minerals. Following this, he refers to the analogy of precious stones in which, according to him, sapphires stand out, and within an array of multi-coloured sapphires, it is the red ruby that is most exceptional as it is able to retain its essence even when thrown into fire or water. It is, therefore, a supreme jewel amongst all precious stones just as the imam is among all creation.

Al-Naysābūrī cites further examples from plants and trees. He begins with wheat, which he believes to be the most nutritionally balanced grain. Of all fruit-bearing trees, the date palm, in his view, is the most advantageous to mankind, be it raw or cooked. He explains that certain plants reach a degree of such refinement that they are used as antidotes for those dying from chronic illnesses. Examples such as these are cited to show the degree of perfection in each range with parallels of excellence drawn among humans. Al-Naysābūrī thus concludes:

> Man is the pinnacle of animals, plants, minerals and [other] realms of nature. Through him, the welfare and affairs of animals and whatever came before became perfected and ordered. Likewise, the imam is the pinnacle and summit of human beings, their quintessence and their perfection.[59]

57. Paragraph [45] of the text and translation.

58. Abu'l-Fawāris, *al-Risāla fi'l-imāma* (ed. and tr. Makarem as *Political Doctrine*, p. 24 of English trans. and p. 5 of the Arabic text), also mentions the encounter of the two lights whereby exalted knowledge from prophets and imams enters the soul to realize its potentiality into actuality.

59. See paragraph [29] of the text and translation.

A number of reasons could have inspired al-Naysābūrī to write on the subject of the imamate. He does not mention al-Ḥākim by name in his treatise but refers to him as the *amīr al-mu'minīn*, the Commander of the Faithful, and feels compelled to comment on 'the time in which we live.'[60] He was certainly not the only one perplexed by the circumstances of the day, for we have two other Ismaili authors, al-Kirmānī and Abu'l-Fawāris, also writing on the subject of imamate. It must be noted, however, that Abu'l-Fawāris does not mention the difficult times in the capital in his *Risāla fī'l-imāma* and is simply keen to discuss the subject of why imamate is a necessity, presenting arguments as to why the Qur'an, the traditions and the *sharī'a* could not substitute for the imam who should be installed by *naṣṣ*. He was an important *dā'ī* in Syria and mentions al-Ḥākim by name in his work which has sixteen chapters to correspond with his imam being the sixteenth imam. He does not mention any doctrines regarding the Druzes and it can, therefore, be safely assumed that his work was written before the beginnings of their movement in 408/1017. Syria was a success for al-Ḥākim, who was able to extend his authority to Aleppo as well. [61] Whilst in Syria, Abu'l-Fawāris was also given the responsibility by Caliph al-Ḥākim to go to Jerusalem, according to Ibn al-Qalānisī.[62]

The internal challenges faced by al-Ḥākim from some of his followers who wished to ascribe divinity to him, could be another reason for undertaking this work. Al-Naysābūrī calls them the *ghulāt* (exaggerators), although they refer to themselves as the *muwaḥḥidūn* (monotheists). Later, they became known in history as the Druzes, taking their name from one of their leaders, Anūshtikīn al-Darzī (lit. 'the tailor').[63] Their preaching and propaganda had led to great unrest

60. See paragraph [83] of text and translation. For sources on al-Ḥākim's reign refer to Daftary, *The Ismā'īlīs*, 2nd ed., pp. 178–191 and p. 579, n. 77, and to Halm, *The Fatimids*, pp. 35–40.

61. Daftary, *The Ismā'īlīs*, 2nd ed., p. 183.

62. Abū Ya'lā Ḥamza Ibn al-Qalānisī, *Dhayl ta'rīkh Dimashq*, ed. H.F. Amedroz (Leiden, 1908), p. 61, cited by Paul E. Walker, 'The Ismaili *Da'wā* in the Reign of the Fatimid Caliph al-Ḥākim', *Journal of the American Research Center in Egypt*, 30 (1993), p. 169.

63. The word *durūz* is a broken plural from *darzī*. For details on their beliefs and theology see Sami N. Makarem, *The Druze Faith* (Delmar, NY, 1974), and his

in Cairo so that even the *majālis al-ḥikma* had to be shut down for a while. However, al-Naysābūrī, like his contemporary al-Kirmānī, rejects the ascription of divinity to al-Ḥākim.[64]

In the early part of the 5th/11th century, the Abbasid caliph al-Qādir (381–422/991–1031) was sufficiently alarmed at the growing popularity of the Fatimids and gave orders to orchestrate the 'Baghdad Manifesto' which denied their 'Alid genealogy. There is also a vicious critique of the Bāṭiniyya in *al-Farq bayn al-firaq* by Abū Manṣūr 'Abd al-Qāhir b. Ṭāhir al-Baghdādī (d. 429/1037) who spent some time in Nīshāpūr, the homeland of our author.[65] The polemics of Abu'l-Qāsim al-Bustī (d. 420/1030),[66] a Zaydī Mu'tazilī authority, against the Ismailis would also seem to be among the many external reasons that led scholars such as al-Naysābūrī, al-Kirmānī and Abu'l-Fawāris to defend the imamate. In al-Naysābūrī's own words moreover:

> 'Proof of the messengership is needed for those who are outside the domain of Islam, while affirming the imamate is necessary for Muslims who are closer to the true believers. The struggle with them through debate and argument has priority over those denying the messenger and the messengership.'[67]

'Isma'ili and Druze Cosmogony in Relation to Plotinus and Aristotle', in Michael E. Marmura, ed., *Islamic Theology and Philosophy: Studies in Honor of George F. Hourani* (Albany, NY, 1984), pp. 81–91. Also see Marshall G.S. Hodgson, 'al-Darazī and Ḥamza in the Origin of the Druze Religion', *Journal of the American Oriental Society*, 82 (1962), pp. 5–20.

64. Paragraph [89] of text and translation. For the split under al-Ḥākim, see Madelung, 'Das Imamat', pp. 116–112, and Daftary, *A Short History*, pp. 99–101.

65. He has a massive chapter in this work on the Bāṭiniyya and why they fall outside the pale of Islam. Unlike al-Shahrastānī, al-Baghdādī's work is a polemic dealing with each sect separately, judging them all from the standpoint of orthodoxy and condemning all those deviating from 'the straight path'. See his *al-Farq bayn al-firaq*, ed. Muḥammad Badr (Cairo, 1328/1910), pp. 265–299.

66. Samuel M. Stern, 'Abu'l-Qāsim al-Bustī', pp. 299–320. See notes in the introduction regarding this in a partial edition by Stern and by Heinz Halm, *Kosmologie und Heilslehre der frühen Ismā'īlīya: Eine Studie zur islamischen Gnosis* (Wiesbaden, 1978).

67. Paragraph [3] of the text and translation.

Al-Naysābūrī was thus responding to the contemporary discourse taking place amongst scholars of different persuasions, on whether or not the imamate was valid on intellectual grounds besides its certitude in the revelation itself. All Muslim scholars view the imamate as a necessity although many scholars, especially the Sunnis, ignore the role of reason, confirming that leadership in Islam is only valid from religious law. Al-Baghdādī for example, argues that it is necessary for the Muslims to have an imam in order to implement ordinances, enforce legal penalties, direct armies, divide revenues and defend the domain of Islam.[68] Al-Naysābūrī's entire final section is devoted to establishing the imamate of the *amīr al-mu'minīn*. Here, besides seeking to prove the imamate of ʿAlī, he also defends the actions of the imam of the time, al-Ḥākim. Before doing that, he has to establish the hierarchy and supremacy of ʿAlī, and in doing so, he enumerates the limitations of the earlier caliphs whose excellence in Sunni sources is gauged according to the sequential order in which they became caliphs.[69] Al-Naysābūrī, on the other hand, uses the criteria of knowledge, *jihād* and piety to demonstrate systematically the excellence of ʿAlī, proving which is the hallmark of his thesis of *tafāḍul* or degrees of excellence.[70] His theory is obviously intertwined with the question of the succession of the Prophet, for if he is not able to determine ʿAlī's excellence, he would not be able to contest

---

68. Abū Manṣūr ʿAbd al-Qāhir al-Baghdādī, *Kitāb uṣūl al-dīn* (Istanbul, 1928), p. 272, cited in Makarem, *Political Doctrine*, p. 56, n. 6, where Makarem has given further sources on the Sunni concept of *imāma*.

69. The *Kitāb al-ʿUthmāniyya* of al-Jāḥiẓ (d. 255/869) argues for the most part for the superiority of Abū Bakr over ʿAlī and is opposed to undue exaltation of ʿAlī. For a time, there were those who held that ʿAlī should come before ʿUthmān, but in the end the ʿUthmāniyya, who were amongst the forerunners of the *Ahl al-sunna wa'l-jamaʿa*, came to accept the view that the chronological order was the order of merit. See the discussion in W. Montgomery Watt, *The Formative Period of Islamic Thought* (Edinburgh, 1973), pp. 166–169. Also compare the views of the early Zaydīs on the imamate of *al-afḍal* (the best) over that of *al-mafḍūl* (the preferred) and how the Batriyya differed in this respect from the Jārūdiyya who were largely influenced by al-Bāqir's school. See A.R. Lalani, *Early Shīʿī Thought: The Teachings of Imam Muḥammad al-Bāqir* (London, 2000), pp. 46–53.

70. See details in section seven of the text and translation. The concept of *faḍl* or excellence also occurs in the Qur'an. See Qur'an, 16: 71 and 17: 70.

the distinction of his descendants, which included his present imam, al-Ḥākim. This, in turn, was bound to the essential question of whether or not the Qur'an and the traditions, in their application to the community, were to be interpreted by the scholars or by the decisions of the imam.

Clearly conditions were extremely difficult in the Fatimid capital, Cairo, where al-Naysābūrī was operating, especially during the latter part of al-Ḥākim's reign.[71] Anti-Fatimid tradition gives a totally distorted image of this Fatimid caliph. Heinz Halm's findings are very pertinent in this respect:

> The Christian chronicler, John of Antioch (Yaḥyā al-Anṭākī), offered, from a distance, a diagnosis of mental disorder. Later Sunni authors maintained that he stopped washing himself for seven years, that he lived in an underground room for three years without ever leaving it and that he worshipped the planets Mars and Saturn. All this is nonsense. Even the reproach that al-Ḥākim was unpredictable and erratic and that he used to countermand instructions he had just given cannot be confirmed from the sources. If we refer to the contemporary annals of Cairo, and above all to al-Ḥākim's edicts (*sijillāt*), as handed down in the sources, we acquire a very different picture.[72]

Al-Naysābūrī is evidently aware of the challenges faced by the imam and in the latter's defence he employs different tactics to illustrate and prove that whatever steps were being taken in and around the empire were for the good of all. He draws on the example of an educator who tolerates hardship from his pupils, coercing them to seek knowledge and learn proper behaviour even though they hate that, dislike the teacher and choose play and laziness. But the teacher also knows that when the child becomes mature, he will realize its benefit and regret his earlier shortcomings and disobedience.[73] Another analogy that the author uses is of a physician healing a

---

71. Sadik A. Assaad, *The Reign of al-Hakim bi Amr Allah* (386/996–411/1021): *A Political Study* (Beirut, 1974).

72. Halm, *The Fatimids*, p. 35. See especially his 'Der Treuhänder Gottes: Die Edikte des Kalifen al-Ḥākim,' *Der Islam*, 63 (1986), pp. 11–72, where he unravels numerous historical reports of al-Ḥākim's edicts.

73. See paragraph [36] of the text and translation.

patient and how he reverts sometimes to medication, at other times to the slitting of wounds, sometimes cauterization and at times even amputation. Al-Naysābūrī speaks of the imam as a compassionate doctor of souls who acts in a similar manner when religious diseases are rife among the people on account of disputes, arbitrary desires and divergent doctrines. He characterizes al-Ḥākim's purpose as 'enjoining good and forbidding evil' (*al-amr bi'l-ma'rūf wa'l-nahy 'an al-munkar)*, this being one of the primary duties of the imam.

Description of the Arabic Manuscripts

As noted earlier in the introduction, 10 manuscripts were available for the present edition of the Arabic text of the *Kitāb ithbāt al-imāma*, all obtained from the Library of The Institute of Ismaili Studies, four of which were chosen for this new edition. A fifth manuscript was consulted during the proof-reading stage.

The following manuscripts were used:

1. A manuscript of 64 folios, 15 lines to a page (12 on the first page) belonging to the Fyzee collection with a shelf mark MS (R) 56 C.1 and copied in 1134/1722 by Malik Khānbhāi Tuhafjī Bhānpūrī. This manuscript has been designated as *alif* and was examined only in a photocopied form. Describing this manuscript in his catalogue of the Fyzee collection, Mu'izz Goriawala mentions that it is partially affected by water and has also been worm-eaten. [74]

2. A manuscript of 61 folios, between 11 to 17 lines to a page (7 on the first page) formerly belonging to the Ismaili Society of Bombay, with a shelf mark MS 91 (Ar) and copied in 1244/1828. This manuscript was completed in Zayn al-Dīn's class and copied by Malik 'Abd al-'Ali Mullā Shaykh-bhāi Bhānpūrī. It has been designated here as *bā*. Adam Gacek has described this manuscript in his catalogue of Arabic manuscripts in the Library of The Institute of Ismaili Studies.[75]

3. A manuscript of 153 pages, 13 lines to a page with 10 lines on the first page, belonging to the Institute's Zāhid 'Alī collection with a

74. Mu'izz Goriawala, *A Descriptive Catalogue of the Fyzee Collection of Ismaili Manuscripts* (Bombay, 1965), pp. 36–37.

75. Adam Gacek, *Catalogue of Arabic Manuscripts in the Library of The Institute of Ismaili Studies* (London, 1984–1985), vol. 1 p. 32.

shelf mark MS. 1212 (Ar I, ZA). It was completed on the night of the 16th of Shābān, 1259/1843 and copied by Mawlanā Najm al-Dīn's servant (*'abd*), Ismā'īl b. Mullā Khān-bhāi Bihārī written at the request of Mullā Ghulām Ḥusaynjī b. Miyān-Khān *'āmil* of Andūr under the supervision of his master, Miyān Sahib 'Abd al-Muḥsīn. This manuscript has been designated with the Arabic letter *tā*.[76]

4. Totalling 134 pages (129 pages in other variants), this manuscript has 14 lines per page with 11 lines on the first page and a shelf mark MS 94 (Ar). No date or name of the copyist is given. It does however appear to be a late 13th/19th century copy and is designated here with the Arabic letter *thā*.[77]

5. A fifth manuscript, MS 1047 (ArI) which the Institute acquired from Syria after the draft of the present edition was complete, was also compared and consulted. This manuscript has an illuminated head-piece on the front page, and has 78 folios with 12 lines per page. Neither the date of completion nor the name of the copyist is given. It is worm-eaten and written in black *naskhī* style with some corrections and additions in the margin. This manuscript is designated as *jīm*.

All these manuscripts are quite recent in date, yet retain an archaic form of spellings, which have been modernized in this edition. The pious benedictions after the names of the prophets and the imams, such as *ṣalla Allāh 'alayhi wa ālihi* and *'alayhi al-salām*, that are abbreviated in the manuscripts have been written out in full in the Arabic edition.

Notes on the Translation

The translation seeks to follow the original text as far as possible, even literally most of the time, except for the benedictions, which have been omitted at times in order to maintain the flow of the account. Also, certain passages of a polemical nature have not been included in the English translation. In addition, to render the text more clearly, punctuations and paragraphs as well as *hamzas*, *shaddas* and certain

76. Delia Cortese, *Arabic Ismaili Manuscripts: The Zāhid 'Alī Collection in the Library of The Institute of Ismaili Studies* (London, 2003), p. 53.

77. Gacek, *Catalogue of Arabic Manuscripts*, vol. 1, p. 32.

vowel marks, especially in the Qur'anic verses, have been inserted. Following the *fuṣūl* in the manuscript, the work has similarly been divided into sections. Paragraph divisions and numbering them is also an editorial addition to facilitate cross-referencing between the Arabic and English texts. The translations of the Qur'anic verses are my own, adapted from several translations including those of ʿAbdullah Yūsuf ʿAlī, Arthur J. Arberry, Marmaduke Pickthall and Mir Aḥmad Ali.

Certain terms in the text presented a challenge with regard to their translation. This is the case especially with the title word, *ithbāt*, which I have translated as 'affirming' and 'affirmation' in the text although it can equally be rendered as 'proof', 'evidence', 'certitude', 'confirming', 'establishing', 'verifying', and other such related words. The other challenging term was *tafāḍul*, which can have several meanings but is here translated as 'degrees of excellence' and used in the title of this study. This word can equally be rendered as 'variation in perfection, merit, superiority, precedence and priority'.

Aḥmad b. Ibrāhīm al-Naysābūrī

Kitāb ithbāt al-imāma

Book on Affirming the Imamate

In the Name of God, the All-Compassionate, the All-Merciful,
From Whom we seek help in all matters

Section One

[1] Praise be to God, who sent messengers and prophets and appointed imams and caliphs as a blessing for His friends (*awliyā'*), a punishment to enemies, a benefit for religion and the world, as well as [being] an edifice (*'imāra*) for this present world and the world to come. I praise Him with the eulogy of one who is aware of the immense value of the bounty brought through them, and who is grateful for it and who fares his way for the sake of God, hastening towards it. I bear witness that there is no deity except God, with the testimony of a worshipper who is aware of the requirements of this profession and who strives to fulfil its obligations. I bear witness [also] that Muḥammad is His worshipper and Messenger, who is preferred over all His messengers and is immune from all mistakes and errors, may God bless him with innumerable and infinite blessings. May God also bless his loyal and truthful legatee ['Alī], the adept in the clarification and the spiritual realities of the Qur'an, and the imams descended from the martyr,[1] to whom belong praise, glory, infallibility and uprightness. May He [also] bless the master of the palace and age [al-Ḥākim] supported by conquest and victory. May the most excellent salutations of God, and the most bounteous blessings and purest greetings be upon him and on the heir-apparent of the Muslims (*walī al-ahd al-muslimīn*)[2] and the vicegerent (*khalīfa*) of the Commander

1. The reference is to al-Ḥusayn b. 'Alī, the martyr of Karbala from whose genealogy descend all imams of the Shi'i Ismailis and Ithna'asharīs.

2. The reference is to al-Ḥākim's cousin, 'Abd al-Raḥīm b. Ilyās, who was appointed as heir-apparent of the Muslims in 404/1013. A *ṭirāz* that exists from the final years of al-Ḥākim's reign explicitly names him as such. See examples of these inscribed cloths made at Tinnīs in the year 410 in *RCEA (Répertoire chronologique d'épigraphe arabe)*, 6, no. 2212, cited in Paul E. Walker, *Exploring an Islamic Empire: Fatimid History and its Sources* (London, 2002), pp. 104–106. There is also evidence from al-Maqrizī, vol. 2, p. 103, of coins minted in his name in 404/1013 as noted by Walker in his article, 'The Ismaili *Da'wa* in the Reign of the Fatimid Caliph

of the Faithful, as long as tongues discourse and darkness and light continue to alternate.

And now:

[2] The imamate is the pole (*quṭb*) and foundation of religion (*aṣāṣ al-dīn*) around which revolve all religious and worldly matters, and [it is] a benefit for this present life and the life hereafter. Through it are governed the affairs of the worshippers, the prosperity of the land and the acceptance of recompense in the abode of return. It is through the imamate that knowledge of God's absolute unity (*tawḥīd*) and of the [revealed] Message is attained based on proof, demonstration and evidence; [as is] the knowledge of the religious law and its foundations, its interpretation (*ta'wīl*) and clarification.

[3] We have said that the imamate is the pole and foundation of religion and have not given precedence to the messengership over the imamate because in the affirmation (*ithbāt)* of the imamate there is affirmation of the messengership.[3] Whoever acknowledges the imam acknowledges the messenger, but not all those who acknowledge the messenger acknowledge the reality of the imam. Proof of the messengership is needed for those who are outside the domain of Islam, while affirming the imamate is necessary for Muslims who are closer to the true believers. The struggle with them through debate and argument has priority over those denying the messenger and the messengership. This is because the summons [to Islam and the messengership] has reached the polytheists and proof has [already] been established for them, and confronting them with the sword is more appropriate as the world can never be deprived of an imam at any given moment or time, while the messenger is present at some times but not at others. Consequently, in affirming the imamate, there is also an affirmation of the messengership.

---

al-Hakim' p. 176. Besides appointing a *walī 'ahd al-muslimīn* in charge of temporal matters, al-Ḥākim also appointed Abū Hishām 'Abbās ibn Shu'ayb as *walī 'ahd al-mu'minīn* to deal with religious affairs. See S. Makarem, 'Al-Ḥākim bi-Amrillāh's Appointment of his Successors', *Al-Abḥāth*, 23 (1970), pp. 319–324. Makarem cites the compendium of Druze Epistles 26 and 74.

3. Al-Naysābūrī is keen to emphasize here that in proving the imamate he is also proving the messengership since the latter is contained within the former.

God, the Exalted, called the imam a messenger when He said: 'And remember in the Scripture, Ismā'īl was indeed faithful in fulfilling his promise while he was a messenger, a prophet.'[4] Likewise, God called the messenger an imam when addressing Abraham: 'Indeed, I am appointing you an imam for all humanity.' This was when he had completed his messengership and God, the Exalted, said: 'And (remember) when His Lord tried Abraham with His commands and he fulfilled them, He said: "I am appointing you an imam for all humanity".'[5]

[4] It is related from Ja'far al-Ṣādiq, peace be upon him, that he said: 'God chose Abraham [initially] as a prophet (*nabī*), then as a friend (*khalīl*), then as a messenger (*rasūl*) and finally said: "I am appointing you an imam for all humanity".'[6] God called Adam a vicegerent (*khalīfa*),[7] and the name 'vicegerent' is one of the names of the imams. God called David, peace be upon him, a 'vicegerent',[8] whilst he was one of the imams in the past cycles and [called] the proofs (*ḥujaj*) 'prophets'.[9] He called Muḥammad and other messengers 'prophets', addressing them as prophets just as He addressed them as messengers.[10] This is because the messenger arrives first at the rank of the imamate. Then, if the times require the establishment of a [new] religious law, he becomes the seventh imam of that cycle, undertaking the promulgation of the religious law.[11] [In this way] the

4. Qur'an, 19: 54.

5. Qur'an, 2: 124. This verse endorses the continuation of imamate in the progeny of Abraham.

6. A longer version of this tradition is transmitted from Muḥammad al-Bāqir, al-Ṣādiq's father, who mentions that God accepted Abraham first as a worshipper (*'abd*), then a prophet (*nabī*), then a messenger (*rasūl*), then a friend (*khalīl*) and finally as an imam over the people. See Muḥammad b. Ya'qūb al-Kulaynī, *al-Uṣūl min al-kāfī* (Tehran, 1388/1968), vol. 1, p. 175. See also Lalani, *Early Shī'ī Thought*, p. 76 n. 75. Note the absence of *'abd* in the text above. Also compare the status of a *khalīl* in al-Naysābūrī's text which precedes that of a *rasūl*.

7. Qur'an, 2: 30.

8. Qur'an, 38: 26.

9. The author here implies the imams when referring to the 'proofs'.

10. Qur'an, 4: 163–164.

11. Each cycle is headed by one who conveys to people what they are able to comprehend. They are called 'proclaimers' (*nuṭaqā'*, pl. of *nāṭiq*) of the divine message who also have the 'silent one' (*ṣāmit*) in charge of interpreting the inner

imam occupies the place of the messenger in his age and time. The messenger, before arising to promulgate the religious law, is one of the imams, having assumed command from a previous imam. After finalizing the religious law, he hands over the command to the [next] imam. The imam is [therefore] present in the world at all times; the world is never deprived of him. The imam espouses and maintains the religious law and its esoteric reality as we mentioned [earlier]. It is now clear that the progression of the religious cycle depends on the imam and that it is the imam's prerogative how he acts on the prophet's law during his time. No one can reach the prophet, nor attain his rank, or arrive at the proper [understanding of] the religious law, which is only changed or replaced by the imam. It is only through the imam that one can attain the inner truth of the religious law, its interpretation and meaning.

[5] Many works [that are] written on affirming the imamate by the elders of the *daʿwa* draw on deduction and evidence cited from well-known Qurʾanic verses revealed regarding the imamate and the imams, peace be upon them, in addition to traditions reported from the Prophet. Those who came before have left nothing in this matter to those who came later and there is not much point in [simply] repeating the same notions using different words. Therefore, we wish to write a treatise on affirming the imamate using evidence (*istishhād*) and deduction (*istidlāl*) from the [outer] horizons (*al-āfāq*) and [our] inner selves (*anfūs*),[12] from politics or governance (*siyāsa*) and norms (*rusūm*) by way of intellect (*ʿaql*), self-evidence (*ḍarūra*), innate constitution (*al-fiṭra*), natural disposition (*al-jibla*), and agreement (*al-ittifāq*) from all religious communities (*ahl kull milla*), as well as from philosophers (*al-falāsifa*) and mathematicians (*ahl al-ḥisāb*). We shall further deduce evidence from the structure of religious duties (*farāʾiḍ)* and practices in a way that has

---

meaning of the message. Thus, the function of the *nāṭiq* is to proclaim the revelation plainly (*tanzīl*), while the imam elucidates its esoteric interpretation (*taʾwīl*), guiding the believers according to the needs of the time. See the Introduction above for details and for the significance of the seventh imam.

12. Qurʾan 41: 53 and later cited in full by the author: 'We shall show them our signs on the horizons and within themselves until it becomes manifest to them that it is the truth.'

not been done by the elders of the *daʿwa*. Then, if it is found to be reasonable, it is due to the excellence of support from the master of the age and the time (*walī al-ʿaṣr waʾl-zamān*). But, if there is any error, then, it is due to my [own] weakness and shortcoming, and that is most proper of me.

Section Two

[6] Thus we say: Indeed the necessity (*wujūb*) of the imamate and the imams, peace be upon them, is essential in natural disposition (*jibla*), and innate constitution (*fitra*), in nature (*tabiʿa*), intellect (*ʿaql*), governance (*siyāsa*), prescription (*waḍʿa*) and norms (*rusūm*).[13] It is obligatory in all revealed law (*sharīʿa*), religion and religious communities, just as the existence of the Creator is necessary in innate constitution, natural disposition, and the intellect in every religious community and religion. But people differed regarding the Creator after His necessity was proved and after [having] accepted His existence. They began drawing conclusions according to their own personal whims and opinions as well as blindly imitating their forefathers and teachers, claiming that the Creator, Whom the innate constitution and natural disposition necessitates, is [actually] either the substance or elements or stars, or sun or something other than that. At times, they describe the Creator with attributes that constitute His similarity, that is, anthropomorphism or that which is akin to polytheism, basing that on their judgement without any [authentic] knowledge. Likewise, with regard to the necessity of the imamate, they fell into disagreement after their commitment to the imam, some insisting that the imam, who is ascertained by intellect and self evidence, is the wise man in every age. This [then] is similar to the [views of] philosophers who call their teachers 'imams' (*aʾimma*), 'sages' (*ḥukamāʾ*), 'head of the scholars' (*raʾs al-ʿulamāʾ*), 'master of the world' (*sāʾis*) and 'the teacher' (*al-muʿallim*).

---

13. Compare with Abu'l-Fawāris' *al-Risāla fi'l-imāma*, ed. and tr. Makarem, as *Political Doctrine*, pp. 22–25 of English trans. and pp. 2–7 of Arabic text.

Section Three

[7] Followers of [all] religions called their past imams 'prophets' and 'sages' in every cycle, whilst [certain] followers of Islam call their usurping, oppressive false pretenders 'imams', calling [also] their scholars and jurists 'imams'.[14] Yet, if you examine them, they all confirm the existence of the imam by necessity (*ḍarūra*), unable to deny its existence.[15] Whoever wants salvation and guidance must lay aside his inclinations and desires and comprehend the deficiency in every false pretender to this designation [*imām*], his lack of knowledge, gnosis or cognition, piety and all other merits and conditions of the imamate. When he [who wants salvation] realizes [the pretender's] lack of knowledge and the triviality of his piety, modesty and his inability to fulfil [any of] the conditions of the imamate, he will [then] deny his imamate until such time that he attains recognition of the true imam (*maʿrifat imām al-ḥaqq*).

[8] We shall now mention some statements from each pretender including his weakness[es] and limitation[s]; we shall [then] return his own principles against him, and repudiate the imamate from those not suited for it. We shall establish the imamate of the true imams, peace be upon them, with proofs and demonstrations. We shall establish the necessity of obeying them, entrusting our affairs to their command and accepting the revelation, the interpretation and the confession of Unity from them, just as we mentioned in *Kitāb al-tawḥīd* (The Book on Divine Unity).[16] All those who know the created beings realize their inability and deficiency, repudiating their divinity until such time that they reject the divinity from all

---

14. In the author's view, only the prophets and imams are entitled to the designation 'imam'.

15. Ḥamīd al-Dīn al-Kirmānī, in his work *al-Maṣābiḥ fī ithbāt al-imāma* (Beirut, 1969), pp. 80–95, enumerates fourteen points to prove the necessity of the imamate. See Makarem, *Political Doctrine*, pp. 37–39, where these points are summarized. For details, see Paul Walker's new Arabic edition and English translation of the *Ithbāt* as *Master of the Age* (London, 2007), pp. 71–79 (English) and pp. 36–45 (Arabic).

16. As observed by Ismail Poonawala in his *Biobibliography*, this work of al-Naysābūrī is in the collection of the late Muṣṭafā Ghālib. See also Cortese, *Ismaili and Other Arabic Manuscripts*, pp. 94 and 96.

created beings. Thus, Divine Unity is left pure, without ascription of human qualities to God (*tashbīh*), and the denial of all attributes to God (*taʿṭīl*).

[9] We also say that God, the Exalted, through His subtle wisdom and extensive power, created for the human body principles, causes and means. He also made all the derivatives and realms of nature manifest in them and in their traces. These would thus become manifest from them in a predetermined manner and in a definite term, until such time that He brought forth from them a body with senses parallel to its principles and corresponding to them. He made those principles and means its sustenance and nourishment through which it survives and from which its corporeal and perceptual reward and punishment are determined. Similarly, He made principles, causes and means for the souls, spirits and religious noetic forms from whose traces they become manifest. [It is] through them that their sustenance, nourishment, survival and reward are determined while [at the same time] their punishment is determined by disrupting their support and distancing them from their origin.

[10] God, may His mention be exalted, made the principles and causes of the body a testimony and proof for principles of the soul as well as for its derivatives and its nourishment, so that the religious creation would be similar to the physical creation, corresponding and parallel to it. Thus, just as the body manifests itself by becoming perfect only through the celestial spheres along with the stars (*kawākib*), and just as it cannot become perfect through the celestial spheres without the stars—even if the stars [themselves] revolve around the spheres—yet, the course of events is [always] influenced by the stars; likewise, the manifestation of the religious noetic forms and the everlasting souls manifest themselves and become perfect only through the influence of the imams, peace be upon them. Their nourishment is from the imams' knowledge, for they (the imams) are the religious stars as the Prophet, may God bless him and his family, said: 'My companions are like the stars, whomsoever you emulate, you will be guided.'[17] This is so even when they act in place of the

17. al-Nuʿmān, *Sharḥ al-akhbār*, vol. 2, pp. 248–249. Note that this *ḥadīth* is not listed in A.J. Wensinck, *A Handbook of Early Muhammadan Tradition* (Leiden,

prophets who are like the celestial spheres. Thus, the course of affairs for all created beings as well as their recourse is towards the imams. If we were to mention the parallelism of the religious celestial spheres with the natural celestial spheres, this epistle would be prolonged and go beyond its scope. Therefore, we shall confine ourselves [only] to certain indications in the introduction of this treatise for those who want to pursue [further] research and understand aspects of what we have not mentioned, if God, the Exalted, wills.

[11] Accordingly, we say that the existence of differences and degrees of excellence in all things that comprise the elements, realms of nature and their derivations are the firmest evidence and proof of affirming the imamate and the imams.[18] This is because God, the Exalted, created all things different and disparate in respect to excellence, relating to all genera and species, and thereafter set for each and every genus and species an upper limit (*ghāya*), a summit (*dhurwa*), an end (*nihāya*) and a virtue (*faḍila*), which none other in that category can attain. He either made those genera and species principles in creation, without which the world of humans cannot do, nor their bodily existence and function be complete; or alternatively, He made them [a source of] nourishment, a remedy, an elegance, an adornment and an indispensable tool. He [thus] placed in all things an advantage (*manfaʿa*) that does not exist in anything else. He powerfully endowed in them a capacity which the creation would necessarily need, and which they can neither avoid nor be able to maintain their physical affairs without it. He also put them to a test and made them seek to acquire that which would remove their deficiency (neediness). Thus, when one cannot find the cure of that neediness in its place, one seeks it [elsewhere] or hastens to [another] place where it may be found.

1971). See also Abū ʿAbd Allāh Jaʿfar Ibn al-Haytham, *Kitāb al-munāẓarāt*, ed. and tr. Wilferd Madelung and Paul E. Walker as *The Advent of the Fatimids: A Contemporary Shiʿi Witness* (London, 2000), p. 9 of the Arabic text and p. 70 of the English.

18. See Abu'l-Fawāris, *al-Risāla fi'l-imāma* (ed. and tr. Makarem as *Political Doctrine*, p. 34 of English trans. and p. 18 of Arabic text), where he says that the judgement of reason assumes and testifies that the disparity of mankind is devised wisdom, that is, a wisdom conceived primordially by God.

As long as one remains in the world of one's body, one cannot for a moment dispense with breathing (*tanāsum*) and seeking to benefit from the elements of one's world, its derivations, realms of nature, vegetation and nourishment, [all of] which are a wisdom from God, the Exalted, and a mark of justice from Him. [This is] so these aspects would be witnesses and ephemeral, obligatory symbols (*al-mithālāt al-jabriyyāt*) for the symbolized realities that are religious, eternal and chosen. The benefit of all symbolized realities comprising principles, realms of nature, nourishment and religious remedies are more deserving, more worthy and more powerful than the obligatory symbols. Their need is more than the need of what is compulsory by nature because their benefit[s] go back to the body, while those of the symbolized realities go back to the spirit and the soul. Therefore, the extent of increase in merit of the intellectual symbolized realities over the natural symbols is according to the extent of the spirit's merit over the body. Furthermore, the merit of the symbolized over the symbol is according to the extent of the merit of the everlasting ones over the perishable ones. The merit in each one of them reflects the deficiency in the other. For whoever is deprived of the physical aspects he is in need of, will not experience destruction from that. Even if there be [such a] destruction, it would [only] be that of his body which undoubtedly will [one day] perish and die. In the absence of the symbolized, religious reality, however, there would be destruction of the soul [which] plunges into perpetual punishment. Therefore, if people's struggle in seeking for what the soul needs was similar to their struggle and desire for seeking what the body needs, then no two people would doubt, stray or ascribe human qualities to God, that is, anthropomorphism (*tashbīh*).

[12] We also say that whatever God, the Exalted, has created along this order in the creation and people's need of it, as we mentioned earlier, is an admonition to them for [the sake of] the symbolized religious reality. It is a witness to everyone who seeks testimony for it and an evidence for whoever asks for [such a] proof. It is an insight for all those who see and reflect on it. It is also a proof against those who deny the symbolized, religious reality of the imams and the hierarchies, as well as their knowledge and benefit, while they accept [proofs of] the benefit from natural elements, planets and the celestial spheres.

Indeed God, the Exalted, has created these elements, means and natural causes so powerfully that no one is able to either deny them or seek testimony against them, change them or even alter them, unlike what they have done with the religious law and with what the Prophet had asked them to bear witness to concerning affirmation of the imamate and the imams—its necessity and devotion to the imams, the necessity of obeying them, condemning those who disobey them, and promising reward to those who obey them—[and] in a manner in which they changed the Qur'an and distorted it. [With regard to this] God, the Exalted, has informed us about in His words: '... changing words from their context while they forgot a portion of what We have reminded them of'[19] and just as God, Whose mention is exalted, has also stated: 'Indeed, forgetfulness is only an excess of disbelief ....'[20] That was not forgetfulness on their part, because they forgot the testimony [intentionally], as though they had neither seen nor heard it.

[13] Furthermore, just as the testimony of the outer horizons and the inner selves is compulsory and not chosen, thus becoming impossible for anyone to either alter or substitute it, likewise the Messenger, may God bless him, made the testimony compulsory, without entailing a choice for the witnesses to change, alter or conceal it. He has threatened whomsoever would change or conceal it with a painful punishment. God, the Exalted, ordered [man] to judge on the basis of the testimony of two witnesses, mentioning in His words: 'If one of them falls into error, the other will remind. And the witnesses must not refuse when they are summoned'.[21] By this, He meant that true judgement in religion and in affirming the imamate and the hierarchies is at the hands of two witnesses, one posited by law and the other compelled by nature. If people deny the legally established testimony, then the one bound by nature, namely the horizons and our [own] inner selves reminds, enforces and verifies the conventional witnesses, just as God, the Exalted, says: 'We shall show them our signs on the horizons and within themselves until it becomes manifest to them that it is the

19. Qur'an, 5: 13.

20. Qur'an, 9: 37.

21. Qur'an, 2: 282.

Truth,'[22] and just as the Prophet, when asked, 'Who is the witness of your prophethood,' answered: 'My witness is every stone and every [piece of] clay.'[23] He then pointed to the testimony of the horizons and the souls. Thus, when legal and natural witnesses testify and intellect becomes the criterion in assessing the witnesses without preference or partiality, then truth swiftly becomes manifest.

[14] Now, we shall mention the differences and degrees of excellence in each principle and realm of nature. We shall also show that the ultimate limit and highest summit in each genus and species points to the imam in every age and time. If these genera and species show proof of the imamate and the imams in a different order from the theme of heptads, such as the seven planets being the testimony for the seven imams and other heptads, that does not prevent there being [another] proof given through the peak and perfection in every genus and species for the imam as we have just mentioned.[24]

[15] The sages among the philosophers mention the ten categories and say that one cannot mention or discuss anything except in reference to these ten: substance (*jawhar*), quantity (*kammiyya*), quality (*kayfiyya*), relation (*iḍāfa*), place (*makān*), time (*zamān*), possession (*jidda*), posture (*nusba*), action (*fā'il*) and affection (*maf'ūl*). The ultimate extent of the ten is the substance upon which all others rest and which excels over all others because the [remaining] nine are established from it. Therefore, the substance that they describe is a proof for the permanent, intellectual, luminous and authentic substance through which all souls are illumined and on which all nine religious accidents (*al-a'rāḍ*) depend.[25] Yet, it is one that has no

---

22. Qur'an, 41: 53.

23. Muḥammad Bāqir al-Majlisī, *Biḥār al-anwār* (Tehran, n.d.), vol. 3, p. 333.

24. Al-Naysābūrī is evidently illustrating here how his work is different from the ones previously written which were based on the theme of the heptads.

25. The author is using the ten Aristotelian categories to explain the position of the imam in relation to the hierarchy of the *ḥudūd* in the *da'wa*. Although he mentions nine 'accidents', in the text he speaks only of seven as proofs (*ḥujaj*), adjuncts (*lawāḥiq*), the summoner (*dā'ī*), the wing (*janāḥ*), licensee (*ma'dhūn*) and motivator (*mukallib*) in relation to the imam who is the *jawhar* or substance See paragraph [21] below.

need of any created thing; it draws benefit from nothing or no one in the world, but rather, everything benefits from it and is in need of it. That is the imam, peace be upon him, and all other ranks in the same manner are below him as the nine 'accidents' are in respect to the 'substance'.

[16] We also say that among the four basic constituents (*al-ʿanāṣir)* from which the first composites (*tarākib*) were composed, two are active and two passive. The two active ones are heat and cold while the two passive ones are dryness and humidity. The ultimate and the noblest among them is heat, from which arises luminosity, light, motion, movement and elevation while the other three are established through it. Heat thus has precedence in origin and in existence. No foundation or realm of nature would be complete without it. Likewise, the imam illumines the souls[26] and from him comes intellectual light (*al-nūr al-ʿaqlī*), motion (*al-ḥaraka*) and elevation (*al-ʿulūw*). No principle or religious realm is complete without him.

Additionally, among the celestial spheres, the most lofty and supreme sphere is the outermost one (*falak al-aflāk)* in which they all orbit. Likewise, the imam in his religion is the supreme religious sphere for all other spheres. All heavenly bodies and religious signs of the zodiac function under his command. If someone were to claim that this is rather a symbol for the *qāʾim* (resurrector), given that the highest principle in the world points to the intellect in respect to the four principles,[27] then we would answer that the imam is the *qāʾim* in his time; he is the proclaimer (*nāṭiq*) in his age and time, and he is the one who assumes the position of the *qaʾim*. The imam's position in his realm is that of the Universal Intellect (*ʿaql al-kullī*).

Section Four

[17] We also say that among the four elements (*al-arkān*), the highest and the noblest is fire which is the summit and peak, [at a level]

26. Literally, 'the imam is the light of the souls'.

27. The author obviously means the four elements he referred to in the section above, referring to heat as the ultimate element and comparing it to the imam.

to which no other element or nature can attain.[28] Likewise, the imam, in his age and time, is the highest religious pillar through whom souls are illumined. It is on this basis that Abraham ordered glorification of the fire if what has been reported from him is true, preventing them from extinguishing and putting it out.[29] However, the indication was towards glorifying the imamate, which no one must put out through the injustice of those who falsely claim its position. The fire worshippers fell into confusion not knowing its symbolized reality. God, the Exalted, related about the adversaries and the usurpers of the position of the imamate in His words: 'They would like to extinguish God's light with their mouths, but God will not allow that [to happen] until He perfects His light even if the unbelievers may detest it.'[30]

[18] We also maintain that there are many planets *(kawākib)*, and among them there are differences and disparities in degrees of excellence. Their peak and summit in nobility and merit is the sun through which physical eyesight draws its light, and through which all plants, animals and newborns grow and become perfect. No plant or newborn will grow without the effect of the sun.[31] Like-

28. For al-Nasafī, these four elements are blended to form the four composites, where ether is the fourth element with earth, water and air, whereas al-Rāzī in his *Kitāb al-iṣlāḥ* identifies ether with fire, comparing it to the *qā'im*'s role with reference to *ta'wīl*. See al-Rāzī, *Kitāb al-iṣlāḥ*, ed. H. Minūchihr and M. Muḥaqqiq. In his *A'lām al-nubuwwa*, however, al-Rāzī enumerates ether as the fifth element. See *A'lām al-nubuwwa*, ed. Ṣalāḥ al-Ṣāwy and G. A'wānī (Tehran, 1977), p. 138. See also Shin Nomoto's dissertation, 'Early Isma'ili Thought on Prophecy', pp. 165ff, for a discussion on ether as the fifth element.

29. The narrative on Abraham's trial has been mentioned in several places in the Qur'an: how he was thrown in the blazing furnace (37: 97–98) and how by God's grace he was not harmed (21: 68–69 and 29: 24), although glorifying the fire is not mentioned.

30. Qur'an, 9: 32.

31. Al-Naysābūrī gives the importance of the sun without entering into a discussion of its numerical significance. Al-Nasafī maintains that the divine 'Word' is more perfect in the fourth *nāṭiq* by virtue of his fourth rank, a position shared by the sun, the fourth planet in the cosmology of his day. Al-Rāzī, although recognizing the significance of number four, holds that the seventh *nāṭiq* is superior, being the *qa'im* whose function is *kashf*, unveiling the inner meanings of past sacred laws. See,

wise, the imam is the sun of the religion through which insight is enlightened and souls are illumined from the light of guidance and wisdom, radiating the hearts of God's friends. It is because of this that some people propose to glorify the sun. However, worshippers of the sun [too] fell into confusion as they only understood the symbol, not recognizing the symbolized reality. It is for this reason the Prophet, may God bless him, indicated the rising of the sun from the west which signals the 'rising' of the imam, peace be upon him, in the Maghrib.[32]

If the physical sun were to depart from its usual orbit and its ascent and descent from its centre, for even a blink of an eye, the entire world would be destroyed; which is impossible [as we know], both rationally and naturally. Therefore, the Prophet's statement holds true only on the basis of esoteric interpretation. In fact, his interpretation has proved right as we have witnessed it with our [own] eyes by the grace and favour of God.[33]

[19] We also say that among the twelve signs of the zodiac, four are most glorious and excellent. One of the four is the peak and the summit in nobility. Likewise, among the twelve proofs (*ḥujaj*),[34] the one who is connected to the imamate is the most excellent, the noblest and the most exalted of them all.

---

especially, Shin Nomoto's paper, 'An Ismā'īlī Thinker on the Prophets in Cosmic Correspondence', Translation of the *Kitāb al-Iṣlāḥ* by Abū Ḥātim al-Rāzī I', *Reports of the Keio Institute of Cultural and Linguistic Studies*, 34, (2002), pp. 97–152.

32. This refers to the rise of the Fatimid Imam al-Mahdī who established the Ismaili state in the Maghrib in 297/909. See pp. 19ff of Hamid Haji's *Founding the Fatimid State: The Rise of an Early Islamic Empire* (London, 2006), a translation of al-Qāḍī al-Nu'mān's *Iftitāh al-da'wa*, where he cites all the primary and secondary references on al-Mahdī.

33. This is an indication that the author is a witness to the rule of the Fatimid dynasty and the state.

34. Here the author is referring to the twelve proofs serving in the twelve *jazā'ir* ('islands' or regions of activity) of the Fatimid caliphate and how the one connected to the imam is the noblest. Earlier, in paragraph [4], he refers to imams as proofs.

Section Five

[20] We maintain that the fourth clime (*iqlīm*), which is parallel to the fourth heaven and parallel to the sun, is the most moderate as well as being the most excellent and noblest of all. In the same manner, the imam is the most excellent in the hierarchy as well as the most glorious of them all, being their peak and apex.[35]

[21] We also say that among the melting mineral substances the most excellent is gold. It is that with which people conduct their transactions. It establishes the value of valuables and is not affected by fire or water nor does it get destroyed. Likewise the imam, peace of God be upon him, is the most excellent religious and intellectual substance in his age and time. Through him the transactions of the creation and their well-being, in a worldly and a religious manner, are completed. Each melting substance has its peak in nobility.

Among the precious stones, the best is sapphire, and among all the white, green, yellow and red sapphires, it is the red ruby which is excellent. No other jewel lasts like the ruby, because it keeps its essence and does not get transformed either by fire or water; it [always] retains its purity, radiance and gravity. It obtains traces from its source that no other substances can. Not even other sapphires, emeralds, the Badakshī stone, the carnelian, agate, diamonds, turquoise or jade, are able retain these qualities. So, the crown among the jewels is the red ruby just as the imam is the peak in all creation in his age and time. He is unique among all the ranks of the hierarchy—among the proofs (*ḥujaj*), the adjuncts (*lawāḥiq*), the summoner (*dāʿī*), the wing (*janāḥ*), the licensee (*ma'dhūn*) and the motivator (*mukallib*).[36]

---

35. Following Aristotelian natural philosophy where 'four' is emphasized in the four elements, seasons, humours and directions. For the symbolism of numbers in medieval Islam, see *Rasā'il Ikhwān al-Ṣafā' wa khullān al-wafā'*, ed. B. al-Bustānī (Beirut, 1957), vol. 1, pp. 51–54 and vol. 3, pp. 178–198, as well as Bernard R. Goldstein, 'A Treatise on Number Theory from a Tenth Century Arabic Source,' *Centaurus* 10 (1964), pp. 135–160, reprinted as 'A Theory on Numbers', in S.H. Nasr and M. Aminrazavi, ed., *An Anthology of Philosophy in Persia, Vol. 2, Ismaili Thought in the Classical Age, From Jābir ibn Ḥayyān to Naṣīr al-Dīn Ṭūsī* (London, 2008), pp. 235–256.

36. These are ranks of the *daʿwa* in the author's time, which since the move of the Fatimids to Cairo in al-Muʿizz's time, became even more organized and

The imam is, therefore, the apex whose status, rank and position no one is able to attain in his age or time. From another angle, the seven jewels are proofs for the seven 'proclaimers' and the seven imams. But this aspect on which we rely [degrees of excellence] for proof is more powerful in its position. That is because the natural symbol is present in every age and time, and therefore the symbolized reality ought to be present in every age and time. For, as the stars, the natural elements, the realms of nature and the substances are present, it is necessary too that the ranks of the hierarchy also must exist in every age and time so that they always influence the souls.

[22] We maintain that there are seven grains that provide human beings with food and nourishment. Their peak and summit is wheat, which is the most balanced in nature and nobility and which [helps] build the body. Likewise it is the imam who is the peak and summit, through whom souls benefit and become nourished. From him is their livelihood and their life, and it is also from him that they receive knowledge.

Section Six

[23] As for the fruit-bearing trees, the peak and summit among them is the date palm. It is similar to human beings who have male and female, and who need mating and impregnation like the animals. In addition, everything in the date palm is beneficial and nothing is wasted; its fruit is eaten at all times, be it raw or cooked. Whilst asleep, whoever dreams that he is plucking dates from a date palm, its interpretation is that he is going to benefit from a certain believer. That believer in reality is the imam who is the head of the believers.

[24] We maintain further that among plants, some mild medicines have reached [such a level of] refinement and excellence that they have become antidotes (*tiryāqan*) for those on the verge of death. Among them some cure chronic diseases while others are lower in degree. The peak and summit among them points to the imam; the

---

extensive. It was referred to as the *daʿwa al-ḥādiya,* the rightly-guided summons or awakening. See Daftary, *The Ismāʿīlīs*, 2nd ed., pp. 211–223, on his synthesis of the Fatimid *dawla* and the Ismaili *daʿwa*.

imam and his word become antidotes for the souls, and a means for their healing as well as their relief from death, illnesses, doubts and discords. The like of fatal poison and harmful things that are to be found among medicines is like the opponents who forcefully usurp the position of the imams, peace be upon them. They are the harmful fatal poisons destroying those who listen to them or accompany them or incline towards them if the imam does not reach them with the great antidote that rescues their souls from destruction. Likewise these opponents are similar to the useless and worthless stones. It is for this reason that God, the Exalted, said: '... pebble-covered hell where you will return',[37] and His words '... and guard yourself against the Fire that has been ignited for the people and the stones that have been prepared for the non-believers'.[38]

[25] We also say that among the animals the horse is the best and among the birds the eagle, while the lion takes the first place amongst beasts of prey. The differences in these [various] species of animals with regard to their disparity in strength, their usefulness and the extent of their ability to accept training and in attaining the summit within their own species, point to the fact there is a peak amongst the genus of animals while amongst the human species the summit is the imam, peace of God be upon him.

[26] We further say that some plants are sweet, delicious and appetizing, and people benefit from these. Some are bitter, having neither benefit nor delicacy. Some bear no fruit and have thorns that harm people. The sweet, pleasant ones are like the imams, and they are a symbol of their speech and knowledge that entice the soul and please the eyes. The bitter, putrid and thorny ones symbolize the leaders of the literalists (*ahl al-ẓāhir*). For that reason God, the Exalted, said: '... The example of a good word is like a good tree whose roots are firmly established and whose branches reach the heavens giving its fruit perpetually (in every season) by the permission of its Lord. So God sets forth similitudes for mankind in order that they may reflect. And the similitude of a bad word is like that of a bad tree uprooted from the top of the earth, having no stability.'[39]

37. Qur'an, 21: 98.
38. Qur'an, 2: 24.
39. Qur'an, 14: 24–26.

[27] We also say that some plants are sweet-smelling, their fragrance refreshes people and they heal them of all diseases and illnesses. The summit of [their] goodness and fragrance is a symbol of the imam and his words that refresh and relax people, while the putrid, repellent, offensive ones are an indication of the imams of error whose speech harms the souls, [and] perhaps even destroys them.

[28] We uphold that the gazelle that gives musk and the bees that provide honey, indeed their chief (*yaʿsūb*) is an indication for the imam. It is for that reason the Prophet, may God bless him, said to the Commander of the Faithful [ʿAlī]: 'You are the chief (*yaʿsūb*) of the believers'.[40] And God, the Exalted, said: 'And Your Lord inspired the bee to choose its homes in the mountains and on the trees and on that which they thatch; then eat from all the fruits and follow the path of your Lord skilfully that He has made smooth for you. From within its bellies a drink of varying colours comes forth in which there is healing for mankind ...' [41]

[29] In the same way, we maintain that humankind is the ultimate among animals and in the realms of nature. The advantage in all that preceded the creation of mankind, from the principles, derivatives and realms of nature, goes back to humankind. The merits of the world and that of the animals, plants and other things are contained in humankind; their benefit, glory, value, goodness are all apparent in mankind. If it were not for mankind, the merit of all things would not become apparent and neither would the order of the world. Nothing would be complete, nor would any benefit accrue from it, nor would anything be preserved from it or from the plants and animals. For it is the human being who utilizes water and irrigates the land bringing it under his rational control, tapping it from valleys, rivers and wells. It is also man who tills the land, cultivates it, makes habitations from it, and irrigates plants and fields with water, bringing the land under rational control.

In addition, it is the human being who utilized the wind and air, and it is man who discovered fire by means of flint and also the crossbreeding of animals that was non-existent. Man grafted

---

40. al-Majlisī, *Biḥār al-anwār*, vol. 38. p. 144.

41. Qur'an, 16: 68–69.

different trees in order that he produces fruits from them that were not available [before] in the world. He extracted jewels from minerals and brought beneficial trees, seeds and fruits under his control and rule. He protected the welfare of animals and plants, as well as their produce, and took animals under his command and control. Man is the pinnacle of animals, plants, minerals and [other] realms of nature. Through him, the welfare of animals and whatever came before became perfected and ordered. Likewise, the imam is the pinnacle and summit of all human beings, their quintessence and their perfection. It is through the imam that the affairs of mankind are ordered. As the benefit of all that preceded human beings goes back to mankind, similarly the benefit of all humanity and their quintessence goes back to the imams, peace be upon them. Human beings learn virtues and knowledge from them, and acquire minds and comprehension from them. It is through them that their welfare is guarded in their worldly and religious matters as well as in their life hereafter. They are guided by the imams towards the recognition of the Creator (*maʿrifa al-Ṣāniʿ*), learning the necessity of gratitude to the benefactor and the manner in which gratitude should be expressed. It is through the imams that mankind recognizes the messengers and how they ought to be obeyed.

[30] Just as the benefit of all animals and everything that preceded them goes back to mankind and man, therefore, became their leader, similarly the benefit of all human beings goes back to the imams, who became their leaders, their commanders and prohibiters. If it were not for the imams and the direction and guidance they give to humanity and the protection of their well-being in this life and in the life hereafter, as well as their encouragement to acquire virtues and avoid vices and animal habits, then there would be no difference between beasts and humans; rather animals would be better. If man did not accept training to acquire virtues for his soul and did not learn to stimulate his intellect from the imams, then he would be in a worse position than animals since animals are not as prone to evil as humans are and animals have numerous benefits. If man did not have intellect and religion he would totally be evil and corrupt. It is on this account that God, the Exalted and Glorious, said: 'For the worst of beasts in the sight of God are the deaf and dumb—those who

understand not'.[42] The Exalted also said: 'they are like cattle nay, more misguided, for they are heedless of warning'.[43]

If there were no humanity, there would be no wisdom in the creation of animals and plants as there would be no benefit in them. Similarly, if it were not for the imams, peace be upon them, there would be no wisdom in creating humanity and their superiority would not become manifest. For indeed, human beings have been created for religion and for the acquisition of virtues and knowledge. So learn knowledge and religion from the imams, peace be upon them, for through them, religion is established and perfected. If the excellence of man were not made manifest through religion, then the value of plants and animals would not become known either, and there would be no wisdom in the creation of humanity, plants and animals. Further, if there were no wisdom in their creation, then there would be no wisdom in the creation of all the worlds.

[31] It is then true to say that all the worlds [the entirety of natural worlds] have been created for humanity, and that humanity has been created for the imams, peace be upon them, and to receive religion from them and become perfect through them, manifest their virtues, their organization and their foundation. So, if all the worlds and all creatures were created for the imams, peace be upon them, and all the benefits of the worlds belong to them, and the rest of the creation depends on them and are like children to them, then what they bestow on the creation is by their favour, generosity and mercy. If they [do] hold back anything, they are not obliged to bestow anything, nor are they indebted for appreciation to them. Whoever takes anything from this world and what it contains, without permission and approval of the imam, [that is] then regarded *ḥarām* or forbidden for them, and is [considered] as usurpation. Thus, God said: 'And that which God bestows on the Messenger from the people of the villages, it is for God and His Messenger'.[44] 'Bestowal' (*fay'*) means the return, and it is for that reason the shadow is called *fay'*, because it returns to the same place from which it comes forth. The whole world comes from the

42. Qur'an, 8: 22.
43. Qur'an, 7: 179.
44. Qur'an, 59: 7.

fortune and the property of the imams and whatever returns to their property is [in fact] a *fay'*, a return.

[32] We further say that since plants surpass the earth by a single spirit, that is, the spirit of growth (*rūḥ al-namā'*), the earth becomes subservient to plants that grow on it, drawing strength from it. Animals surpass plants by another additional spirit to the spirit of growth, [that is] the spirit of sensation (*rūḥ al-ḥiss*), and so they subdue the earth, stepping out on it and the plants, as they eat them. Since humans surpass animals with the spirit of articulated speech or reason (*rūḥ al-nuṭq)*, they are in charge of the earth as they build, sow and plant on it, bringing it under their wisdom and control. They also eat the plants and fruits, using what they like and burning what they want. Man also subdues the animals, riding on those he needs, slaughtering [some], milking [others] and shearing their wool, employing them as he wants, and even forcefully, to the dislike of animals.

So when the imam undertakes the charge, he is endowed with additional spirits as well as powers and purity that no ordinary human being possesses. Thus, the pinnacle of purity in the human animal is combined in the imam along with the subtlety and refinement of nature. The peak of the sensuous animals, their choicest parts, the furthest felicity of the celestial spheres, the balance of nature and the subtlest influence of the entire celestial spheres and stars, are so combined that he [the imam] becomes the quintessence of the whole world. Then, the subtleties of the spirit of reason, pure thought and the entire intellectual spirit, unite in the imam and the total sanctified spirit (*rūḥ al-quds*). Man only possesses a portion from this spirit, no more than what he acquires from the imam and [no more than] on whom he chooses to bestow by his grace. Connected to this is the creative spirit (*rūḥ al-ibdā'*), which is the perfect seventh spirit prepared by God for humanity in the world of reward. It is the spirit of Oneness (*rūḥ al-waḥda*).

[33] These are some of the merits that are bestowed on him by God, the Exalted, in addition to what he acquires solely by way of purity, good character, generosity, giving, forbearance, courage and other qualities that cannot be enumerated by the likes of us, in addition to being free from all impurity, shame and defect. So, when God

gathered in the imams these faculties, merits and spirits in addition to what man is endowed with, He subjected all humanity to them [the imams] giving them control over all that preceded mankind, such as animals, plants, earth, minerals, and made all that subservient to the imams, just as humans dominate animals ruling over them because of an additional weak spirit, and just as animals control plants by having one additional weak spirit, and plants dominate the earth by still another additional weak spirit. Furthermore, the great number of spirits [existing] in the imams, peace be upon them, [determines] the extent of their control and dominion over humanity, entitling them to rule over them convincingly in line with the requirements of faculties and spirits. This is in view of what we mentioned earlier concerning human beings. In effect, it is not for humans to remove themselves from the imam's domain and reign, just as it is not for animals to remove themselves from the control of man. Those animals who refuse to be under the control of man, like the beasts of prey with no benefit or merit, are judged by reason and law that it is acceptable to kill, destroy and annihilate them because they refuse to obey human beings and remain under the control of their supremacy.

In the same manner, those who distance themselves from the imam's obedience turn out to be like beasts, wild beasts whose killing, destruction and annihilation becomes lawful. This is on account of their rejection of the imams' rule according to the religious law, intellect, nature and politics.[45]

But whoever obeys the imams, peace be upon them, and submits to their rulings in the world will escape from the sword and punishment in this world, and live in peace, well-being and justice. It is obligatory upon the imam, peace be upon him, by the norm of kingship, nature, policy and law, to protect the well-being of mankind, just as man, when controlling animals, protects their well-being, nourishment and cultivation. Whoever submits to the imams' rule over their own spirits and physical bodies will be saturated with knowledge and wisdom invigorating them and allowing them to

---

45. See Daftary, *The Ismāʿīlīs*, 2nd ed., pp. 178–191, where he describes other serious revolts including that of Abū Rakwa Walīd b. Hishām who claimed pedigree from the Umayyads of Spain.

compete among other people, so that they will live in the tranquillity of knowledge [and enjoy] its fragrance. They will come out of this abode of works to the abode of recompense, in an upright form, fully prepared to accept the recompense and eternal life.

Whoever submits to their rule physically but not spiritually will fall into the torture of ignorance, perplexity, doubt, disagreement and regret, and will return to the abode of recompense with a crooked form, unprepared to accept recompense and will remain in torture or punishment.

[34] We further say that human beings, at all times and in all moments look after the well-being of animals, protecting them from whatever harms them and leading them to what benefits them. Man protects their watering and grazing places as well as their time of reproduction and their bearing of offsprings, protecting them from any means of destruction and from places that would harm their eating and drinking. Many times the cattle covet that which harms them, but man prevents this, protecting their well-being, even if it be against the will of the animals.

Likewise the imam, peace be upon him, protects the outcome of human affairs, their well-being, all their conditions, means, transactions and their hidden interests out of compassion for them. If it were not for the imam, man would have no orderliness in his worldly affairs nor would he have [any] safety or escape from harm from those stronger than him, nor would he have security from disputes or from punishment in the hereafter. Further, man tolerates pain from animals, having patience with their bad behaviour in expectation of their improvement, and because judgement of wisdom requires that he who has knowledge is not allowed to destroy, harm or annihilate any living creature without good reason, but rather, he is obliged to save them from destruction. Similarly, wisdom dictates that property must be protected and prevented against destruction, and must not be excluded from human use. Likewise the imam, peace be upon him, tolerates the bad conduct of people and bears pain and hardship from them since rules of sovereignty and wisdom of judgement deem it necessary to guide the ignorant and protect their welfare, preventing them from perdition and annihilation in the hope that they will eventually revert to good conduct and achieve salvation. The imam does not look at their bad manners owing to their ignorance, nor at their lack of obedience, rather does he look at them with an eye of mercy.

[35] We also say that man tolerates pain and hardship from his young children and prays for them in the hope that they will realize their human potential and be rightly guided. In the same manner the imam, peace be upon him, tolerates pain and hardship from humans out of mercy and compassion, like the compassion of parents for their children. He spends on them in worldly and religious matters, hoping that they would be rightly guided and saved.

[36] We say further that the teacher tolerates hardship on account of young boys and coerces them to learn the sciences and proper behaviour, while the child hates that, disliking the teacher and choosing play and laziness. The teacher cares about the child and tolerates that from him, knowing that if the child were to know what benefit he will achieve he would not hate the teacher. He also knows that when the boy reaches the age of maturity, he will realize the benefit of that and gain pleasure, regretting his [former] shortcomings and disobedience to the teacher. Likewise the imam, peace be upon him, pushes mankind to their own worldly and religious good while they dislike that, objecting to the way in which he deals with them. Eventually, when the benefit in that dawns upon them, they regret their disobedience.

[37] We also say that since man is created out of various opposing natures, he is not free of natural sickness, illness and diseases. The influence of time, place, celestial spheres and stars, the effects of nourishment and other opposing elements in nature, over-indulgence, lack of eating, exhaustion, sexual intercourse and other reasons, [all] influence illness and diseases. Yet people were ignorant of medicine. If they had remained uninformed and ignorant despite the multitude of these illnesses, most people would have died and perished, causing destruction of the world. But God, the Exalted, created cures in the face of each illness and inspired prophets and imams, peace be upon them, so that they realized the advantage of medicines, recognizing the poisons and illnesses. They taught mankind, opening up for them the method of medicine so that they began to build upon that foundation and improved it through experience and practice, just as they made progress in all trades, crafts and sciences such as engineering,

agriculture, navigation and others until there arose among mankind physicians to treat people, collecting medicines from far and distant lands. They struggled in that area, some for its profit and some for the welfare of mankind, treating people at times with good, sweet things and at others with hot and bitter things. Perhaps the patient hates the bitter and foul smelling thing that cures him, yet the physician makes him drink it, willingly or unwillingly, assuring him of the goodness of its result, warning and frightening him of death if he did not do so, or cajoling him to bear the hardship. At times, he prevents the patient from eating and drinking while the patient longs for it. But the doctor orders him to refrain from eating that which he likes and which was agreeable for him when he was healthy. He may make him drink what is hard on him and affects his weakness, while he is in danger of death. If he fails to cure him with medication, he orders for him splitting, slitting the wound, cauterization or amputation of some limbs in the hope of saving others.

One who is intelligent will bear with that, as he becomes convinced [of the result] and knows that the doctor is more knowledgeable than him with regard to his well-being, and that he is a trustworthy guarantor who only wants his welfare and recovery. But if he is not intelligent, he will hate the doctor, detesting him while the doctor shows human understanding when he sees a man of cold constitution with an illness. If he does not treat him he would be dead, and so owing to his kindness and compassion he straps the patient, forcing him to drink [the medicine]. Perhaps the patient abuses him, getting agitated and intending to beat him up, but the doctor tolerates him out of compassion realizing that if he knew and was intelligent enough he would not resist his cure. The doctor does not get distracted by requiting his bad behaviour but rather is kind to him and treats him until he recovers his health.

[38] In the same manner, when religious diseases increase due to disputes among people and because of their arbitrary desires, inclinations towards leisure, comfort and disclosures, innovation, aspirations, different doctrines, conflicting statements, diverse opinions, the lower self [inciting men to evil], while the night is dark and the path is obscure, and people are ignorant of the medicine of the souls and its cure and the protection of its health and

of harmful conditions and things from which they need to protect themselves, ignorant of the ways and the religious paths, [then] humanity needs a guide and a physician to treat their illnesses and show them their right actions, saving their spirits with gentleness, compassion, advice, affection, toleration and cajoling [people] many times more than the toleration and compassion of the medical doctors. There must be no greed in their treatment, or drawing of any benefit, averting any harm. These guides must be most reliable and trustworthy for the souls and religions, more than the reliability of general physicians of the body, being more expert, experienced and knowledgeable.

[39] For indeed, the risk and danger in the treatment of the soul are more than those of treating the body, for mistakes in it can be more severe. The requirement of this is intellectually inevitable just as the requirement of a medical doctor is compulsory and inevitable. This knowledgeable, compassionate doctor for the souls is the imam, peace be upon him, in all ages and times. If it were not for the mercy, compassion and kindness of the imams, peace be upon them, towards the creation, they would perish in their worldly and religious affairs, [both] in this life and the life hereafter. They, peace be upon them, treat the created beings with subtle kindness, tolerance and gentleness. They do not look at their deficiency in obedience nor at their bad manners nor at their evil actions, but they look at them with an eye of mercy, endeavouring to protect their health and cure their illnesses at times by means of a balanced and delicate diet, in order to protect their [spiritual] health through subtle sciences that strengthen the soul and at other times by discontinuing the nourishment so that it is neither nauseous nor heavy. At other times, they force them to drink a bitter, foul smelling medicine so as to remove the bad germs (*al-kaymūsāt*). Still at other times, they order them to go on a diet until they become extremely weak, cheering them and warning them, just as the Commander of the Faithful [al-Ḥākim] is doing with these people, while they in all circumstances desire corruption, and even though he does not see any good in them, he is still patient with the pain they have caused. We pray that he allows us to be among those who benefit from the treatment of the imam of the time, peace be upon him, and not allow us to be among those who require burning

or amputation of limbs by his turning away from us. If it were not for the mercy of the imams, there would not remain a single person on the face of the earth just as God has said: 'If God took humanity to task for what they deserve, He would not leave a [single] living creature on the surface of the earth ...'[46]

[40] We also say that wise men and men of insight, in building the world, consider it to be [similar to] actions of God in His creation of the world, its environment and in preserving human welfare. When they see a good fertile land, they know that it will accept the planting of seeds and the growth of plants. [When they] see water in distant deep valleys or underground, they struggle to bring it forth from those valleys and from under the ground by digging canals and wells, reverting water to those lands. They do not see any wisdom in leaving these good fertile lands unused and wasted or leaving [aside] the water unutilized, out of compassion for the creatures, as well as for safeguarding their welfare and the environment of the world.

Likewise when the imams, peace be upon them, see people ready to accept the seed of wisdom and knowledge, although being very far from being able to receive it, the imams put great effort in digging canals through preparatory religious exercises on many an occasion. People would be perhaps unaware of the reason for that religious exercise until they realize its wisdom and become prepared and able to accept it. Perhaps, when the imams are unable to make them reach that level by exercise, they place the wisdom in many dense symbols, either in words or actions so that people can accept these symbols and gradually arrive at their meaning, and [the imams] elevate them to that level of understanding.

[41] In this manner, it is requisite to believe in the supreme leadership or the imamate of the imam of the time, and know that he is the head of the world and the vicegerent of God over His creation, and not to object to any of imams' commands, prohibitions, actions and teachings, and to know, in general, that all of that is wisdom and welfare for the creation. The correct aspect of that may be problematic for the believer at times. In the end, its benefits will become clear to him, just as many of the things that were not known before become

46. Qur'an, 35: 45.

apparent and clear, and just as in much of the *sharīʿa*, the faithful do not know the purpose of the Legislator and the wisdom in it and disapprove of that. Those whom God provides with the recognition of its meaning know the wisdom in it, just as many of those who see things in the world whose wisdom they do not understand, think that there is no benefit in it or in its creation, realize later that there is wisdom in it, which they are unable to deny.

There are numerous things whose creation they [people] see as harmful and destructive, having no wisdom in it or any benefit, but when they realize its wisdom they become calm and content from their protest. Whoever recognizes the Wise One (*al-Ḥakīm*) and acknowledges that He is wise, it is inevitable that he knows and acknowledges that everything the Wise One does is [full of] wisdom and that He would not do anything that has no wisdom and that He would not command or prohibit or say anything except out of wisdom. Futile action is not permissible for the Wise One; if it were permissible for the Wise One to do, say, command or forbid anything that has no wisdom, then that would be a vain act which is not permissible for the Wise One. Whoever does anything whose doing or not doing is the same will be foolish and depart from the domain of wisdom.

[42] Further, if it is not permissible for the Wise One to perform an action whose existence or non-existence would be the same, how is it then possible for the imam to perform an action while wisdom is in another or in its opposite or that the welfare is in something other than it, while he, the imam, is absolutely wise and whose bestowal of wisdom on any one of his servants makes them wise? Whoever performs an action without wisdom and goodness, his action is corrupt and futile, and may God save us from those who believe that of the imam of the time. [This would then mean that] the individual has distanced himself from wisdom and if he departs from wisdom, he has [then] departed from the domain of his imamate, and that is departure from the faith, may God protect us and all believers from any [such] doubt, idea or belief as this. May He bestow upon us contentment and unquestioning submission (*taslīm*).

[43] We also say that the freely-grazing livestock who have their own benefits and excellence must inevitably have a shepherd to tend them, look after and protect them, and choose their feeding and

drinking places, safeguarding them from thieves and beasts. If it were not for the fact that there was someone to undertake that, they would perish, being unable to manage their affairs for themselves, nor be able to defend themselves against beasts of prey, nor manage their affairs for their own good and well-being.

So, likewise, people are like sheep; if there is no shepherd to protect them, they would perish. The imam is their shepherd safeguarding their worldly and religious affairs and preventing them from worldly and religious enemies. If they were to relinquish that [role], not even two [people] would remain, nor would a single individual escape from punishment. It is in this manner that people in the countries are called subjects (*raʿīya*), because they are under the custody of their shepherd, while the shepherd in reality is the imam, the other claimants being wolves devouring the cattle.

[44] We maintain that the example of the world is that of the [human] body. If the body were to have no head, it would be a decayed cadaver of no use. Similarly, if there were no head, leader or master (*sāʾis*) in the world, guiding the worldly and religious affairs, people would become beasts devouring each other. The world would not exist even for a single day and there would be no wisdom in the creation of the world. The imam is [indeed] the head of world, its leader and master.

[45] Further, we say that there are disparities (*tafāwut*) and differences in degrees of excellence (*tafāḍul*) in the organs of the body; the foremost and the best among them is the head. It is in the head that the face [is situated and] by which each human being is recognized and distinguished from others. Among the internal organs, the best one is the brain, which is their chief, being the source of the intellect. So, likewise, the imam has a position in the world similar to the head and in relation to the organs, similar to the brain. Around him revolve all affairs of the creation just as all actions pertaining to the body revolve around the brain. Amongst the faculties in man and the spirits, the best is the intellect, and the imam is the Universal Intellect (*ʿaql al-kullī*) in the world from and in whom all people of the world become united.

[46] As we mentioned earlier, leadership in nature is present in everything. It is present in animals and in birds, such as the stallion protecting and disciplining the females. Thus the rooster protects

its fowl, disciplining it. Every genus protects its young and children according to its capacity and defends its female, the weak among the genus as well as the female and the young ones according to their need for benefit and learning from those above. The crane obeys its leader and the bee obeys its chief.

[47] Indeed God, the Exalted, created the world and made the creatures as we mentioned earlier to a certain extent, according to this classification, disparity and difference in degrees of excellence, having more or less strength, nobility or inferiority, so that they would know that in each species and genus there is a peak, summit and chief in nobility and merit. Likewise, it is necessary that the whole of mankind also have a peak and summit in nobility and merit that will be their leader and guide in the world. It has thus been shown that headship and leadership is necessary in nature and creation as well as within natural disposition and intuition, and that those who deny the revelation and religion are not able to deny the leadership, headship and authority of the world, either rationally or in witnessing it with [their own eyes] as it is obligatory and necessary. It is, therefore, mandatory that that leader should be the best among them all, the most noble, the most perfect, the most knowledgeable and the most pure according to the arguments that we have mentioned [earlier] from creation and nature, and that the foremost is the imam in everything as well as the chief and the head. The name 'supreme leader' (*al-imām)* cannot be placed on the one who is led (*al-ma'mūm)* nor the name 'the excellent' (*al-fāḍil)* on the 'one preferred' (*al-mafḍūl*), nor the name 'one who supersedes' (*al-sābiq)* on 'one who is preceded' (*al-masbūq).* Moreover, people from all communities and religions, as well as philosophers, atheists and those who deny God all attributes, affirm that the leader of the world ought to be one who is the best among them, the most perfect in merit, and the most knowledgeable of all the people. There is no leader in the world of this description except for the imams, peace be upon them.

[48] We also say that the philosophers divided politics or authority (*siyāsa*) into three categories: the authority of the individual (*siyāsat al-khāṣṣa*), the authority of the family (*siyāsat al-ḥāmma*) and

the authority of the general (*siyāsat al-ʿāmma*).[47] The authority of the special is the governance of the individual himself and the authority of the family is the governance by a man of his family and dependents, while the authority of the general is governance of managing cities and provinces. The governance of the individual himself must be such that he stops his self from all vices, bad traits, bestial habits and blameworthy lusts, and that he governs his own self with the governance of a resolute person, his own self against his own self. Thus he punishes his soul when it errs through reproach and repentance, and rewards it when it does well by praise, happiness and by being consistent in doing that. The governance of one's own family is that the individual manages his own household and his dependents by protecting their welfare, encouraging them to acquire virtues and pleasing character, punishing those who err by reprimanding and [through] other such ways, and rewarding those who do good by praise and such other ways.

[49] The governance of generality is by man governing cities, protecting the welfare of their livelihood and preventing them from reprehensible morals and bad deeds. He protects all their positions and punishes those who err by reprimanding, while rewarding those who do well by praising, protecting and governing the affairs of their religion and the hereafter. This is what they call politics or authority, which is found neither in the world nor among those who [falsely] claim the imamate, nor among the rulers, and nor among their scholars. This attribute is not to be found anywhere except in the imams from the family of Muḥammad, may God bless them, and there is no one in the world who is able to undertake this responsibility except them.

The philosophers agree that he who does not undertake the governance of his own self should not have the governance of managing his family. He who does not have a good management of his own family does not deserve the name governance of the generality, in any way. [But] the literalists (*ahl al-ẓāhir*) and their rulers and

47. These qualities are also mentioned by the author in his other work, *al-Risāla al-mūjaza*, which he composed for the etiquette of *dāʿī*s working for the Fatimid imams. See also Klemm's book on al-Mu'ayyad fī'l-Dīn al-Shīrāzī entitled *Memoirs of a Mission*.

scholars do not have this qualification. Those who sat in place of the imams and called themselves by their names can not govern themselves, or their families, or the people; they are those whom we see today engaged in amusement, moral depravity and corruption. The qualification with which the philosophers describe the political leader is not held by any of their rulers. It is perhaps clear that the author of this classification aimed at encouraging obedience to the imam, for he described the imam by the attribute of the ruler so that they would look for a ruler with this qualification and description.[48] Whoever does not have this description would not be accepted until they find the true imam.

[50] We also say that since people are ignorant at the time of their birth, having no knowledge, and as knowledge does not come to them from nature, nor does speech, [therefore] they need teaching. The proof that knowledge does not come forth from nature is that if knowledge did come from nature, then people would naturally be scholars and be able to speak naturally, just like the braying of donkeys and the barking of dogs, for it is obvious that they need no teaching for that. There is also no difference between the braying of donkeys and the barking of dogs in [different parts of the world such as] Hind, Sind, Rūm [Anatolia] and in the land of the Arabs.

Further, if speech and knowledge came naturally, then, as mentioned earlier, it would certainly mean that people would need no teaching for that. People would be equal in that respect with no difference between one another, [just] as mentioned earlier regarding the braying of donkeys being no different in different places. People, [therefore], do need teaching, one learning from the other until they reach the one who has had no teaching from anyone but who received it through inspiration, not through teaching. This deficiency in people and their need for teaching necessitates a teacher, which in turn necessitates an ultimate end for the teachers, that is, the prophet and the imam, peace be upon them. That is among the most cogent

48. It is fairly certain that al-Naysābūrī was referring to an excerpt in al-Fārābī's *Taḥṣīl al-saʿāda*, ed. Jaʿfar Āl Yāsin, pp. 92–93; see Muhsin Mahdi's English translation, *Alfarabi's Philosophy of Plato and Aristotle*, pp. 46–47, where there is a description of the imam, philosopher and legislator as a single entity.

or convincing proofs for the confirmation of the imamate and the messengership.[49]

[51] We also say that God, the Exalted, created human beings deficient and ignorant in order to make them accept knowledge and wisdom. If He had left them on their own there would be no obligation upon them and there would be no work, reward or punishment and there would have been no wisdom in creating them. Thus, when God inspired prophets and imams giving them wisdom and knowledge, they [in turn] informed mankind, explaining to them their guidance and their path to the Truth, imposing obligations, commands and prohibitions upon them.

Further, if it were not for the imams, humanity would not be responsible and there would be no guarantor or proof over them. Therefore, the imams are God's proofs unto His creation at all times from the very beginning of their responsibility as well as when they fall into disagreement. If mankind fell into sectarian disagreement, arguing with one another by adducing a verse of the Qur'an, a tradition or analogical reasoning, then there would be no proof established for any of them against the other. If there were no imam in the world to save them from disagreement, confusion or perplexity and guiding them to the Truth, there would be no proof from God against the creatures, but indeed the proof would be from the creatures against God. For they would say: 'We have not found anyone to guide us to the truth from falsehood.' Therefore, through the imam the proof of God is established unto the people, just as God, the Exalted, said: 'Say, to God belongs the most apparent proof.'[50]

[52] We also say concerning the rules and regulations that are attributed to the sages, that the sages in reality are the imams, peace be upon them. From them people acquired the principles of all disciplines of knowledge and wisdom such as arithmetic and geometry. There is a purpose for each one of them and an end which points to the imam. The end among the geometric shapes such as squares, triangles, arcs and all other shapes is the circle. The circle is the best

49. This argument of the author illustrates the need for the imam as a supreme teacher against those who asserted in that milieu that reason alone was sufficient as a basis for true knowledge.

50. Qur'an, 6: 149.

and most perfect of them all. It is the foundation of all shapes from which it is possible to form the square, the triangle and the arc.

When the circle is divided, a square emerges and arcs remain on the edges. If we take the horizontal and the vertical lines, there will be four triangles; all other shapes are derived from the circle and all shapes are contained within it. The position of shapes is similar to the world and the creation. Among the shapes, the circle is made a proof and evidence for the imam, who is the circle of the religion (*dāʾirat al-dīn*), and all the *ḥudūd* (ranks of the hierarchy) are contained within his command and prohibition while they all benefit from him. The circle is in no need of any shape, while all other shapes need it, just as the imam is in no need of other ranks in the hierarchy in his age and time, whereas [all] the ranks need him; he encompasses them all.

[53] We also say that the origin and cause of numbers is the number one. It is the most perfect of numbers, being independent of the number two and what is above, up to a thousand. The thousand and what is below need the number one.[51] The imam is the one who is unique in his age and time; all ranks of the hierarchy need him while he is independent of everyone. If some people think of the number one as an indication of the Creator of the creatures, then this assumption is wrong because the number one is the cause of mathematics and the foundation of numbers, while the number two is one plus one and similarly the three. But the one is indeed the imam in his rank and position, being unique. No one else among the creatures in his age and time share his position.

[54] We also say that the dot, which the mathematicians mention has no parts to it [and] is the origin of the line, its surface and the body, is an indication for the imam whose rank or status no one can attain and who cannot be truly recognized. No one can describe his attributes properly; rather they attest their own weakness.

[55] Further, we say that among all the days Saturday is the most

51. See Abū Yaʿqūb Isḥāq al-Sijistānī, *Kitāb al-yanābīʿ*, tr. Paul E. Walker in his *The Wellsprings of Wisdom: A Study of al-Sijistānī's* Kitāb al-yanābīʿ (Salt Lake City, UT, 1994), p. 55, where he designates the number one as the Intellect, using the same argument, that every number is only a single number, even though multiplicity exists within it.

important and amongst all the months, Ramaḍān is the best. Within the hours, there is one hour in which the supplication (*du'ā'*) is answered. Every genus and species in the world, be it created or posited certainly has a peak and a summit in nobility and merit, which none can attain. That points to the imam as we mentioned earlier. If we were to mention everything that should be entered in this chapter, this treatise would go beyond its limit. What we have mentioned should suffice for those who contemplate, and it will be possible for him to make analogical deductions from the principles and branches we have mentioned. However, we shall mention, by adducing evidence [aspects] from the obligatory religious duties *(farā'iḍ)* and their structure, some points in brevity (*nukatan 'alā al-ikhtiṣār*).

[56] We also say that in the ritual prayer and its arrangement, its prescribed standing and direction of the *qibla*, and in the standing of the imam [prayer leader] in front of [all] the rows, are a powerful indication for affirming the imamate. That is because the Prophet may God bless him, first ordered [the Muslims] to face the *qibla*. The *qibla* is derived from *qabāla*, which means 'face to face' and whoever faces it, points his face directly to it, and that is the imam. It is said that to be before (*amāma*) something means [being] in front of it and, [therefore], preceding it.[52] That is the opposite of back, behind and after. The word *imām* derives from one meaning and the imam of the prayer is thus called an imam for this reason because he precedes the worshippers. The indication to the *qibla* is an indication for the imam, and [the Prophet] commanded people to follow and obey him in all [forms] of worship and to accept his direction. When a man faces what is in front of him during prayers, he is facing the *qibla* with respect to the imam in all his worship and obedience to him. Then, if an individual's prayer is with his imam—as the Prophet mentioned that the congregational prayer is

---

52. The word *imām* is derived from the root *amma-ya'ummu*, to lead the way or to be led by one's example. It is the same root from which the words *umm* (mother) and *umma* (community) are derived in Arabic. See Muḥammad b. al-Mukarram Ibn Manẓūr, *Lisān al-'Arab* (Beirut, 1955–1957); al-Zābidī, *Tāj al-'arūs* (Cairo, 1306–1307/1888–1889); E.W. Lane, *An Arabic-English Lexicon* (Cambridge, 1984); and A.R. Lalani, 'Imām-imāma', in *The Qur'ān: An Encyclopaedia*, ed. Oliver Leaman (London and New York, 2006), pp. 289–294.

equal to twenty-seven prayers said by an individual on his own—its merit is because it is with the imam while he is facing him, following him and being led by him in intention and action. That is an indication that the entire [aspect of] obedience is being led by the supreme imam (*al-imam al-aʿẓam*)—guided, followed and led by him so that 'obedience' has excellence. Then the Prophet, may God bless him, ordered them to align in rows, so that there was no difference [between anyone] in their arising; this is an indication that it is not permissible for the hearts of those who are led and guided by the imam to be different, and nor should this be the case in their actions or their speech.

[57] The Prophet, may God bless him, ordered them to follow the imam of the prayers, even if the recitation, arising or prostration became prolonged and not to go against him in gestures or in intention. This was the case even when the worshipper agrees [only] with the imam's action and not his intention, his prayer would [still] not be accepted. If one who is led is negligent, the imam removes his negligence. It is evident from all this that if the obedience of the partial (*juzʾī*) imam, who is not an absolute imam, is made obligatory, [and] the reward of that worship is increased, then how about the obedience of the supreme (*aʿẓam*) imam who is an imam in all revealed law (*sharīʿa*) and esoteric interpretation (*taʾwīl*)? Further, if it is not permissible to oppose the imam in any of the prayer actions, then how can it be permissible to oppose the supreme imam in his commands and prohibitions in the life of a believer? He [the believer] remains ever [under the patronage] of the *daʿwa* in the prayer as long as he is included in the allegiance (*walāya*) of the imam. If he opposes him in an action, intention or in decision, he will indeed have anulled his prayers and departed from the norm of the worshipper, just as when the worshipper resolves to oppose the imam, his prayer, bowing, prostration, standing and sitting are worthless, and his action is futile and he must restart the prayer. Then how about the obedience to the supreme imam, which God has made absolutely obligatory? The Prophet has said: 'The imam is the one responsible [for those who follow him]',[53] and it certainly does not mean the imam of the

53. This has been cited in Lane's *Lexicon* under *dh-m-n* in a fuller version

prayer, for he requires someone who can vouch for him. Indeed, the indication is to the supreme imam, peace be upon him, who guarantees the purification of those led by him from doubt, suspicion, confusion, forgetfulness, and guarantees his salvation as long as he is guided by him, following him. The Prophet indicated the position of the imam preceding everyone and commanded them not to compete with the imam in the recitation of the Qur'an, and he said: 'When he prostrates you should prostrate, when he bows you bow and when he recites you listen, and when he says the salutations (*taslīm)* then you should say it too.'

[58] All these are indications for the obedience to the imams, peace be upon them, and for their glorification in all matters, and the permanence of their position in their time, the necessity of obeying them, and the submission (*taslīm*) of the command (*al-amr*) when he concludes [his affair] to whomsoever he submits it. Even if there were no proof for the imam and for his obedience in the *sharīʿa* except for in the prayer, that would be sufficient. Thus, the Prophet explained that the imam absolves worshippers from their negligence in prayer, which means that the imam relieves their slips, and seeks forgiveness for them. As God, the Exalted, said: 'If only when they wronged themselves, they had come to you seeking forgiveness of God and the Prophet, they would have surely found God Most Forgiving and Merciful.'[54]

If the imam were to remove forgiveness and acceptance of repentance from this *umma* (community), they would surely perish for they are most in need of forgiveness. Rather, all that remains in effect, in every age and time, for those who come to the imam, is for the imam to seek forgiveness for them, and God will forgive them just as he did for those people.

[59] We also say that the Friday prayer is not acceptable without the sermon (*khuṭba*) [delivered] on the pulpits (*manābir*). People pray

---

although there the reference is to the leader of prayer, which our author seems to refute.

54. Qur'an, 4: 64. The Shiʿa relate this verse to the concept of *shafāʿa* in the doctrine of *imāma*. See A.J. Wensinck [D. Gimaret] '*Shafāʿa*', in *EI2*, vol. 9, pp. 177–179 and Meir M. Bar-Asher, *Scripture and Exegesis in Early Imami Shiism* (Leiden, 1999), pp. 180–189.

behind the imam so that they realize that obedience to the imam is not lifted from any created being anywhere. Furthermore the pilgrimage in its entirety is a proof for the affirmation of the imamate. The pilgrimage is an intention, and the intention must be for a known matter so that when the intention is mentioned with full knowledge (*maʿrifa*) it becomes a known intention that needs no explanation. That is an indication for the intention towards the imam.

The Kaʿba, in some esoteric interpretations, is a proof for the imam. Its being placed in a desert with no civilization around it so that it can only be reached with great difficulty, and its location in a place that has no planting or trees deprived of worldly benefit are such so that the worshippers should know that what is symbolized by it (*mamthūl*) also can be attained only by great effort and difficulty as well as injury from enemies. They should also know that aiming for the imam and seeking him must not be for worldly purpose, greed, pleasure or worldly dignity but visiting the imam must only be out of pure faith. If he faces hardship, tiredness, attacks from enemies, fatigue or other such things, then his heart must not constrict but he must patiently endure. Then he will see and recognize as such in its symbol (*mathal*), which is the pilgrimage. Then its circumambulation, touching or accepting it (*istilām*), the indication of it, the running to it, the throwing of stones, the wearing of white garments (*iḥrām*) and giving up of perfume and sex, all that is an indication for the affirmation of the imamate and obedience to him in all different conditions, seeking guidance and protection of their souls while discarding reprehensible doctrines and corrupt beliefs.

[60] We also say that the most emphatic proof for the necessity of the imamate is in the obligation of alms (*zakāt*), in its religious duties, its safekeeping and in its distribution. That is because God, the Exalted, commanded the Prophet to take almsgiving (*ṣadaqa*) from them when He said: 'Take alms (*ṣadaqa*) from their wealth, purify them and cleanse them through it and pray for them. Your prayers will indeed bring them tranquillity.'[55]

55. Qur'an, 9: 103. Both *zakāt* and *ṣadaqa* are used for alms, although it is *zakāt* that is paired with *ṣalāt* (prayer) in the Qur'an. *Zakāt* is obligatory alms, while *ṣadaqa* is broader and usually refers to voluntary almsgiving. They are often used synonymously.

Then the Prophet explained the obligations of *zakāt*, its amount and how it should be collected. He himself collected it until they knew how it should be given and how it should be collected. He who sat in place of the imams also collected the *zakāt*, claiming that collecting alms belonged to him and arguing against the *umma* with this verse and through the actions of God's Messenger, may God bless him. He waged war against the Banū Ḥanīfa for that reason and killed them.[56] Those who sat in place of the imams after him also collected the alms until this matter reached their leaders who took offence [to this], kept the alms money for themselves and prevented it being collected on behalf of the imam.

Is it any wonder then to see the condition of this community? They affirm that the verse [in question] is abrogating (*nāsikh*) in judgement and recitation, yet it is not abrogated (*mansūkh*) and that the Prophetic *sunna* continues to require collection of alms. How did they make allowance for changing the rule in the verse and of God's command and changing the *sunna* [of the Prophet] and the *sunna* of those whose imamate they claim? The only intention for changing that was their denial of the imams' status and the existence of imamate in the Prophet's family (*ahl al-bayt*), may God bless him and his family. God, the Exalted, had explained in regard to alms (*zakāt*) and the manner of collecting it, the position of the imamate and the imams by forbidding *ṣadaqa* to the Prophet so that they would not accuse him of taking them. Likewise, He forbade them to the Prophet's family so that they would know that the imam among them is the one who takes the position of the Prophet, may God bless him and his family, in collecting the alms, and that they [the imams] are trustworthy in this regard.[57]

[61] If people had been entrusted to discharge the duty of almsgiving and its distribution themselves, God would have commanded them to do so, just as He commanded them with regard to prayer, fasting and other obligatory duties. But He did not order them to distribute the *ṣadaqa*, [instead He] commanded the Prophet,

56. The author is referring to Abū Bakr and the *ridda* wars undertaken during his time. Banū Ḥanīfa was the tribe of Khawla, another wife of ʿAlī and mother of Muḥammad al-Ḥanafiyya.

57. See note below in paragraph [63].

may God bless him, to do so. If it were permissible for the people to do it themselves, then that would have been permissible during the Prophet's time when they were far more steadfast in religion, in their certainty of faith, as well as in having more integrity. How is it [then] that later on they have become trustees of almsgiving? Why is it also permissible for them that the prayer, which is more preferable than almsgiving, is to be behind their imams and such other duties, but [that] it is not acceptable to give their imams alms? Further, why is it that they are trustworthy with regard to shedding of blood and sexual offences and with respect to all other aspects of property and yet not reliable and trustworthy with regard to alms?

If people were truthful regarding what they say about their imams being untrustworthy with regard to alms, then they are not actually imams but embezzlers. If they are embezzlers, it is not permissible to pray behind them or [for them to conduct] any other duties such as *jihād* and pilgrimage or give rulings in respect to sexual offences, shedding of blood and property. If these people are lying in what they say and claim, then their scholars who put forward religious opinions (*fatwā*) in that regard are liars too, since they are those who bear witness to their leadership, and the testimony of liars is not acceptable.

God, the Exalted, also commanded the Prophet, may God bless him and his family, to purify the believers and pray for them when He said: '... purify them and pray for them; your prayers will indeed bring them tranquillity'.[58] Thus, He made purification for them and prayer upon them a means of [their] tranquillity, and the prayer was [compensation] for the alms He took from them.

If He had given compensation for almsgiving to the people present in the time of the Prophet, may God bless him, and had not given it to those who came after them, even though they are more in need of it than those present in the time of the Prophet, may God bless him, then that would [indeed] be injustice against those who came after that age. God is above injustice [with regard] to His worshippers and He, may His name be exalted, does not command an obligation and provide a compensation (*'iwaḍan*) for it in this world or the hereafter, except that He made the compensation in general. Rather, [the

58. Qur'an, 9: 103.

aspect of] purification, prayer, and tranquillity perpetually remain with whosoever comes to the imam and gives alms (*zakāt*) from his property, be it in public or in private. The imam then purifies him and prays for him. If the imam were [in fact] necessary only for this, [then] that would be sufficient. His distribution of alms to those entitled to it is because he knows those to whom it ought to be given and those for whom it is not permissible to be given and he [also] knows when there is no one in a category of people entitled to alms for the portion that ought to be given. The imam [therefore] is the one who protects the treasury of the Muslims, distributing it according to the needs of religion and time.

[62] We also say that *jihād* is one of the principles of religion and that it is only permissible to wage war under the banner of an imam. No command for waging war can be established except from the imam, the reason being that the imam first needs to protect the treasury (*bayt al-māl*) of the Muslims which is under his guarantee, and protect the border towns as well as the Muslim army, and rescue the Muslim prisoners of war from the hands of the infidels by giving ransom. Moreover, it is only permissible to send out an army under a commander appointed by the imam or by someone appointed by the imam. The imam is more knowledgeable of the times of peace and agreement or treaties, and it is he who concludes the treaties. Then when he takes the prisoners of war, he knows whom to forgive, whom to seek ransom for and whom to put to death. He is more knowledgeable about the ways in which to take the land tax (*kharāj*) and money so that it is a means of benefit and support for the Muslims. The imam also knows the rebel and it is also through the imam that a party (*fi'a*) becomes the party of the truth because it is with him. The rebel is the one who departs from the obedience of the imam, and then it is permissible for the imam to wage war and fight, or to make peace and armistice. Al-Shāfiʿī said: 'If it were not for the Commander of the Faithful, ʿAlī b. Abī Ṭālib, peace be upon him, we would not have known how to wage war against rebels nor would we have been able to tell the difference between the rebel and the rightful believers.'[59]

59. al-Shāfiʿī, *Kitāb al-umm*, ed. M. Zuhrī al-Najjār (Beirut, 1393/1974), vol. 4, pp. 223–226.

[63] Thereafter, there is the fifth (*khums*) that God gave specifically to the Prophet's family and to the imams in place of the alms (*ṣadaqa*) which he forbade them.[60] All benefits from alms and *zakāt* as well as their requirement are linked to the imam. Furthermore, there are the *ʿīd* feasts and the month of Ramaḍān, where the imam preserves and accepts the testimony of the witness, and from among the opponents, whether they hold that fasting and breaking of the fast is done by sighting the moon or by the one appointed by the imam. The two feast prayers and the Friday prayer are not acceptable in congregation without a sermon (*khutbā*) from the imam and his presence or by someone whom the imam appoints, even if four [people] in the congregation are reduced to two because of the imam's sermon.

[64] Then the execution of legal punishments (*ḥudūd*): Only the imam or the one whom the imam designates may carry out legal punishments. For example, cutting off hands, flogging, stoning, imprisonment, indemnity for injuries (*ʿarsh al-jirāḥāt*) and judgement concerning them can only be carried out by [orders of] the imam. If these rules were the only proof for the imamate in the Messenger's family, then that would be sufficient. For, the opponents agree that whoever has no authority (*walāya)* cannot be allowed to give judgement on legal punishments. Therefore, if a man sees another killing someone unjustly, it is not up to him to kill that person. And if he were to see someone stealing, it is not for him to cut his hand off, stone him or do other such things. The extent of this goes so far that most people agree that it is not for the slave's owner to carry out legal punishments or to chastise him; only the imam should chastise him and carry out legal punishments.

It is not possible to abolish legal punishments because if they were [to be abolished], people would perish and countries would be ruined. If people were allowed to carry out legal punishments, everyone would intend to kill or hit and then claim that the person had

60. The Prophet and his family are forbidden to benefit from either *zakāt* or *ṣadaqa* as these are collected as a means of purification for the believers. As a compensation, God reserves for the family of the Prophet a fifth (*khums*) of *ghanima* (booty) and *fay'*, property received by Muslims without waging war (Qur'an 8: 41).

killed someone else or stolen money that necessitated him to carry out the legal punishment. Yet how can someone who [himself] requires twenty legal punishments every day rule on legal punishments, and how can he be permitted to carry them out? If he were allowed to do those, then that would certainly be permissible for every oppressor or rebel. It would mean perdition for the people. Rather, when a rebellious party carries out legal punishments and destroys peoples' lives and the imam has power over them, he fines them for whatever damage they caused to the righteous party, preventing the wrongdoers from destroying the people and damaging their property.

Then, they claim that all was done according to a legal rule enjoined upon them. But God, the Exalted, has clarified this in His words: 'Do you command people to do good and forget it yourselves?'[61] God, the Exalted, warned that whoever needs to be commanded to do good and be prevented from evil is not allowed to command people to do good and forbid evil. God has also explained in another verse that 'enjoining good and forbidding evil' (*al-amr bi'l-maʿrūf wa nahy ʿan al-munkar)*, is a duty of the imams, peace be upon them, when He said: 'You are the best community (*umma*) that has been raised for the people. You enjoin good conduct and forbid evil.'[62] They are the equitable leaders (*a'imma al-wasaṭ*) who are witnesses over the people.

How can one command good if he does not practice it himself and how can he forbid evil if he himself loves evil and commits it every day a hundred times? How is it permissible for their imams when they commit the very things that necessitate legal punishment every day, that is, their [acts of] lust and desire? And when they draw close to themselves those who love doing that and who join them in it? How can they forbid such acts while they see them as elegant, victorious, convivial, charming and refined? Whoever does not join them in drinking and debauchery, they will neither draw him near, nor employ him, for he would be disagreeable to them. Is that not a lesson for those who are led by them and an incitement for them to [tread the path of] corruption and debauchery?

61. Qur'an, 2: 44.
62. Qur'an, 3: 110.

[65] We also say: It is agreed that legal judgement between people regarding bloodshed, sexual offences and property is only permissible for he who knows the cases and the legal opinions in their regard, who knows the legal norms, the Qur'anic revelation and its meaning, [including] the abrogating and the abrogated verses (*al-nāsikh wa'l-mansūkh*), the analogical deduction (*qiyās*) in their view, and who fulfills its conditions, such that he is trustworthy in [giving judgements on] bloodshed, property and sexual offences. Does anyone among the usurpers claiming the imamate fulfill these conditions? Rather, all of them need those so-called jurists, who it is claimed, possess knowledge, but who do not have its reality. They give them the frail possessions of this world and appoint them governors of provinces, allowing them to sit in their public sessions. If an incident takes place, they ask [the jurists], and what do you say? So, one will say, 'According to Abū Ḥanīfa, this person should be killed', while the other will say, 'According to al-Shāfi'ī, he should not be killed'. Still another will say, 'According to Mālik, this woman should be divorced', while yet another will say, 'According to Aḥmad b. Ḥanbal, the woman is not forbidden to him'.[63] [The usurpers] gave the leadership of religion to [the jurists] so that they may judge according to their [own] desires and opinions, in order that they would leave the leadership of the world to [the usurpers] and give false testimony for them. Thus, they [the jurists] disgraced themselves in agreeing. I do not know about whom I should marvel—should it be about him who shamelessly claimed the imamate while having no knowledge of religion whatsoever or of its legal norms, so that he needs the like of these scholars? If they were scholars, and the order and judgement were according to their statements, then they would be the imams, not the one who [falsely] claims the imamate, whilst being a mere idol set up having no authority whatsoever, neither benefiting nor harming anyone. Or should I marvel about him who adheres to his leadership and rewards their ignorance and shame? Thus, their imam is like the one who is led, and the one who is led is like their imam.

---

63. Abū Ḥanīfa (d. 150/767), Mālik b. Anas (d. 179/796), al-Shāfi'ī (d. 204/820) and Aḥmad b. Ḥanbal (d. 241/855) are founders of the four major Sunni schools of jurisprudence (*madhāhib*).

[66] If their imams do not have legal judgement and authority (*walāya*) because they have no knowledge and because they do not fulfil its conditions, having neither modesty nor integrity, then most of those who uphold the doctrine of choice (*ikhtiyār*)[64] uphold that if the imam is unjust and immoral [in this manner], then he forfeits the imamate, and in the view of some, ought to be removed. Likewise, if the judge among them were to betray [the people's trust], he should be removed and similarly, the legal guardian should [also] lose his guardianship. Some also say: The community is obliged to remove the imam if he is unjust and immoral. Al-Shāfiʿī said: 'The sinner has no legal guardianship such that if he had a daughter he would have no guardianship and no right to give her in marriage; rather, it is the judge who would give her in marriage while he has no guardianship over his daughter.'[65] And also, according to all [these jurist-imams], the testimony of the sinner is not to be accepted. Thus, by agreement (*ittifāq)* and consensus (*ijmāʿ*), their imams are not among those who can exercise legal reasoning (*ijtihād)* in religion, nor be among those who can give their daughters in marriage, or be among those whose testimony is accepted, and nor be among those allowed to carry out legal punishments.

Indeed, they [usurpers] have been well-known and infamous offenders, and those who remain of them followed their way. How could he who has these attributes be the Commander of the Faithful, the vicegerent (*khalīfa*) of the Lord of the worlds and the imam to whom obedience is obligatory? Moreover, if they do not possess the right of guardianship, legal judgement and testimony, how can those whom they appoint have guardianship, and how can testimony be accepted from those whom they commend? Furthermore, how can their testimony be acceptable when they say that such and such a person is good for judgement, witnessing and guardianship? Is there anything in this world more amazing than those people, the contradiction of their judgements, the principles of their belief (*madhhab)* and their

64. The doctrine of *ikhtiyār* or choice is one which Sunnis maintain in determining the imam while the Shiʿa hold that the imam is appointed by designation (*naṣṣ*), which is hereditary. See chapter 4 of Lalani, *Early Shīʿī Thought*, for al-Bāqir's views on this.

65. al-Shāfiʿī, *Kitāb al-umm*, vol. 4, p. 225.

doctrine? And is there anyone more infamous than their imam and the one led by him?

[67] If we were to mention all the contradictions and disgraces in their principles, we would need to prolong this treatise and go beyond its scope and intention. In what we have said, there is a refutation of their imamate and an explanation that all they have done and are doing is falsehood, injustice and transgression. That is sufficient shamefulness and ignominy for them. If their imamate is false, as we have mentioned, and it is true that the imamate is one of the principles of religion (*uṣūl al-dīn*), and that it is an inevitable necessity and that all revealed laws and norms are linked to the imam, thus the imamate is [then] true of the pure imams from among the progeny of Ṭāhā and Yāsīn,[66] who are protected from corruption and oppression, lying and transgression, and purified of all filth and blame. What we have mentioned by deduction and from the religious law is sufficient.

Now we shall mention the necessity of the imamate on the basis of the past cycles and [the fact] that there has never been a time or period that has been deprived of a true imam to whom obedience is obligatory.

Section Seven

[68] We say that if it were acceptable that there be creatures on earth without there being an imam or caliph, then that should have been acceptable during the time of Adam, peace be upon him, when there were [only] angels. At that time God, the Exalted, said: 'Indeed, I am placing a vicegerent on earth. They said: "Are You going to create one that will corrupt and shed blood on it while we glorify Your praises and regard You holy?" He said: "[Surely], I know what you know not".'[67] God, may He be glorified, clarified in that passage that there would never be a time when the earth is deprived of an imam, even if all the people were impeccable and saintly, so that they would realize

66. Two *sūras* in the Qur'an are named after them, *sūra* 20 *Ṭā Hā* and *sūra* 36 *Yā Sīn*.

67. Qur'an, 2: 30.

how indispensable the imam is when they are ignorant—and most of them are corrupt. God, the Exalted, also made plain in that passage that if it was acceptable for the imam to be chosen (*ikhtiyār)*, then the angels certainly would have been given the choice. He would not have contradicted them because they were immune from inclinations, false desires and cravings for the world and for domination. Since that was not acceptable for them, it is not acceptable for those below them. This meaning is concealed in the verse of God, the Exalted, when He said regarding the rights of the parents: 'Do not even say "fie" to them or tell them off.'[68] Therefore, God has forbidden hitting or abusing them, which is [even] more extreme.

God, the Exalted, has indeed mentioned the story of the past communities and the prophets in order that they should know that the same would happen in the cycle of the Prophet [Muḥammad] as it did in other cycles. The Prophet said: 'My community will experience exactly what happened among the Banū Israel.'[69] He also said: 'You will follow the footsteps of those before you, step by step in an identical manner (*qudhdha bi-qudhdha*), to the extent that if they were to enter the hole of a lizard, you too would enter it.'[70]

[69] In the story of Adam, there is an indication that the imamate and the caliphate are not acceptable by choice or consultation. If that were permissible, then the choice of the angels would have been more appropriate and their consultation would have been more suitable because they were immune from jealousy and rebellion. In it, there is also an indication that it is not for people to say whether such and such person is suitable for the imamate or not, and that they prefer one to the other. God, the Exalted, informed those who did not like Adam about the error of their speech, reproached them and rebuked them, showing them the falsehood of their words. He mentioned this in the Qur'an so that they would learn a lesson from it and

68. Qur'an, 17: 23.

69. See A.J. Wensinck, *Concordance et indices de la tradition musulmane* (Leiden, 1936–1969), vol. 1, p. 95, citing al-Tirmidhī, tradition 18 in section on '*īmān*'.

70. See al-Muslim b. al-Hajjāj, *Ṣaḥīḥ Muslim*, *Kitāb al-ʿilm*, tr., A.H. Siddiqi (Lahore, 1976), vol. 4, p. 1403. I would like to thank Dr Moojan Momen for this reference.

would argue about the imamate or about whomsoever God and His Messenger chose for the imamate as they did. In the appointment of [Adam's] son to the imamate, there is an indication that the world can never be devoid of an imam. All people agree and accept the imams in the period of Adam but deny them in the period of Muḥammad, may God bless him. God, the Almighty and Glorious, has explained in His words: 'Such was our way (*sunna*) in the case of Our messengers whom We sent before you (Muḥammad). And you will not find in Our way any change.'[71] God also said: 'You will certainly not find any change in Our way (*sunna*).'[72] What is meant is the *sunna* of the imamate, not the *sunna* of religious practices such as prayer, fasting and others. For the Prophet, may God bless him, has indeed changed the *sunna* of all the prophets regarding acts of worship (*'ibādāt)* but not the *sunna* of the imamate.

[70] We also say that when Noah invited people to the ark out of compassion, he was fully aware that those who stayed behind would perish and be drowned, by their own choice and by their belief that their welfare would be in something else. The explanation of that is that every people who have been summoned by their prophet and imam to a matter and have abstained from it and denied it, were destroyed for it. The ark was nothing but the imam himself and Noah's invitation of the people was to the imam, just as the Prophet said: 'The likeness of my family (*ahl al-bayt*) among you is like Noah's ark; whoever comes aboard will be saved and whoever remains behind or stays away will be drowned.'[73]

Noah, peace be upon him, appointed his son Shem (Sām) to the legateeship and the imamate by designation (*naṣṣ*) and appointment (*tawqīf*), and thereafter [it continued] one after the other until the time of Abraham, peace be upon him. The [opponents] accept the imams in the cycle of Noah, but denied them in the family of

71. Qur'an, 17: 77.

72. Qur'an, 33: 62.

73. The story of Noah's ark occurs in the Qur'an in several places including 29: 15. References to this tradition in Sunni sources can be found in Wensinck, *Concordance*, under *th-q-l*. Also see al-Qāḍī al-Nu'mān, *Da'ā'im al-Islām*, ed. A.A.A. Fyzee (Cairo, 1951–1961), revised and annotated by Ismail K. Poonawala as *The Pillars of Islam* (New Delhi, 2002–2004), vol. 1, pp. 37 and 100.

Muḥammad, even though the *sunna* has not been replaced or altered and the people cannot do without an imam.

[71] When Abraham, peace be upon him, appeared he ordered the glorification of the fire. If what has been said about this is true, then that was an indication for the glorification of the light of the imamate (*nūr al-imāma*), as we have already mentioned.[74] Then Abraham and Ismāʿīl, peace be upon them, built the House (the Kaʿba), commanding the people to glorify it, this being an indication that the imamate was to be in Abraham's house and progeny. He urged the people to glorify the imamate and venerate and obey [the imams of] his family.

[72] When Moses, peace be upon him, arose, he ordered the people to face toward Jerusalem. Since Moses had no children or family in whom the imamate could continue, he pointed to Jerusalem (*bayt al-muqaddas*) saying: 'Whoever possesses the sanctified spirit among the Banū Israel is your imam and your direction of prayer (*qiblatakum*).' Then Jesus, peace be upon him, appeared. He did not have a family or children, and it is reported that he ordered people to face toward the east. If this is true, then his command to face toward the east meant turning towards the place where the light of the imamate rises. This means that whoever radiates that light shall be your imam and your direction of prayer.

When the Prophet [Muḥammad], the seal of the prophets, may God bless him and his family, appeared, he ordered people to turn their faces from Jerusalem to the Kaʿba as the direction of prayer for Muslims. The Kaʿba was built by Abraham and Ismāʿīl, peace be upon them. The Prophet ordered this as an indication that the direction had returned to the house of Abraham, which is the family of Ismāʿīl. This means that the imamate had returned to the children of Ismāʿīl who are the children of the Prophet Muḥammad, may God bless him. He ordered people to glorify the House and perform the pilgrimage to it, which no other prophet had ordered, as an exhortation to the people about the superior excellence of the imams from the family of Muḥammad above all other imams in past cycles. Can there be anyone more iniquitous in the world than this community who accepted the

74. See note on this in paragraph [17] above.

imams from all the prophetic periods, affirming that the world cannot be deprived of an imam, and [affirming] that there was never an imam in the previous cycles by choice (*ikhtiyār*), but [who now] deny the imamate of Muḥammad's family, reject designation (*naṣṣ*) and call for choice? God, the Exalted, also said: 'And your Lord creates whom He wills and chooses what is good for them.'[75] If the imamate were by choice, then every people would choose whom they wanted. The elders have mentioned the discussion of designation and choice. We have stipulated that we shall mention what the elders have not mentioned in the books on affirming the imamate. What we have mentioned is sufficient. We shall [now] establish that the imam must be the most excellent, the most knowledgeable and the noblest [of mankind].

[73] We say that the virtues that God, the Exalted, has mentioned and by which He preferred some people over others consist of three kinds (*ashyā'*):[76] knowledge, *jihād* and piety, as God, the Exalted, said: 'God has preferred those who strive and struggle over those who sit back by a great reward in stages or degrees of rank.'[77] His words also [read]: '[Say to them, O Muḥammad,] "Are those who know and those who do not, equal"[78].' Similarly His words: 'Those who have been given knowledge have degrees of rank,'[79] and also His words: 'The most noble among you in the presence of God is the most pious among you.'[80]

... As for *jihād*, the elite (*khāṣṣ*) as well as the Muslims in general (*'āmm*) know that these men did not wage war for even a single day on their own. The wars fought by the Commander of the Faithful ['Alī] are well known and famous. The only disgrace in the holy war had been their flight from the battle of Ḥunayn when 'Umar failed to obey the order and recommendation of the Prophet to protect the mountain and his incurring the blame of the Muslims, while the Prophet and 'Alī were fighting and killing the enemies until they were routed.[81]

75. Qur'an, 28: 68.
76. lit. 'things'.
77. Qur'an, 4: 95–96.
78. Qur'an, 39: 9.
79. Qur'an, 58: 11.
80. Qur'an, 49: 13.
81. See the battle of Ḥunayn described in *Kitāb al-jihād* in al-Nu'mān,

As for piety (*taqwā*) … where there is no knowledge, there can be no piety, for piety comes through knowledge, when one knows what belongs to him and what [belongs] to others. It has been reported from Muḥammad b. al-Ḥasan, Abū Ḥanīfa's companion, that some God-fearing man (*muḥtasabin*) asked him to compile a book on asceticism. He therefore compiled a book on trading and when asked about it, he replied: 'Whosoever does not master jurisprudence, buying and selling, how could he [understand and] consume lawful things? Whosoever does not consume lawful things has no asceticism.' Therefore, it is correct according to the verses of the Qur'an we have mentioned, that the imamate belonged to the Commander of the Faithful, peace be upon him, because he had precedence (*sābiq*) in virtues, being the most knowledgeable, the most pious, and the one who fought most [in the cause of Islam].

[74] We further say that those people [who ruled] did not claim any excellence, knowledge or piety for themselves. Rather, their companions did this for them. Indeed, Abū Bakr was the first to climb the pulpit and say: 'You have appointed me, although I am not the best amongst you.'[82] If he was telling the truth, then those claiming superior excellence for him are liars; if he was lying in what he said, then a liar cannot be an imam. If they say that he said that out of humility, then we say that there is a [time and] place for humility. The Prophet, may God bless him, himself used to mention his rank and status for which God had singled him out and did not lower himself. That did not amount to arrogance. Thus, he said: 'I am the master of the Arabs, without boasting', 'I am the master of humanity without boasting' and 'I am the most eloquent of the Arabs without boasting.'[83]

Daʿāʾim, tr. Fyzee, rev. Poonawala, *Pillars*, vol. 1, pp. 459 ff. See also Ingrid Mattson, 'Ḥunayn', *Encyclopaedia of the Qurʾān*, vol. 2, p. 466, where further primary and secondary sources are given.

82. These words are cited in a number of sources with some variations. See Abu'l-Fawāris, *Risāla fī'l imāma* ed. and tr. Makarem, *Political Doctrine*, p. 37 of English trans. and p. 23 of Arabic text with an extensive note on pp. 79–80. See also al-Nuʿmān, *Kitāb al-walāya,* in *Daʿāʾim* tr. Fyzee, rev. Poonawala, *Pillars*, vol. 1, p 105, n. 294.

83. This tradition of the Prophet is reported on the authority of ʿAlī and is

The Commander of the Faithful, ʿAlī b. Abī Ṭālib, peace be upon him, said: 'Ask me before you lose me.'[84] He also said: 'If a cushion were to be folded for me to sit on, I would pass judgement on the followers of the Torah according to the Torah, on the followers of the Bible according to the Bible, and on the followers of the *Furqān* (Qur'an) according to the *Furqān*.'[85] Many such examples can be recounted but this does not constitute arrogance or negate humility. The words of Abū Bakr, 'I have been put in charge of you although I am not the best amongst you' are an indication that God and His Messenger had neither given him preference, nor indicated him [as his successor] in ordering him to lead the prayer or anything else. … He [Abū Bakr] confirmed about himself

---

part of a long tradition on the merit of the *āyāt al-kursī*, the famous verse of the throne, Qur'an. 2: 255. See M.M. Ayoub, *The Qur'an and its Interpreters* (Albany, 1984), vol. 1, pp. 247–249, citing al-Faḍl b. al-Ḥasan al-Ṭabarsī (Ṭabrisī), *Majmaʿ al-bayān*, ed. H. al-Rasūlī al-Maḥallātī (Beirut, 1380/1961), vol. 2, p. 299: "ʿAlī also said, "I heard the Apostle of God say, 'O ʿAlī! The master of humankind is Adam, the master of the Arabs is Muḥammad, nor is there pride in this. The master of the Persians is Salmān, the master of the Rūm [Byzantine] is Ṣuhayb [a Christian convert among the Companions of the Prophet], and the master of Abyssinia is Bilāl. The master of the mountains is al-Ṭūr [Mt. Sinai] and the master of trees is al-Sidr [the lote tree]. The master[s] of the months are the sacred months and the master of the days is Friday. The master of all speech is the Qur'an, the master of the Qur'an is *sūrat al-baqarah*, and the master of *al-baqarah* is the throne verse. O ʿAlī, it consists of fifty words, every word containing fifty blessings.'""

84. This is a very popular *ḥadīth* of ʿAlī and is reported in different versions by various scholars; see al-Qāḍī al-Nuʿmān, *Sharḥ al-akhbār*, ed. S.M. Ḥusaynī al-Jalālī, 2nd ed. (Qumm, 1414/1993), p. 91. Al-Ḥasan b. Muḥammad al-Mayhadhī relates its longer version in his letter to the people of Rayy. See *Risāla ila jamāʿat ahl al-Rayy* in *Majmūʿat al-tarbiya*, vol. 2, fol. 177r, MS I and p. 349 MS A. Also, see *Nahj al-balāgha*, vol. 6, p. 174, cited in Makarem, *Political Doctrine*, p. 22 in Arabic and p. 37, n. 85 in English.

85. Abū Jaʿfar Muḥammad al-Saffār, *Baṣā'ir al-darajāt*, ed. Mīrzā M. Kūchabāghī, Tabriz, 1380/1960, pp. 132–135; Ibn Abi'l Ḥadīd, *Sharḥ nahj al-balāgha*, ed. M.A. Ibrāhīm (Cairo, 1961), vol. 12, pp. 196–197; Muḥammad Hādī al-Amīnī, *al-Ghadīr* (Tehran, 1396/1976), vol. 6, pp. 193–194; al-Majlisī, *Biḥār al-anwār*, vol. 35, pp. 391–392. In some sources, this *ḥadīth* is cited together with the one above, that is, 'Ask me before you lose me.' Al-Naysābūrī treats them together. Al-Shahrastānī also does the same in his *Tafsīr al-Shahrastānī*, known as *Mafātīḥ al-asrār wa maṣābīḥ al-abrār*, ed., M. ʿAlī Ādharshab (Tehran, 1376Sh./1997), vol. 1, p. 200.

all that was to be expected of him, and so he said: 'Put me right.' Putting someone right is necessary [only] with regard to monstrous and major sins, since smaller ones can be cancelled by seeking forgiveness ...

[75] When 'Umar ascended the pulpit after Abū Bakr, he said: 'The oath (*bay'a*) to Abū Bakr was a *falta*, a hasty, unconsidered decision, but God has averted its evil from us. Whoever repeats the like of it, kill him.'[86] In saying this, he expounded the falsehood of what the literalists claim regarding Abū Bakr's appointment [by the Prophet] to lead the prayer that it made his imamate obligatory and that this was an indication for his imamate.[87] Moreover, ['Umar's statement] contains a refutation of what they claim in the traditions, such as the saying: 'Follow the two who come after me, Abū Bakr and 'Umar.' ...

[79] Now we shall mention some merits of the lord of the age and time (*walī al-'aṣr wa zamān*), the Commander of the Faithful (al-Ḥākim), although someone like me will never attain the status that would enable him to mention his true merits, just as God, the Exalted, said: 'They have not valued God according to His true value.'[88] But I shall say this according to my little knowledge and ability, and the Commander of the Faithful is the most worthy to accept his servant's excuse; just as when God, the Exalted, with the multitude of His bounties unto His servants, asked them to be grateful for the blessings, and they were unable to give thanks

86. See Ibn Isḥāq, *al-Sīra*, vol. 4, pp. 307–308; al-Balādhūrī, *Ansāb al-ashrāf*, vol. 1, pp. 581, 584 and 590–591; Aḥmad b. Ibn Wāḍīḥ al-Ya'qūbī, *Ta'rīkh*, vol. 2, p. 148, cited in al-Nu'mān, *Da'ā'im*, tr. Fyzee, rev. Poonawala, *Pillars*, vol. 1, p. 105; see also al-Ṭabarī, *The History of al-Ṭabarī*, Vol. IX: *The Last Years of the Prophet*, tr. by Isma'il K. Poonawala (Albany, NY, 1990), pp. 189ff; Abu'l-Fawāris, *Risāla fi'l-imāma*, ed. and tr. Makarem as *Political Doctrine*, p. 37 of English trans. and p. 23 of Arabic text with notes 87 and 88 on p. 80).

87. On the basis of 'Umar's statement, the author is here providing a counter argument to the literalists' view who consider the Prophet's order to have Abū Bakr lead the prayer before his death as an indication of his imamate. See Wilferd Madelung, *The Succession to Muḥammad: A Study of the Early Caliphate* (Cambridge, 1997), pp. 24–26 citing reports from al-Ṭabarī, vol. 1, pp. 1810–1812, and concludes that 'in the eyes of Muḥammad the leadership of the prayer had no significance for the succession.'

88. Qur'an, 6: 91.

equal to the bounties, [but] He forgave them being content with their saying '*al-ḥamdulillah*' (praise be to God).[89] This was a lesson for His creatures, such that whenever gratitude to a benefactor is incumbent on them, and they are unable to express gratitude equal to the bounty, they should do so according to their capacity and should not relinquish giving thanks entirely, because of their inability to give him what he deserves.

We say further that God, the Exalted, made the earth radiant with His light as He has promised and told us in His words: 'And the earth shines by the light of her Lord ...',[90] that is, the earth of the outer reality [shines] through the justice of the Commander of the Faithful, and the earth of the inner meaning [shines] through knowledge and explanation.

[80] We say that as in every species, genus, root, branch and law, there is a peak and summit in nobility, merit, rank, degree and position which nothing else can attain. In the same way, it is incumbent that the imams, peace be upon them, [too] have a peak, summit and an utmost degree which no one else has previously attained. That peak and utmost degree is the Commander of the Faithful ['Alī]. He is the peak of all peaks and the utmost limit over which there is no other limit. Since the wisdom of the world and of the animals and plants in it appeared in the rise of human beings and their welfare became complete through humanity, and the benefit of all of them goes back to mankind and it is through the imams, peace be upon them, that the merits of human beings have become complete and wisdom appears in creation, and the benefit of all human beings goes back to the imams, likewise, through the Commander of the Faithful, all affairs (*umūr*) of the prophets, legatees and imams became complete, their order (*amr*) was organized and perfect wisdom became manifest in their disposition, and in their laws and their esoteric interpretations. He, peace be upon him, is like the head and they are like the body. They are like the body while the Commander of the Faithful is like the spirit. Not [a single] body is complete without the spirit. The Commander of the Faithful is like the heart while [all] others who

89. Qur'an 1: 1.

90. Qur'an 39: 69.

have passed away are like the limbs. It is through the fusion of the spirit and life to the heart that all limbs receive life and recompense. Each nail, hair and limb receives its share of reward, of recompense by means of the heart. This is the sensual knowledge, which is the recompense of the action that occurs from the embryo in its womb (*dār ʿamalihi*)[91] during its stay in the six stages from the sperm to the final creation.

Likewise, it is through the Commander of the Faithful that people gain recompense and acceptance of life in the seventh stage. He, peace be upon him, is the one who awakens the desire in every one to become him, and he is the one through whom God promised creatures the fulfilment of reward on His day. As God said of the Judgement: '... And you will be paid only that which you have earned fairly on the Day of Resurrection. Whoever is removed from the Fire and allowed to enter Paradise, will indeed be triumphant.'[92] God commands the creation to believe in Him and in His Day [of Judgement] when He said: '...They believe in God and the Last Day ...'[93]

[81] Just as the entirety of humankind exists because it is the final realm of nature (*mawālid*) in the world, having accepted all that existed before in the previous realms and exceeding it by things in which other realms had no share, and just as the imams acquired all the merits that existed in human beings, being their peak, summit and quintessence, and they were able to accept what was not in the power of mankind, and the benefit of all those who preceded them reaches the imams, likewise, the Commander of the Faithful, peace be upon him, gathers in himself all the merits of those who preceded him and all their benefit and knowledge comes to him, and he exceeds that many times over. Just as the power and merit of the Prophet existed because he gathered in himself the merits of those in the previous cycles, all their knowledge and more, in the same way, the Commander of the Faithful, peace be upon him, gathers in himself the merits of all the prophets, imams and the sages who preceded him in the previous cycles, and exceeds them

91. lit. 'the abode of his actions.'

92. Qur'an, 3: 185.

93. Qur'an, 3: 114.

in things of which they were incapable. If he did not rise in this position, there would not have been the perfection of wisdom in their rise, peace be upon them. The Commander of the Faithful, peace be upon him, is therefore the sum of everything in the worlds today, spiritual, physical and conventional (*waḍʿi*). It is because of him that these [different] worlds have been created, and all of them are his agents and propagators until His Day [of Judgement]. He is the one who arose in the world for the perfection of the Creator's vicegerency in the universe among humanity. Indeed, we have said that he is the perfector (*mutimm*) of all those who passed away. Some may say that this is the description of the final *qāʾim* and that the Commander of the Faithful, peace be upon him, is not the final one. We reply that the Commander of the Faithful [al-Ḥākim], peace be upon him, is the *qāʾim* in his time and period and that he is the *qāʾim* of all those who preceded him, the perfector of them all. He is the sixth through whom the command of the seventh will be perfected.[94] He will finish what the seventh requires, just as the Prophet, may God bless him, established all that the *qāʾim* would require, to become the perfector of what the Prophet established and arranged. The Commander of the Faithful, peace be upon him, is the ninth in a different calculation.[95] The command of the seventh [al-Muʿizz][96] who passed away is perfected through the ninth [al-Ḥākim], just as the perfection of the seven members, their order and function become manifest through the nine, that is the four natures and the five senses, and [just as] the perfection of the human creature is in nine months. [This] calculation is based on the figure of nine.[97] Life in the hereafter is based on four spiritual

94. Al-Ḥākim was the sixth Fatimid caliph, al-Mahdī being the first, just as the Prophet Muḥammad was the sixth great prophet after Adam, Noah, Abraham, Moses and Jesus.

95. The Imam-Caliph al-Ḥākim was the ninth imam in the cycle from Muḥammad b. Ismāʿīl meaning the three hidden imams of *dawr al-satr* and the five imam-caliphs of the Fatimid period, making him the ninth.

96. Al-Muʿizz was the second *mutimm* (perfector) of the second series of seven imams, as he was the fourteenth imam, Muḥammad b. Ismāʿīl being the first.

97. '... The perfect resides wholly in the ninth [imam] ... In him the

natures and five spiritual senses, as God said: 'Indeed, the abode of the hereafter—that is life, if only they knew'.[98]

[82] The Commander of the Faithful [al-Ḥākim], peace be upon him, is the second by a different calculation. The order at the beginning of each cycle is perfected by the second. He is also the sixth through whose sword God will conquer the whole world, just as He conquered through the Prophet, may God bless him, the sixth one from Adam. The Commander of the Faithful, peace be upon him, arose in the world perfecting vicegerency (*khilāfa*) of the Creator of the universe among His creatures. He deals with the creation in all circumstances, in the same way as God, the Exalted, deals with His creatures in respect to their constitution and their sustenance and in the abundance of His mercy on them. Each one of those who arose before him carried out a small portion of this, but the Commander of the Faithful, peace be upon him, carried out the whole. The vicegerent is one who carries out among those over whom he has been appointed, everything done by the one who appointed him.

Indeed, Adam like all other vicegerents was called 'vicegerent' (*khalīfa*) because he was the first of those who undertook the vicegerency. Those who came after him carried out some of the conditions of the vicegerency and so they were called by that name. Whoever carries out a part of a duty is called by its name. The Commander of the Faithful, however, performs the worldly and the religious vicegerency in reality. When the Prophet, may God bless him said, 'The ruler is the shadow of God on earth'[99] he indeed meant the Commander of the Faithful, peace be upon him, because the shadow of something is that which imitates what casts the shadow with all that is in it. There is no one who deals with the creatures as God, the Exalted, does except for the Commander of the Faithful, peace be upon him. The Prophet, may God bless him, also said: 'Indeed God, the Exalted,

---

parturition is accomplished, the coming of light is done, and the concealed one and hidden one appear. In al-Ḥākim, God established His Will in the world, and the wisdom of the Just was realised.' See the translation of Muḥammad ibn 'Alī al-Ṣūrī, *al-Qaṣīda al-ṣūriyya*, p. 68, cited in Makarem, 'Al-Ḥākim bi-Amrillāh's Appointment', p. 321.

98. Qur'an, 29: 64.

99. al-Majlisī, *Biḥār al-anwār*, vol. 3, p. 306.

establishes (*naza'a*) as proof through the ruler more than what He establishes through the Qur'an,' and the Commander of the Faithful, peace be upon him, is the one through whom God established what He does not establish through the Qur'an.

[83] The philosophers have said that philosophy is to seek to resemble God (*al-tashabbuh bi'l-bāri'*), glory be to Him, according to human capacity. Seeking to resemble the Creator, glory be to Him, means dealing with mankind in the same way that God, may His mention be exalted, deals with them, and to interact with them and with his own self in the same way that God acts with him and mankind and in accordance with their nature. The philosophers have stolen this speech from the 'people of the truth' (*ahl al-ḥaqīqa*),[100] although except for the Commander of the Faithful, none of them have been able to carry out the real meaning of this phrase. Indeed, all his treatment of the humankind is in accordance with God's treatment of them in the nature of the world, in sustenance and in other such things. We shall now mention a small amount of that which is appropriate for the time in which we live.

[84] We shall begin first by saying that the compassion, mercy, bounty and forgiveness of the Commander of the Faithful [al-Ḥākim], as well as his tolerance towards the misbehaviour of people out of lack of their obedience are impossible for me to describe. They are all in following God's actions towards humanity, following God's command and adopting His manners.

Surely, God by His bounty bestows blessings upon people, be they pious or impious, believers or unbelievers. If He bestowed material benefit[101] on the believers and denied it to the unbelievers, that would mean that people's faith was [only] because of the world, not because of God or His religion. On the other hand, if He denied it to all the believers and gave it only to the unbelievers, most people's belief (*īmān*) would surely revert to unbelief (*kufr*). He thus gave it to some unbelievers and denied it to others, just as He gave it to some believers and denied it to others. He gave it to each of them at some times and denied it to them at others. Likewise, the Commander of the Faithful

100. Al-Naysābūrī is referring to his own community.

101. lit., 'gave the world'.

bestows worldly benefit on the Muslims and the unbelievers and denies it to them too. He bestows it on the believers and hypocrites, and denies it to them too. He gave it to all of them sometimes and denied it at others. If he gave everything to the believers, then surely their faith would be mostly for the sake of the world, but if he were to deny all the believers at all times, they would surely become despondent and their good intention would weaken. Consequently, the Commander of the Faithful, for a certain period of time bestowed blessings on the believers, such as no one else bestowed and he also withheld from them for some time for their benefit in order that they would not become like those about whom God has said: 'Nay, indeed man certainly becomes rebellious, considering himself self-sufficient'.[102]

Indeed, God gave worldly goods to the pious and the impious [alike], so that the deeds of the pious would not [just] be for the sake of this world, nor would restraint from immorality be [only] for the sake of this world, nor restraint from disobedience only because of worldly benefit, such that they would be deprived of reward in the world to come; rather, they would be exclusively for the sake of religion and God. Likewise, the Commander of the Faithful peace be upon him, gives worldly benefits to the righteous as well as the immoral alike.

[85] Indeed God, the Exalted, has given the temporal world to those who obey and those who disobey out of wisdom on His part, in order that obedience be not for the sake of the world, nor restraint from disobedience because of it; rather it should be purely for the sake of God. Similarly, the Commander of the Faithful gives the obedient and the disobedient alike, following the actions of God, the Exalted, in order that humanity's obedience to Him is not for worldly advantage, and the reward of the hereafter not be excluded from them.

Surely God gives worldly goods to the worshipper as well as the non-worshipper, lest the worship of the creatures be for the sake of worldly benefit. Similarly, the Commander of the Faithful engages with his people not looking at their imperfections and disobedience, but looking at them with a merciful eye. God, the Exalted, has given worldly benefit to the simpleton and the ignorant, and has given it to the learned and the intellectual, while also withholding it from

102. Qur'an, 96: 6–7.

both of them. Likewise, the Commander of the Faithful gives to the simpleton and the ignorant, the learned and the intelligent alike, on account of his wisdom and his virtue. If he were to give to the learned and the intelligent [only] and to withhold from others, then the people's acquisition of knowledge would only be for the sake of this world, and their use of reason and acquisition of virtues would also only be for this world, leaving the ignorant and the simpleton in despair. But God has [equally] given the world to the simpleton and the ignorant.

He has also given worldly benefit to the wrongdoer and the just, to the generous and the miser, to the noble, to the depraved and the lowly, to those possessing every virtue and those lacking it, equally giving them all out of His wisdom, mercy and grace. Likewise, the Commander of the Faithful treats all of them equally, following the actions of God, the Exalted, and His mercy upon His creatures, in order that everyone may obtain their fair share of His bounty and kindness.

[86] Moreover God, the Exalted, has concealed the affairs of the world and how His creatures may benefit from it, as well as their path in approaching it in all respects. He has concealed from mankind both the means and the actions needed to acquire worldly benefits, such that one becomes rich, while the other has nothing to eat,[103] one becomes wealthy from trade and commerce, while the other goes bankrupt, one becomes rich from agriculture, while the other loses even his seeds, and one becomes self-sufficient from hunting, while the other is impoverished. All this is on account of the exceeding wisdom so that He would not provide [easy] access to the world, while all other accesses become void and disorder pervades the creation and corrupts the world. Similar is the interaction of the Commander of the Faithful, peace be upon him, with mankind in that respect in this world. He conceals the means to that such that one seeks it by some means whereupon he gives it to him, while the other who seeks it by the same means is denied. If they knew a particular means by which they could obtain worldly goods from the Commander of the Faithful, then, all other means would become certainly futile. All those

103. lit., 'to find no bread'.

who lacked that would despair of his mercy, becoming deprived, and there would be no merit in that.

[87] The interaction of the Commander of the Faithful, peace be upon him, with regard to his proximity with people close to him and his distance from them are similar. If the Commander of the Faithful were to remove the hypocrites and bring the believers close [to him], then surely all people would become believers because he brought them close to him, not because of the religion. Similarly, if he were to keep his distance from all believers at all times, they would then avoid him and anxiety would crop into their hearts, either because of the perceived anger from the Commander of the Faithful or because of a slip on their part that necessitated that. Thus, he deals with them according to what is appropriate to the prevailing times and conditions —awakening desire, alarm, removing them or bringing them close, granting and denying, punishing and forgiving—all this is following the actions and characteristics of God, the Exalted, so that people would perpetually be both in fear and hope, neither feeling secure lest they become bold, nor despairing so as to become despondent. In all this he follows the manners of God, the Exalted, towards His creation, just as He, may He be glorified, gives abundantly to all, including those who do not fear poverty and exhaustion of wealth; similarly the Commander of the Faithful also gives to those who do not fear poverty and exhaustion of wealth, exceeding the generosity of human beings.

[88] Those who look through the eye of reality at the actions of the Commander of the Faithful in the religion and worldly matters will find that everything he does with the creation, commanding [good] and forbidding [evil], granting and denying, are all parallel to the actions of God, the Exalted. But people are baffled regarding that because they look at his actions on the basis of those of [ordinary] human beings and of what they have heard. They compare the actions of the Commander of the Faithful with those of other people and the actions of other rulers, and with what they have heard, seen and understood. They regard that as being in opposition to what they are accustomed to, and so have fallen into perplexity, confusion and speculation. If they view it in relation to God's actions with His creation, then all that would be easier for them. It is difficult for them

only because, ever since the time of Adam to this day of ours, no one has done anything like that. If anyone did act in this manner at any time, it was only a small portion of it as is reported in the actions of the sage [Khiḍr][104] with Moses, peace be upon him. Moses was not patient about Khiḍr's actions as he saw them in relation to his own action, knowledge and intellect. If he had viewed them in relation to God's actions, then that would have certainly been contrary to what actually happened to him. Another instance is what has been reported about David's judgement and God's command in regard to the perplexing and astounding story of the owner of the vineyard[105] and the owner of the bull. Similarly God, the Exalted, has warned in His words: 'On the day when the summoner calls them to a painful end … their eyes will be lowered in humiliation'.[106] God also said: 'They were called to prostrate while safe and secure.'[107] It is amazing that if they cannot endure these worldly actions; how can they then endure the affliction by religious actions and by things that are far more difficult than that? Indeed, all that is found in two extreme positions does not exist at the centre and what is in the centre does not exist in the regions. Yet people pass judgement on the issues according to what they see in the centre, while themselves being at the extremities. It is for that reason they become confused and baffled, unable to bear or endure it.

[89] We also say that gifts of the [other] monarchs are perceived by people as being given because of a service, relationship, an obligation,

---

104. Usually Khiḍr, but more correctly, Khaḍir. The author is referring to the archetypal story of Moses and his initiator, identified later as al-Khaḍir, in the *sūra* of the cave (18: 60–82).

105. Qur'an, 21: 78–79. This is when David and his son Solomon gave judgement regarding the damage caused to the field (vineyard) when some sheep wandered in and devoured the tender shoots of all the plants causing incredible damage. As king, David passed the ruling that the owner should retain the sheep in compensation but Solomon, who at the time was only eleven years old, suggested that the owner could benefit from the sheep with regard to its milk, wool and the ewes before returning them. These judgements were inspired by God as mentioned in the Qur'an. See details in *The Glorious Qur'ān: Translation and Commentary* by 'Abdullah Yūsuf 'Alī, 3rd ed. (Lahore, 1938), p. 839.

106. Qur'an, 54: 6–7.

107. Qur'an, 68: 43.

out of love, need, seeking a benefit or averting harm. [They could also be given] for other reasons that necessitate it, such as fearing calamity, in expectation of good [fortune], or in fear of someone's tongue, in seeking praise or exaltation and glorification, in desire of gratitude or benevolence, as a reward to an official or as a means of sustenance. All that is done on the basis of appraisal and assessment, while gifts from the Commander of the Faithful are beyond all that, because gifts given for the reasons cited above are not called generosity, virtue or beneficence. Rather, they are given either in payment of an obligation for something in the past or as an advance payment for something in the future. Delay of obligations and fulfilment of rights is blameworthy and miserly, and likewise, the action of advancing money for the sake of future benefit is not considered generosity or virtue. Also, whatever is given in connection with indebtedness is not considered generosity, nobility or virtue. The gifts of God, glory be to Him, exceed all that, for there is nothing that God is obliged to give anyone, nor does God seek any reward from any of His creatures. In the same manner, the Commander of the Faithful does not give to anyone for the reasons cited, nor does he demand compensations for that. God, the Exalted, said regarding the Commander of the Faithful, ʿAlī b. Abī Ṭālib: 'We do not desire either reward or gratitude from them.'[108] Rather, he bestows upon them spontaneously out of generosity, nobility and virtue, following the actions of God, the Exalted, with His Creation.

If they viewed the actions of the Commander of the Faithful in this way, they would not fall into confusion. However, some of them perceive him with short-sightedness, judging his actions to be similar to those of other human beings, while others look at him with exaggeration, claiming divinity for him.[109] The actions of the Commander of the Faithful are indeed beyond both these two viewpoints. Rather, he is the Universal Vicegerent of God among His worshippers (*al-khalīfat al-kullī lillāh taʿāla ʿala ʿibādihi*).

[90] Just as God, the Exalted, concealed the reasons for creating the world from mankind and explained the reasons of religion and

108. Qur'an, 76: 9.

109. Al-Naysābūrī is obviously referring to the Druzes, who in his view exaggerated al-Ḥākim's position, while referring to themselves as the *muwaḥḥidūn* (monotheists). See the Introduction above.

the means of attaining it, He also explained ways of attaining His pleasure, clarifying it through the words of His Prophet. He gave knowledge and wisdom to those who deserved it and denied it to those who did not, and 'He made before them a barrier and behind them a barrier',[110] establishing signposts of guidance and the summons of the proof and the guide to the bounty of the hereafter. He disclosed ways of attaining to it and opened its gates, so that whoever deserves it attains it and he who does not misses it in utmost wisdom. Likewise, the Commander of the Faithful concealed the means of attaining worldly fortune through him, giving it to both, those who deserve and those who do not. He explained the means of attaining religion, knowledge and wisdom, and bestowed them upon those who deserved it, neither withholding them nor being miserly. He bountifully bestowed favours upon people, giving more than anyone could ever give in any time or age. He also withheld [favours] from the undeserving ones, differentiating between the people of the truth (*ahl al-ḥaqq*) and the people of falsehood (*ahl al-bāṭil*), following the actions and ways of God, the Exalted, in the governance of the world and religion, and in the building of this present world and the world to come.

[91] We ask God to bestow upon us gratitude for what He has blessed us with in words, deeds and in intention, and that He grant us success in obedience to the lord of the age and time (*walī al-ʿasr wa'l-zamān*), peace be upon him. May He provide us with the means of struggling on his behalf with our hands, tongues and hearts. May God open up the entire world[111] for him and with his sword purify the earth of polytheism (*shirk*), unbelief *(kufr)* and hypocrisy (*nifāq*) through his bounty and generosity.

This worshipper begs and desires the blessings of the Commander of the Faithful, peace be upon him, and seeks 'the supreme command' (*al-amr al-ālī)* to examine what the servant has gathered and compiled, and to give him permission for that which is sound and correct, and draw his attention to mistakes in it, so that the servant can be thankful to him in increasing his insight and certainty, and so

110. Qur'an, 36: 9.

111. lit., 'the east and the west of the world'.

that this would become [a means of] guidance and evidence for those who seek to be guided and a proof against those who deny.[112]

Praise be to God, the praise of the thankful one, the mindful and the pious, and prayers upon His Messenger, our master Muḥammad, and all his progeny.[113]

112. This suggests that al-Naysābūrī had submitted his work to the Imam al-Ḥākim for his blessings as well as for rectifying his mistakes, although it is difficult to determine from the text itself whether or not any such corrections were received and incorporated before the work became public.

113. The following is added in manuscript *alif*: 'God is sufficient for us, blessed is His *wakīl*, and blessed is the *mawlā* and blessed is the *helper*. There is no power except in God, the Supreme, the Great. This book has been completed by the help and favour of God and the support of His *walī*, peace be upon him, on Friday afternoon, the 27th of Rabī' II, 1134/14 February 1722, May God protect it. This book on *Ithbāt al-imām* [*imāma*] has been completed by the Grace of God, the Bountiful Ruler (*mālik al-manān*), by the help of His friends, owners of knowledge and explanation (*'ilm wa'l-bayān*).'

Select Bibliography

Primary Sources: Manuscripts of al-Naysābūrī

al-Naysābūrī, Aḥmad b. Ibrāhīm. *Kitāb ithbāt al-imāma*. Fyzee collection. Ms. (R) 56 C.1. Library of The Institute of Ismaili Studies.

The following variants of al-Naysābūrī's above work used in this study are also housed at the Institute's Library:

——The Ismaili Society of Bombay, Ms. 91 (Ar.).

——Zāhid ʿAlī Collection, Ms. 1123 (Ar I, ZA).

——Zāhid ʿAlī Collection, Ms. 1212 (Ar I, ZA).

——Ms 92 (Ar.), [copied in 1317/1899].

——Ms 93 (Ar), [copied in 1313/1895].

——Ms 94 (Ar.), [no date].

——Ms 911 (Supp.Ar.), [copied in 1355/1936].

——Ms 946 (Supp.Ar.), [copied in 1310/1892].

——Ms 1047 (Ar I), [no date].

——*Kitāb istitār al-imām wa tafarruq al-duʿāt fi'l-jazā'ir li-ṭalabi-hi* (with Muḥammad al-Yamanī's *Sirāt al-ḥājib*), Ms 1008 (Ar I). Library of The Institute of Ismaili Studies, ed. W. Ivanow in *Bulletin of the Faculty of Arts, Egyptian University*, vol. 4, 1936, Cairo, 1939), pp. 89–133; English tr. W. Ivanow, in his *Ismaili Tradition Concerning the Rise of the Fatimids*. London, etc., 1942, pp. 157–183.

——*Risāla al-mūjaza al-kāfiya fī adab al-duʿāt* in Ḥaṣan al-Bharūchī's *Kitāb al-aẓhar*, II, 100–162, cited in Poonawala's *Biobibliography*, pp. 91–92. Ms. 705 (Ar I). Library of The Institute of Ismaili Studies. This *risāla* is also available in Ḥātim al-Ḥāmidī's *Tuḥfāt al-qulūb* and cited in Poonawala, p. 405.

——*Kitāb al-tawḥīd*, preserved in a collection of manuscripts from Syria, Ms. 154/994, p. 1. See Delia Cortese, *Ismaili and Other Arabic Manuscripts:*

A Descriptive Catalogue of Manuscripts in the Library of The Institute of Ismaili Studies. London, 2000, pp. 94 and 96.

Other Manuscripts

al-Mu'ayyad fi'l-Dīn al-Shīrāzī [attr.]. *al-Ibtida' wa al-intihā'*, copied in 14th/20th century. Ms 1250 (Arı, ZA). Library of The Institute of Ismaili Studies.

Ja'far b. Manṣūr al-Yaman, Abu'l-Qāsim. *Kitāb al-shawāhid wa'l-bayān fi ithbāt amīr al-mu'minīn wa'l-a'imma*. Ms.734. Library of The Institute of Ismaili Studies. See Adam Gacek, *Catalogue of Arabic Manuscripts in the Library of The Institute of Ismaili Studies* (London, 1984), vol. 1, pp. 118–119.

Published Primary Sources

'Abd al-Jabbār, Qāḍī. *al-Mughnī fi abwāb al-tawḥīd wa'l-'adl*, ed., 'Abd al-Ḥalīm Maḥmūd et. al., vol. 20, Cairo, n.d.

Abu'l-Fawāris Aḥmad b. Ya'qūb. *al-Risāla fi'l-imāma*, ed. and tr., Sami N. Makarem as *The Political Doctrine of the Ismā'īlīs*. Delmar, NY, 1977.

al-Baghdādī, Abū Manṣūr 'Abd al-Qāhir. *al-Farq bayn al-firaq*, ed. M. Badr, Cairo, 1328/1910. English trans. *Moslem Schisms and Sects*, part I, tr. K.C. Seelye. New York, 1929; part II, tr. A.S. Halkin. Tel Aviv, 1935.

al-Dhahabī, Muḥammad. *Ta'rīkh al-Islām*, ed. 'A. Tadmurī. Beirut, 1987–1994.

al-Fārābī, Abū Naṣr. *Alfarabi's Philosophy of Plato and Aristotle*, tr. Muhsin Mahdi. Ithaca, NY, 1963.

——*Taḥṣīl al-sa'āda*, ed. Ja'far Āl Yāsīn. Beirut, 1983.

——*Al-Fārābī on the Perfect State: Abū Naṣr al-Fārābī's Mabādī' ārā' ahl-al-madīnah al-fāḍilah*, ed. and tr. Richard Walzer. Oxford, 1985.

Ibn Abi'l-Ḥadīd. *Sharḥ nahj al-balāgha*, ed. M.A. Ibrāhīm. Cairo, 1961.

Ibn al-Athīr, 'Izz al-Dīn. *al-Kāmil fi'l-ta'rīkh*, ed. C.J. Tornberg. Leiden, 1851–76; repr. Beirut, 1965–1967.

Ibn al-Dawādārī, Abū Bakr b. 'Abd Allāh. *Kanz al-durar wa jāmi' al-ghurar*, part 6, *al-Durra al-muḍiyya fi akhbār al-dawla al-Fāṭimiyya*, ed. Ṣ. al-Munajjid. Cairo, 1961.

Ibn al-Haytham, Abū 'Abd Allāh Ja'far. *Kitāb al-munāẓarāt*, ed. and tr. Wilferd Madelung and Paul E. Walker as *The Advent of the Fatimids: A*

Contemporary Shi'i Witness. London, 2000.

Ibn Khallikān, Abu'l-'Abbās Aḥmad. *Wafayāt al-a'yān*, ed. Ihsān 'Abbās. Beirut, 1968–1972.

Ibn Manẓūr, Muḥammad b. al-Mukarram. *Lisān al-'Arab*. Beirut 1955–1957.

Ibn al-Nadīm, Abu'l-Faraj Muḥammad. *Kitāb al-fihrist*. Cairo, n.d.; English trans., *The Fihrist of al-Nadim*, tr. Bayard Dodge. New York, 1970, 2 vols.

Ibn al-Qalānisī, Abū Ya'lā Ḥamza. *Dhayl ta'rīkh Dimashq*, ed. H.F. Amedroz. Leiden, 1908.

Ibn Taghrībirdī, Abu'l-Maḥāsin Yusūf. *al-Nujūm al-ẓāhira fi mulūk Miṣr wa'l-Qāhira*. Cairo, 1348–1391/1929–1972.

Ibn al-Ṭuwayr, Abū Muḥammad al-Murtaḍā. *Nuzhat al-muqlatayn fi akhbār al-dawlatayn*, ed. Ayman F. Sayyid. Beirut, 1992.

Idrīs 'Imād al-Dīn b. al-Ḥasan. *'Uyūn al-akhbār wa-fūnūn al-āthār*, vols. 4–6, ed. Muṣṭafā Ghālib. Beirut, 1973–1978.

Ja'far b. Manṣūr al-Yaman, Abu'l-Qāsim. *Kitāb al-kashf*, ed. R. Strothmann. London, etc., 1952.

——*Kitāb 'ālim wa'l-ghulām*, ed. and tr. James W. Morris as *The Master and the Disciple*. London, 2001

al-Kirmānī, Ḥamīd al-Dīn Aḥmad. *Kitāb al-riyāḍ*. ed. 'Ārif Tāmir. Beirut, 1960.

——*Rāḥat al-'aql*. ed. M. Kāmil Ḥusayn and M. Muṣṭafā Ḥilmī. Leiden and Cairo, 1953; ed. Muṣṭafā Ghālib, Beirut, 1967.

——*Majmū'at rasā'il al-Kirmānī*, ed. Muṣṭafā Ghālib. Beirut, 1983.

——*al-Maṣābīḥ fī ithbāt al-imāma*, ed. and tr. Paul E. Walker as *Master of the Age: An Islamic Treatise on the Necessity of the Imamate*. London, 2007.

al-Kulaynī, Muḥammad b. Ya'qūb. *al-Uṣūl min al-kāfī*. Tehran, 1388/1968.

al-Majdū', Ismā'īl b. 'Abd al-Rasūl. *Fahrasat al-kutub wa'l-rasā'il*, ed. 'Alī Naqī Munzawī. Tehran, 1345Sh./1966.

al-Majlisī, Muḥammad Bāqir. *Biḥār al-anwār*. Tehran, n.d.

al-Maqrīzī, Taqī al-Dīn Aḥmad b. 'Alī. *Kitāb al-mawā'iẓ wa'l-i'tibār bī-dhikr al-khiṭaṭ wa'l-āthār. (al-Khiṭaṭ)*. Būlāq, 1270/1853–1854.

—— *Itti'āẓ al-ḥunafā' bi-akhbār al-a'imma al-Fāṭimiyyīn al-khulafā'*, vol. 1, ed. Jamāl al-Dīn al-Shayyāl, vols. 2–3, ed. Muḥammad Ḥilmī M. Aḥmad. Cairo, 1967–1973.

al-Māwardī, 'Alī b. Muḥammad. *al-Aḥkām al-Sulṭāniyya wa'l-walāyat al-dīniyya*, Cairo, 1936; 3rd edition, Egypt, 1393/1973. English trans., *The Ordinances of the Government*, tr. Wafaa H. Wahba. Reading, 1996.

al-Musabbiḥī, al-Mukhtār ʿIzz al-Mulk. *al-Juzʾ al-arbaʿūn min akhbār Miṣr.* Part 1 (historical), ed. Ayman F. Sayyid and Th. Bianquis. Cairo, 1978.

Muslim b. al-Hajjāj. *Ṣaḥīḥ Muslim*, ed. H.M. al-Masʿūdī. Cairo, 1349/1930.

al-Nawbakhtī, al-Ḥasan. *Kitāb firaq al-Shīʿa,* ed. H. Ritter. Istanbul, 1931.

al-Naysābūrī, Aḥmad b. Ibrāhīm. *Kitāb ithbāt al-imāma*, ed. Muṣṭafā Ghālib. Beirut, 1984.

al-Nuwayrī, Shihāb al-Dīn Aḥmad. *Nihāyat al-arab fī funūn al-adab*, vol. 25, ed. M.J.ʿA. al-Ḥīnī and ʿAbd al-ʿAzīz al-Ahwānī. Cairo, 1984.

al-Nuʿmān b. Muḥammad, al-Qāḍī Abū Ḥanīfa. *Daʿāʾim al-Islām*, ed. A.A.A. Fyzee, 2 vols. Cairo, 1951–1961. English trans., A.A.A. Fyzee, revised and annotated by Ismail K. Poonawala as *The Pillars of Islam*. New Delhi, 2002–2004.

——*Asās al-taʾwīl*, ed. ʿĀrif Tāmir. Beirut, 1960.

——*Sharḥ al-akhbār fī faḍāʾil al-aʾimma al-aṭhār*, ed. S.M. Ḥusaynī al-Jalālī, 2nd ed. Qumm, 1414/1993.

——*Iftitāh al-daʿwa*, tr. Hamid Haji as *Founding the Fatimid State: The Rise of an Early Islamic Empire*. London, 2006.

al-Qummī, ʿAlī b. Ibrāhīm. *Tafsīr al-Qummī,* ed. Ṭayyib al-Musawī al-Jazāʾirī. Beirut, 1968.

al-Qummī, Saʿd b. ʿAbd Allāh. *Kitāb al-maqālāt waʾl-firaq*, ed. M.J. Mashkūr. Tehran, 1342Sh./1963.

Rasāʾil Ikhwān al-Ṣafāʾ wa-khullān al-wafāʾ, ed. B. al-Bustānī. Beirut, 1957.

al-Rāzī, Abū Ḥātim. *Aʿlām al-nubuwwa*, ed. by Ṣalāḥ al-Ṣāwy and G. Aʿwānī. Tehran, 1356Sh./1977.

——*Kitāb al-iṣlāḥ*, ed. Ḥ. Mīnūchihr and M. Muḥaqqiq. Tehran, 1377Sh./1998.

——*Kitāb al-zīna*, part 3, ed. ʿAbd Allāh S. al-Samarrāʾī, in his *al-Ghuluww waʾl-firaq al-ghāliya.* Baghdad, 1988.

al-Saffār, Abū Jaʿfar Muḥammad. *Baṣāʾir al-darajāt,* ed. Mīrzā M. Kūchabāghī. Tabrīz, 1380/1960.

al-Shāfiʿī. *Kitāb al-umm*, ed. M. Zuhrī al-Najjār. Beirut, 1393/1974.

al-Shahrastānī, Abuʾl-Fatḥ Muḥammad. *Mafātīḥ al-asrār wa maṣābīḥ al-abrār* (*Tafsīr al-Shahrastānī*), vol. 1, ed. M. ʿAlī Ādharshab. Tehran, 1376Sh./1997.

al-Shayyāl, Jamāl al-Dīn, ed. *Majmūʿat al-wathāʾiq al-Fāṭimiyya.* Cairo, 1958.

al-Sijistānī, Abū Yaʿqūb Isḥāq. *Kitāb al-yanābīʿ*, ed. and partial French trans. by H. Corbin in his *Trilogue Ismaélienne*. Tehran and Paris, 1961; tr. Paul E. Walker in his *The Wellsprings of Wisdom: A Study of al-Sijistānī's* Kitāb al-yanābīʿ. Salt Lake City, UT, 1994.

——*Kitāb ithbāt al-nubuwwa*, ed. 'Ārif Tamir. Beirut, 1966.
——*Kitāb al-iftikhār*, ed. Muṣṭafā Ghālib. Beirut, 1980; ed. I.K. Poonawala. Beirut, 2000.
——*Kashf al-maḥjūb*, ed. H. Corbin. Tehran and Paris, 1949; partial English trans. by H. Landolt, in S.H. Nasr and M. Aminrazavi, ed. *An Anthology of Philosophy in Persia*. Oxford, 2001, vol. 2, pp. 71–124.
al-Ya'qūbī, Aḥmad b. Ibn Wādīḥ. *Ta'rīkh*, ed. vols. 1 and 2. Beirut, n.d.

Secondary Sources

Afsaruddin, Asma. *Excellence and Precedence: Medieval Islamic Discourse on Legitimate Leadership*. Leiden, 2002.
al-Amīnī, Muḥammad Hādī. *al-Ghadīr*. Najaf 1972; Tehran, 1396/1976.
Amir-Moezzi, M.A. *The Divine Guide in Early Shi'ism*, tr. David Streight. Albany, NY, 1994.
Arjomand, Said Amir. 'The Crisis of the Imamate and the Institution of Occultation in Twelver Shi'ism: A Sociohistorical Perspective' in Etan Kohlberg, ed., *Shī'ism*, pp. 109–133.
Assaad, Sadik A. *The Reign of al-Hakim bi Amr Allah* (386/996–411/1021): *A Political Study*. Beirut, 1974.
Ayoub, M.M. *The Qur'an and its Interpreters*. Albany, 1984.
Bar-Asher, Meir M. *Scripture and Exegesis in Early Imami Shiism*. Leiden, 1999.
Bianquis, Thierry. 'Al H'ākim bi Amr Allāh ou la folie de l'unité chez un souverain Fāt'imide', *Les Africains*, 11 (1978), pp. 107–133.
Bosworth, Clifford E. *The Ghaznavids: Their Empire in Afghanistan and Eastern Iran* 994–1040. 2nd edition, Beirut, 1973.
——'Marwān b. al-Ḥakam', *EI2*, vol. 6, pp. 621–623.
Brett, Michael. 'The Mim, the 'Ayn, and the Making of Ismā'īlism', *Bulletin of the School of Oriental and African Studies*, 57 (1994), pp. 25–39.
——'The Realm of the Imām: The Fāṭimids in the Tenth Century', *Bulletin of the School of Oriental and African Studies*, 59 (1996), pp. 431–449.
Bruijn, J.T.P. de. 'al-Kirmānī', in *EI2*, vol. 5, pp. 166–167.
Bryer, David R.W. 'The Origins of the Druze Religion', *Der Islam*, 52 (1975), pp. 47–84, 239–262; 53 (1976), pp. 5–27.
Bulliet, Richard W. *The Patricians of Nishapur: A Study in Medieval Islamic Social History*. Cambridge, MA, 1972.
Canard, Marius. 'Da'wa', *EI2*, vol. 2, pp. 168–170.
——'Fāṭimids', *EI2*, vol. 2, pp. 850–862.

Corbin, Henry. 'Divine Epiphany and Spiritual Birth in Ismailian Gnosis', in *Man and Transformation: Papers from the Eranos Yearbooks*, vol. 5. Princeton, NJ, 1964, pp. 69–160; reprinted in Henry Corbin, *Cyclical Time and Ismaili Gnosis*, tr. Ralph Manheim and James W. Morris. London, 1983, pp. 59–150.

——*History of Islamic Philosophy*, tr. L Sherrard with Philip Sherrard's assistance. London, 1993.

Cortese, Delia. *Ismaili and Other Arabic Manuscripts: A Descriptive Catalogue of Manuscripts in the Library of The Institute of Ismaili Studies*. London, 2000.

——*Arabic Ismaili Manuscripts: The Zāhid 'Alī Collection in the Library of the Institute of Ismaili Studies*. London, 2003.

Crone, Patricia. *Medieval Islamic Political Thought*. Edinburgh, 2004.

Daftary, Farhad. *The Ismā'īlīs: Their History and Doctrines*. Cambridge, 1990; 2nd ed., Cambridge, 2007.

——*A Short History of the Ismailis: Traditions of a Muslim Community*. Edinburgh, 1998.

——*Ismaili Literature*. London, 2004.

——'The Earliest Ismā'īlīs', *Arabica*, 38 (1991), pp. 214–245.

——'Diversity in Islam: Communities of Interpretation', in Azim A. Nanji, ed., *The Muslim Almanac*. Detroit, 1996, pp. 161–173.

——ed., *Mediaeval Isma'ili History and Thought*. Cambridge, 1996.

——The Ismaili *Da'wa* outside the Fatimid *Dawla*', in *L'Égypte Fatimide, Son art et son histoire*, ed. Marianne Barrucand. Paris, 1999, pp. 29–43.

——'Intellectual Life among the Ismailis: An Overview', in F. Daftary, ed., *Intellectual Traditions in Islam*. London, 2000, pp. 87–111.

——'The Medieval Ismailis of the Iranian Lands', in Carole Hillenbrand, ed., *Studies in Honour of Clifford Edmund Bosworth*, Vol. II, *The Sultan's Turret: Studies in Persian and Turkish Culture*. Leiden, 2000, pp. 43–81.

Daiber, Hans. 'Abū Ḥātim ar-Rāzī (10th century A.D.) on the Unity and Diversity of Religions' in J. Gort et al., ed., *Dialogue and Syncretism: An Interdisciplinary Approach*. Grand Rapids, MI, 1989, pp. 87–104.

Sayyid, Ayman F. *al-Dawla al-Fāṭimiyya fī Miṣr: Tafsīr jadīd*. Cairo, 1413/1992; 2nd ed., Cairo, 2000.

Fyzee, Asaf Ali Asghar. 'A Collection of Fatimid Manuscripts', in N.N. Gidwani, ed., *Comparative Librarianship: Essays in Honour of Professor D. N. Marshall*. Delhi, 1973, pp. 209–220.

Gacek, Adam. *Catalogue of Arabic Manuscripts in the Library of The Institute of Ismaili Studies*. London, 1984–1985.

Ghālib, Muṣṭafā. *al-Imāma wa qā'im al-qiyāma*. Beirut, 1981.

——*Mafātīḥ al-ma'rifa*. Beirut, 1402/1982.

Goldstein, Bernard R. 'A Treatise on Number Theory from a Tenth Century Arabic Source,' *Centaurus* 10 (1964), pp. 135–160. Reprinted as 'A Theory on Numbers', in S.H. Nasr and M. Aminrazavi, eds., *An Anthology of Philosophy in Persia, Volume 2, Ismaili Thought in the Classical Age, From Jābir ibn Ḥayyān to Naṣīr al-Dīn Ṭūsī*. London, 2008, pp. 235–256.

Goriawala, Mu'izz. *A Descriptive Catalogue of the Fyzee Collection of Ismaili Manuscripts*. Bombay, 1965.

Haji, Hamid. *A Distinguished Dā'ī under the Shade of the Fāṭimids: Ḥamīd al-Dīn al-Kirmānī* (d. c. 411/1020) *and his Epistles*. London, 1419/1998.

Hajjar, Sami G. and Brzezinski, Steven J. 'The Nizārī Ismaili Imām and Plato's Philosopher King', *Islamic Studies*, 16 (1977), pp. 303–316.

Halm, Heinz. *Kosmologie und Heilslehre der frühen Ismā'īlīya: Eine Studie zur islamischen Gnosis*. Wiesbaden, 1978.

——*Das Reich des Mahdi Der Aufstieg der Fatimiden*, Munich, 1991; English trans. M. Bonner, *The Empire of the Mahdi: The Rise of the Fatimids*. Leiden, 1996.

——*The Fatimids and their Traditions of Learning*. London, 1997.

——'Der Treuhänder Gottes: Die Edikte des Kalifen al-Ḥākim', *Der Islam*, 63 (1986), pp. 11–72.

——'The Cosmology of the Pre-Fatimid Ismā'īliyya', in F. Daftary, ed., *Mediaeval Isma'ili History and Thought*. Cambridge, 1996, pp. 75–83.

——'The Isma'ili Oath of Allegiance ('*ahd*) and the 'Sessions of Wisdom' (*majālis al-ḥikma*) in Fatimid Times', in F. Daftary, ed., *Mediaeval Isma'ili History and Thought*. Cambridge, 1996, pp. 91–115.

——'Abū Ḥātem Rāzī', *Encyclopaedia Iranica*, vol. 1, p. 315.

Hamdani, Abbas. 'The Dā'ī Ḥātim Ibn Ibrāhīm al-Ḥāmidī (d. 596/1199) and his Book *Tuḥfat al-Qulūb*', *Oriens*, 23–24 (1970–71), pp. 258–300.

—— 'Evolution of the Organisational Structure of the Fāṭimī Da'wah: The Yemani and Persian Contribution', *Arabian Studies*, 3 (1976), pp. 85–114.

——'Shades of Shī'ism in the Tracts of the Brethren of Purity', in Peter Slater and Donald Wiebe, eds., *Traditions in Contact and Change*. Waterloo, ON, 1983, pp. 447–460, 726–728.

——'Fāṭimid History and Historians', in M.J.L. Young et al., ed., *Religion, Learning and Science in the 'Abbasid Period*. Cambridge, 1990, pp. 234–247, 535–536.

——'A Critique of Paul Casanova's Dating of the *Rasā'il Ikhwān al-Ṣafā*" in F. Daftary, ed. *Mediaeval Isma'ili History and Thought*. Cambridge, 1996, pp. 145–152.

Ḥasan, Ḥasan Ibrāhīm and Ṭāhā Aḥmad Sharaf. *al-Mu'izz li-Dīn Allāh al-Fāṭimī*. Cairo, 1948; 2nd ed., Cairo, 1963.

Hodgson, Marshall G.S. 'al-Darazī and Ḥamza in the Origin of the Druze Religion', *Journal of the American Oriental Society*, 82 (1962), pp. 5–20.

—— 'Ḥudjdja: In Shī'ī Terminology', *EI2*, vol. 3, pp. 544–545.

Ḥusayn, Muḥammad Kāmil. *Ṭā'ifat al-Durūz*. Cairo, 1962.

'Inān, Muḥammad 'Abd Allāh. *al-Ḥākim bi-Amr Allāh wa-asrār al-da'wa al-Fāṭimiyya*. 2nd ed., Cairo, 1959.

Ivanow, Wladimir. *Ismaili Tradition Concerning the Rise of the Fatimids*. London, etc., 1942.

—— *The Alleged Founder of Ismailism*. Bombay, 1946.

—— 'The Organization of the Fatimid Propaganda', *Journal of the Bombay Branch of the Royal Asiatic Society*, NS, 15 (1939), pp. 1–35.

—— 'Ismailis and Qarmatians', *Journal of the Bombay Branch of the Royal Asiatic Society*, NS, 16 (1940), pp. 43–85.

Jiwa, Shainool. 'Fāṭimid-Būyid Diplomacy during the Reign of al-'Azīz Billāh (365/975–386/996)', *Journal of Islamic Studies*, 3 (1992), pp. 57–71.

Kikuchi, Tatsuya. 'Ḥamīd al-Dīn al-Kirmānī's Theory of Intellect', *Bulletin of the Society for Near Eastern Studies in Japan*, 38 (1995), pp. 45–60.

Klemm, Verena. *Die Mission des fāṭimidischen Agenten al-Mu'ayyad fī d-dīn in Šīrāz*. Frankfurt, 1989.

—— *Memoirs of a Mission: The Ismaili Scholar, Statesman and Poet al-Mu'ayyad fi'l-Dīn al-Shīrāzī*. London, 2003.

Knapp, Bettina L. 'The Kaliph Hakim and History as a Cyclical Happening', *Nineteenth-Century French Studies*, 5 (1976–77), pp. 79–93.

Le Strange, Guy. *The Lands of the Eastern Caliphate*. London, 1966.

Lev, Yaacov. 'The Fāṭimid Imposition of Ismā'īlism on Egypt (358–386/969–996)', *Zeitschrift der Deutschen Morgenländischen Gessellschaft*, 138 (1988), pp. 313–325.

Lalani, Arzina R., *Early Shī'ī Thought: The Teachings of Imam Muḥammad al-Bāqir*. London, 2000. Persian tr. F. Badrei, Tehran, 2002. Arabic tr. S. Kassir. London, 2003.

—— 'Ja'far al-Ṣādiq,' in *Encyclopaedia of Religion*, ed. Lindsay Jones, 2nd edition, Detroit, 2005, vol. 7, pp. 4760–4762.

—— ''Alī ibn Abī Ṭālib', pp. 28–32; 'Imām-imāma', pp. 289–294; 'Shī'a', pp. 586–592; 'Naṣṣ', pp. 448–451; 'Walī-walāya-wilāya', pp. 682–686, in *The*

Qur'ān: an Encyclopaedia, ed. Oliver Leaman, London and New York, 2006.
——'Aḥmad b. Ibrāhīm al-Naysābūrī', in *Biographical Dictionary of Islamic Philosophy*, ed. Oliver Leaman, London and New York, 2006. vol. 2, pp. 158–160.
Madelung, Wilferd. *Der Imam al-Qāsim ibn Ibrāhīm und die Glaubenslehre der Zaiditen*. Berlin, 1965.
——'Das Imamat in der frühen ismailitischen Lehre', *Der Islam*, 37 (1961), pp. 43–135.
——'Aspects of Ismā'īlī Theology: The Prophetic Chain and the God Beyond Being', in S.H. Nasr, ed., *Ismā'īlī Contributions to Islamic Culture*. Tehran, 1398/1977, pp. 53–65.
——'The Shiite and Khārijite Contribution to Pre-Ash'arite *Kalām*', in Parviz Morewedge. ed., *Islamic Philosophical Theology*, Albany, NY, 1979, pp. 120–139.
——'Imāmism and Mu'tazilite Theology', in his *Religious Schools and Sects in Medieval Islam*. London, 1985.
——'The Fatimids and the Qarmaṭīs of Baḥrayn', in Farhad Daftary, ed., *Mediaeval Isma'ili History and Thought*. London, 1996, pp. 21–73.
—— *The Succession to Muḥammad: A Study of the Early Caliphate*. Cambridge, 1997.
——'A Treatise on the Imamate of the Fatimid Caliph al-Manṣūr Bi-Allāh', in Chase Robinson, ed., *Texts, Documents and Artefacts: Islamic Studies in Honour of D.S. Richards*. Leiden and Boston, 2003, pp. 69–77.
——'Cosmogony and Cosmology: vi. in Isma'ilism', *Encyclopaedia Iranica*, vol. 6, pp. 322–326.
——'Imāma', in *EI2*, vol. 3, pp. 1163–1169.
——'Ismā'īliyya', in *EI2*, vol. 4, pp. 198–206.
——'Madjlis: In Ismā'īlī Usage', in *EI2*, vol. 5, p. 1033.
——'Shī'a', in *EI2*, vol. 9, pp. 420–424.
Mājid, 'Abd al-Mun'im. *al-Ḥākim bi-Amr Allāh al-khalīfa al-muftarā 'alayh*. Cairo, 1959.
Makarem, Sami Nasib. *The Doctrine of the Ismailis*. Beirut, 1972.
——*The Druze Faith*. Delmar, NY, 1974.
—— 'The Philosophical Significance of the Imām in Ismā'īlism', *Studia Islamica*, 27 (1967), pp. 41–53.
——'The Hidden Imāms of the Ismā'īlīs', *Al-Abḥāth*, 22 (1969), pp. 23–37.
——'Al-Ḥākim bi-Amrillāh's Appointment of his Successors', *Al-Abḥāth*, 23 (1970), pp. 319–324.

——'Isma'ili and Druze Cosmogony in Relation to Plotinus and Aristotle' in Michael E. Marmura, ed., *Islamic Theology and Philosophy: Studies in Honor of George F. Hourani*. Albany, NY, 1984, pp. 81–91.

Mattock, J.N. 'Maḳūlāt', in *EI2*, vol. 6, pp. 203–205.

Momen, Moojan. *An Introduction to Shi'i Islam*. New Haven, 1985.

Nanji, Azim. 'Transcendence and Distinction: Metaphoric Process in Ismā'īlī Muslim Thought', in D. B. Burrell and B. McGinn, ed., *God and Creation: An Ecumenical Symposium*. Notre Dame, IN, 1990, pp. 304–315.

——'Ismā'īlī Philosophy', in S.H. Nasr and O. Leaman, ed., *History of Islamic Philosophy*. London, 1996, vol. 1, pp. 144–154.

——'Portraits of Self and Others: Isma'ili Perspectives on the History of Religions', in F. Daftary ed., *Mediaeval Isma'ili History and Thought*. Cambridge, 1996, pp. 153–160.

Nasr, S. Hossein, ed. *Ismā'īlī Contributions to Islamic Culture*. Tehran, 1398/1977.

Nasr, S. Hossein and M. Aminrazavi, ed. *An Anthology of Philosophy in Persia, Volume 2: Ismaili Thought in the Classical Age, From Jābir ibn Ḥayyān to Naṣīr al-Dīn Ṭūsī*. London, 2008.

Nomoto, Shin. 'Early Ismā'īlī Thought on Prophecy according to *Kitāb al-Iṣlāḥ* by Abū Ḥātim al-Rāzī (d. ca. 322/934–5)', PhD dissertation, McGill University, 1999.

——'An Ismā'īlī Thinker on the Prophets in the Cosmic Correspondence: Translation of the *Kitāb al-Iṣlāḥ* by Abū Ḥātim al-Rāzī I', *Reports of the Keio Institute of Cultural and Linguistic Studies*, 34 (2002), pp. 97–152.

Peterson, Daniel C. 'Ḥamīd al-Dīn al-Kirmānī on Creation', in Ahmad Hasnawi et al., eds., *Perspectives Arabes et médiévales sur la tradition scientifique et philosophique Grecque*. Louvain and Paris, 1997, pp. 555–567.

Poonawala, Ismail K. *Biobibliography of Ismā'īlī Literature*. Malibu, CA, 1977.

——'Al-Sijistānī and his *Kitāb al-Maqālīd*', in Donald P. Little, ed., *Essays on Islamic Civilization Presented to Niyazi Berkes*. Leiden, 1976, pp. 274–283.

——'Ismā'īlī *ta'wīl* of the Qur'ān', in Andrew Rippin, ed. *Approaches to the History of the Interpretation of the Qur'ān*. Oxford, 1988, pp. 199–222.

al-Qāḍī, Wadād. 'An Early Fāṭimid Political Document', *Studia Islamica*, 48 (1978), pp. 71–108.

Ritter, Carl F. 'The Early Fatimid Mosque of al-Hakim, 990–1010', *Oriental Art*, 27 (1981), pp. 303–315.

Sanders, Paula. 'The Fāṭimid State, 969–1171', in M.W. Daly, ed., *The Cambridge History of Egypt*: vol. 1, *Islamic Egypt*, 640–1517, ed. Carl F. Petry. Cambridge, 1998, pp. 151–174, 560–561.

——'Fatimids', in *Dictionary of the Middle Ages*. New York, 1985, vol. 5, pp. 24–30.

al-Shayyāl, Jamāl al-Dīn. 'The Faṭimid Documents as a Source for the History of the Faṭimids and their Institutions', *Bulletin of the Faculty of Arts, Alexandria University*, 8 (1954), pp. 3–12.

Siorvanes L., *Proclus: Neoplatonic Philosophy and Science*. New Haven and London, 1996.

Smoor, Pieter. 'Fāṭimids', in *Encyclopaedia of Arabic Literature*, ed. J.S. Meisami and P. Starkey. London, 1968, vol. 1, pp. 224–226.

Sourdel, Dominique. 'Dār al-Ḥikma', in *EI2*, vol. 2, pp. 126–127.

Stern, Samuel M. *Fāṭimid Decrees: Original Documents from the Fāṭimid Chancery*. London, 1964.

——*Studies in Early Ismā'īlism*. Leiden and Jerusalem, 1983.

——'Heterodox Ismā'īlism at the Time of al-Mu'izz', *Bulletin of the School of Oriental and African Studies*, 17 (1955), pp. 10–33. Reprinted in Stern, *Studies in Early Ismā'īlism*, pp. 257–288.

——'Abu'l-Qāsim al-Bustī and his Refutation of Ismā'īlism', *Journal of the Royal Asiatic Society* (1961), pp. 14–35. Reprinted in Stern, *Studies in Early Ismā'īlism*, pp. 299–320.

——'Cairo as the Centre of the Ismā'īlī Movement', in *Colloque international sur l'histoire du Caire*. Cairo, 1972, pp. 437–450. Reprinted in Stern, *Studies in Early Ismā'īlism*, pp. 234–256.

——'The Earliest Cosmological Doctrines of Ismā'īlism', in Stern, *Studies in Early Ismā'īlism*, pp. 3–29.

Surūr, Muḥammad Jamāl al-Dīn. *al-Dawla al-Fāṭimiyya fī Miṣr*. Cairo, 1965–1966.

Tāmir, 'Ārif. *al-Ḥākim bi-Amr Allāh, khalīfa wa imām wa muṣliḥ*. Beirut, 1402/1982.

——*al-Imāma fi'l-Islām*. Beirut, n.d. [1964]; 2nd ed., Beirut, 1419/1998.

Tritton, Arthur S. 'Theology and Philosophy of the Isma'ilis', *Journal of the Royal Asiatic Society* (1958), pp. 178–188.

Vadet, J.C. 'Ibn Mas'ūd', *EI2*, vol. 3, pp. 873–875.

van Ess, Josef. *Chiliastische Erwartungen und die Versuchung der Göttlichkeit. Der Khalif al-Ḥākim (386–411)*. Heidelberg, 1977.

Vatikiotis, Panayiotis J. 'Al-Hakim bi-Amrillah: The God-King Idea Realised', *Islamic Culture*, 29 (1955), pp. 1–8.

Walker, Paul E. *Early Philosophical Shiism: The Ismaili Neoplatonism of Abū Yaʿqūb al-Sijistānī*. Cambridge, 1993.

—— *Ḥamīd al-Dīn al-Kirmānī: Ismaili Thought in the Age of al-Ḥākim*. London, 1999.

—— *Exploring an Islamic Empire: Fatimid History and its Sources*. London, 2002.

—— 'An Ismaʿili Answer to the Problem of Worshiping the Unknowable, Neoplatonic God', *American Journal of Arabic Studies*, 2 (1974), pp. 7–21.

—— 'The Ismaili *Daʿwa* in the Reign of the Fatimid Caliph al-Ḥākim', *Journal of the American Research Center in Egypt*, 30 (1993), pp. 161–182.

—— 'The Ismāʿīlī Daʿwa and the Fāṭimid Caliphate', in M.W. Daly, ed., *The Cambridge History of Egypt*: Volume 1, *Islamic Egypt, 640–1517*, ed. Carl F. Petry. Cambridge, 1998, pp. 120–150, 557–560.

Watt, W. Montgomery. *The Formative Period of Islamic Thought*. Edinburgh, 1973.

Wensinck, A.J. *Concordance et indices de la tradition musulmane*. Leiden, 1936–1969.

—— *A Handbook of Early Muhammadan Tradition*. Leiden, 1971.

Wilkinson, John Craven. *The Imamate Tradition of Oman*. Cambridge, 1987.

Zimmermann, Fritz. 'The Origins of the So-called *Theology of Aristotle*', in *Pseudo-Aristotle in the Middle Ages: The Theology and Other Texts*, ed. J. Kraye, W.F. Ryan and C.B. Schmitt. London, 1986. pp. 110–240.

Index

كتاب إثبات الإمامة

كتاب إثبات الإمامة

تأليف

أحمد بن إبراهيم النيسابوري

تحقيق

الرزينة ر. لالاني

بسم اللّٰه الرحمٰن الرحيم

وبه نستعين في جميع الأمور[١]

[١] الحمد للّٰه باعث الرسل والأنبياء، وجاعل الأئمة والخلفاء، نعمة للأولياء، ونقمة[٢] على الأعداء، وصلاحاً للدين والدنيا، وعمارة للآخرة والأولى. أحمده حمد من عرف عظيم قدر النعمة بهم وشكر عليها، وهاجر في اللّٰه وسارع إليها، وأشهد أن لا إِلٰه إلا اللّٰه وحده،[٣] شهادة عبد عارف بحدودها، ومجتهدٍ في أداء حقوقها، وأشهد أن محمداً عبده ورسوله[٤] المفضل على الرسل، والمعصوم من كل الخطايا والزلل، صلى اللّٰه عليه، صلاة لا يُحصى عددها، ولا ينقطع أمدها، وعلى وصيّه الوفي[٥] الصادق، صاحب البيان والحقائق، وعلى الأئمة من ولد الشهيد، أولي الثناء والتمجيد، والعصمة والتسديد، وعلى صاحب القصر والعصر، المؤيد بالفتح والنصر، أفضل سلام اللّٰه عليه وأنمى بركاته، وأزكى تحيّاته، وعلى ولي عهد المسلمين، وخليفة أمير المؤمنين، من[٦] اللّٰه أطيب السلام، ما نطق الألسن بالكلام، واختلف النور والظلام.

[١] وبه نستعين...الأمور: -، ب، ث؛ في جميع الأمور: -، ت.

[٢] ونقمة: نقمة، ب.

[٣] وحده: -، ب، ت، ث، ج.

[٤] ورسوله: -، ب، ث.

[٥] الوفي: الوافي، ا، ب، ت.

[٦] من: عليه من، ب.

[٢] أما بعد[١] فإنّه لمّا كانت الإمامة هي قطب الدين وأساسُه، والتي يدور عليها جميع أمور الدين والدنيا، وصلاح الآخرة والأولى، والتي بها[٢] ينتظم أمور العباد،[٣] وعمارة البلاد، وقبول الجزاء في دار المعاد، وبها يوصل إلى معرفة التوحيد والرسالة، بالحجّة والبرهان والدلالة، وإلى معرفة الشريعة وبنيانها،[٤] وتأويلها وتبيانها.

[٣] وإنمّا قلنا: إنّ الإمامة هي[٥] قطب الدين وأساسه، ولم نقدّم الرسالة على الإمامة، لأن في إثبات الإمامة إثبات الرسالة، والمُقرّ بالإمام مقرٌّ بالرسول، وليس كل من أقرّ بالرسول[٦] أقرّ بحقيقة الإمام، ولأن[٧] إثبات الرسالة يُحتاج إليه مع الخارجين من دار الإسلام، وإثبات الإمامة يُحتاج إليه مع المسلمين، وهم أقرب إلى المؤمنين، والمجاهدة معهم باللسان والمناظرة أولى من المناظرة مع المنكرين للرسول والرسالة، لأن من بقي من المشركين قد بلغت إليهم الدعوة، وقامت عليهم الحجة، والمناظرة معهم اليوم بالسيف أولى، ولأنّ الإمام هو الذي لا يخلو العالم منه في كل وقتٍ وزمانٍ،[٨] والرسول يكون في وقت دون وقت، ولأن في إثبات

---

[١] أما بعد: -، ب.

[٢] بها: -، ب، ث.

[٣] العباد: العبادة، ب.

[٤] وبنيانها: وبيانها، ب.

[٥] هي: -، ا.

[٦] بالرسول: بالرسل، ا، ت، ث.

[٧] ولأن: لأن، ت.

[٨] وزمان: + وأوان، ب، ث.

الإمامة إثبات الرسالة، وقد سمّى اللّٰه تعالى الإمام رسولاً في قوله تعالى: ﴿ وَٱذْكُرْ فِى ٱلْكِتَـٰبِ إِسْمَـٰعِيلَ إِنَّهُۥ كَانَ صَادِقَ ٱلْوَعْدِ وَكَانَ رَسُولاً نَّبِيًّا ﴾[١] وقد سمّى[٢] الرسولَ إماماً في قوله تعالى لإبراهيم ﴿ إِنِّي جَاعِلُكَ لِلنَّاسِ إِمَاماً ﴾، وهذا كان بعد إتمام[٣] الرسالة حيث قال اللّٰه تعالى: ﴿ وإِذِ[٤] ٱبْتَلَىٰٓ إِبْرَاهِيمَ رَبُّهُۥ بِكَلِمَـٰتٍ فَأَتَمَّهُنَّ قَالَ إِنِّى جَاعِلُكَ لِلنَّاسِ إِمَاماً ﴾.[٥]

[٤] ويروى[٦] عن جعفر الصادق[٧] سلام اللّٰه عليه أنّه قال: اتخذ اللّٰه إبراهيم نبياً ثم اتخذه خليلاً ثم اتخذه رسولاً، ثم قال: إِنِّي جَاعِلُكَ لِلنَّاسِ إِمَاماً، وسمّى اللّٰه آدم خليفة واسم الخليفة[٨] من أسماء الأئمّة، وسمّى اللّٰه داود عليه السلام خليفة، وكان من الأئمّة في الأدوار الماضية والحُجج[٩] أنبياء، وسمّى محمّداً صلّى اللّٰه عليه وآله وسلم وسائر الرسل أنبياء وخاطبهم بالأنبياء كما خاطبهم بالرسول، ولأن[١٠] الرسول أولاً[١١] يبلغ

---

[١] سورة ١٩ مريم ٥٤.

[٢] وقد سمّى: وسمّى، ب.

[٣] إتمام: تمام، ث.

[٤] وإِذِ: وإذا، ث.

[٥] سورة ٢ البقرة ١٢٤.

[٦] ويروى: وروي، ث.

[٧] الصادق: بن محمد، ب؛ بن محمد الصادق، ت.

[٨] الخليفة: الخلافة، ا، ب، ت، ث.

[٩] والحجج: الحجج، ب؛ + (حاشية) ظ وسمى، ت.

[١٠] ولأن: لأن، ب؛ ولا من، ت.

[١١] أولاً: إلا، ت.

إلى درجة الإمامة ثمّ إذا أوجب الوقت وضع شريعةٍ ويكون سابع أئمة ذلك الدور يقوم بوضع الشريعة، ولأن الإمام يقوم مقام الرسول في وقته وزمانه، ولأن الرسول قبل قيامه بوضع الشريعة كان من جملة الأئمة وتسلم الأمر من الإمام، وبعد فراغه من الشريعة سلّم الأمر إلى الإمام، والإمام قائم في العالم في كل وقت وزمان لا يخلو العالم منه، والإمام يحفظ الشريعة وحقائقها كما ذكرنا. وإذ قد صحّ وتبين أن مدار الدين على الإمام وإن كان الإمام يعمل في شريعة النبي في دوره فلا يوصل إلى النبي صلى اللّٰه عليه وآله وسلم ومنزلته وإلى شريعته الصحيحة[١] التي لم تغير ولم تبدل إلا من جهة الإمام، ولا يوصل إلى حقيقة الشريعة وتأويلها ومعانيها إلا من جهته.

[٥] وقد كثرت التأليفات في إثبات الإمامة لشيوخ الدعوة من طريق الاستدلال والاستشهاد من آي القرآن المعروفة المنزّلة في شأن الإمامة والأئمّة سلام اللّٰه عليهم والأخبار المروية عن النبي صلى اللّٰه عليه وآله وسلم، ولم يدَعِ المتقدمون في ذلك شيئاً للمتأخرين وليس في تكرير المعاني بتغيير[٢] الألفاظ كثير[٣] الفائدة. فأردنا[٤] أن نؤلف رسالة في إثبات الإمامة على طريق الاستشهاد والاستدلال من الآفاق والأنفس والسياسة

---

[١] شريعته الصحيحة: شريعته الصحيحة وتأويلها، ا؛ شريعة صحيحة وتأويلها، ب.

[٢] بتغيير: بتغير، ا، ت.

[٣] كثير: كثيرة، ا.

[٤] فأردنا: وأردنا، ا، ب، ث.

والرسوم ومن طريق العقل والضرورة والفطرة والجبلة[١] والاتفاق من أهل كل ملة ومن الفلاسفة وأهل الحساب، ثم نستشهد من ترتيب الفرائض والسُّنن من وجه لم يستشهد[٢] به شيوخ الدعوة. فإن كانت مرضية فبحُسن موادّ ولي العصر والزمان لعبيده، وإن كان فيها خطأٌ فمِن عجزي وتقصيري وهو أولى بي.

فصل[٣]

[٦] ونقول: إن وجوب الإمامة والأئمة سلام الله عليهم ضروري في الجبلة والفطرة[٤] والطبيعة[٥] والعقل والسياسة والوضع والرسوم، وواجب في كل شريعة ودين وملة كما أن[٦] وجوب الصانع ضروري في الجبلة والفطرة[٧] والعقل وفي كل ملة ودين، ولكن الناس اختلفوا في الصانع[٨] بعد وجوبه والتزامهم[٩] ذلك، وحكموا بأهوائهم وآرائهم وتقليد آبائهم وأستاذيهم أن الصانع الذي التزمه الجبلة والفطرة هو الجوهر أو العناصر أو الكواكب أو الشمس أو غير ذلك، أو وصفوا البارئ بصفةٍ تكون

---

١ الفطرة والجبلة: الجبلة والفطرة، ب.

٢ يستشهد: يستشهدوا، ا، ب، ت، ث.

٣ فصل: -، ث.

٤ الجبلة والفطرة: الفطرة والجبلة، ب.

٥ والطبيعة: -، ا، ت، ث.

٦ أن: -، ا، ب، ث.

٧ الجبلة والفطرة: الفطرة والجبلة، ب.

٨ الصانع: صانع، ا.

٩ والتزامهم: إلزامهم، ب.

تشبيهاً أو شركاً من جهة حكمهم بغير علم، كذلك في وجوب الإمامة وقعوا في اختلاف بعد التزامهم الإمام حتى قال بعضهم: إن الإمام الذي أوجبه العقل والضرورة هو الحكيم في كل زمان، مثل الفلاسفة فإنهم يسمون أستاذيهم أئمة وحكماء ورأس العلماء وسائس العالم والمعِّلم.

فصل

[٧] وأهل الأديان يسمون الأئمة الماضين أنبياء وحكماء في كل دور، وأهل الإسلام يسمون[١] المدّعين الظلمة المتغلبين أئمة ويسمون علماءهم وفقهاءهم أئمة، والجميع إذا تفحصت[٢] عنهم مقرّون بالإمام[٣] ضرورة لا يمكنهم إنكار وجوبه. فمن أراد النجاة والهدى[٤] ينبغي له[٥] أن يدع الميل والهوى[٦] ويعرف عجز كل مدّعٍ[٧] لهذا الاسم ونقصانه في العلم والمعرفة والتّقى وسائر الفضائل وشروط الإمامة، فإذا وقف على نقصان علمه وقلة ورعه وصيانته وعجزه عن القيام بشرائط الإمامة نفى عنه الإمامة حتى يبلغ إلى معرفة إمام الحق.

[١] يسمون: + الأئمة، ب.

[٢] تفحصت: تفصحت، ت.

[٣] بالإمام: بالإمامة، ا، ب، ت، ث.

[٤] والهدى: والهداي، ب.

[٥] له: -، ث.

[٦] والهوى: والهواي، ب.

[٧] مدع: مدعي، ا، ب، ت، ث.

[٨] ونحن[١] نذكر طرفاً من كلام كل مدّعٍ[٢] وعجزه ونقصانه ونردُّ عليه أصوله وننفي الإمامة عن كل من لا تليق به الإمامة، ونثبت إمامة أئمة الحق سلام الله عليهم بالحجة والبرهان، ونثبت وجوب الطاعة لهم والائتمار بأمرهم وقبول الشرع والتأويل والتوحيد منهم كما ذكرنا في كتاب التوحيد أن من عرف المخلوق ووقف على عجزه ونقصانه ينفي عنه الإلهية إلى أن ينفي الإلهية عن جميع المخلوقين، فيبقى[٣] التوحيد مجرَّداً من[٤] غير تشبيه ولا تعطيل.

[٩] ونقول: إن الله تعالى بلطيف حكمته وسعة قدرته[٥] خلق لجسد الإنسان أصولاً وعللاً وأسباباً وجعل جميع الفروع والمواليد مبروزة[٦] فيها وفي آثارها، يظهر[٧] منها بتقدير[٨] مقدَّر وأجل معلوم، إلى أن أظهر منها جسداً حساساً محاذياً لأصوله وموازياً لها، وجعل بتلك الأصول والأسباب قوامه وغذاءه، وبها يكون بقاؤه ومنها يكون ثوابه وعقابه الجسداني الحسّي. كذلك جعل للأنفس والأرواح[٩] والصور الدينية

---

[١] ونحن: -، ث.

[٢] مدع: مدعي، ا، ب، ت، ث.

[٣] فيبقى: فيبقى له، ت

[٤] من:-، ب، ت، ث.

[٥] قدرته: وقدرته، ب.

[٦] مبروزة: مرموزة + (حاشية) مبذورة، ب؛ مبزورة، ث.

[٧] يظهر: تظهر، ب، ث.

[٨] بتقدير: + (حاشية) ظاهر، ا.

[٩] والأرواح: وللأرواح، ث.

العلمية أصولاً وعللاً وأسباباً تظهر من آثارها الأنفس والأرواح والصور الدينية[١] وبها يكون قوامها وغذاؤها وبقاؤها وثوابها، وبانقطاع مادتها ومخالفتها لأصلها يكون عقابها.

[١٠] وجعل تعالى ذكره[٢] أصول الجسد وأسبابه شاهداً على أصول النفس[٣] ودليلاً عليها وعلى فروعها وغذائها لتكون الخلقة الدينية كالخلقة الجسدانية[٤] موازياً محاذياً[٥] لها،[٦] فكما أن الجسد لم يظهر ولم يتم إلا بالأفلاك[٧] والكواكب ولم يتم بالأفلاك[٨] دون الكواكب، وإن كانت الكواكب تدور في الأفلاك فمجاري الأمور على تأثير الكواكب، كذلك ظهور الصور الدينية والعلمية والأنفس الباقية إنما تظهر وتتم بتأثير الأئمة سلام الله عليهم ومن علومهم يكون غذاؤها وهم النجوم الدينية. كما قال النبي صلى الله عليه وآله وسلم: أصحابي كالنجوم بأيّهم اقتديتم اهتديتم، وإن كان تصرفهم في موضع[٩] الأنبياء الذين هم مثل الأفلاك،

---

[١] العلمية...والصور الدينية: -، ت.

[٢] ذكره:-، ا، ث.

[٣] النفس: الأنفس، ت.

[٤] الجسدانية: الجسمانية، ت.

[٥] محاذياً: محازياً، ا، ت، ث: مخازياً، ب.

[٦] لها: -، ا، ب، ت، ث.

[٧] بالأفلاك: الافلاك، ا، ث.

[٨] بالافلاك: بأفلاك، ت.

[٩] موضع:+ (حاشية) موضوع، ا؛ موضوع، ب؛ مواضع، ث.

وتكون مجاري أمور الخلق ورجوعهم إلى الأئمة[١] سلام الله عليهم. ولو ذكرنا موازاة[٢] أفلاك الدين مع أفلاك[٣] الطبيعة لطالت الرسالة وخرجت عن حدّها. ولكن[٤] اقتصرنا على إشارة منها في ابتداء الرسالة ليبحث[٥] من أراد أن يقف على غير ما ذكرنا إن شاء الله تعالى.

[١١] ونقول:[٦] إن التفاوت والتفاضل[٧] في كل شيء من الأصول والمواليد والفروع من آكد الدليل[٨] والحجة على إثبات الإمامة والأئمة عليهم السلام.[٩] وذلك أن الله تعالى خلق الأشياء متفاوتة متفاضلة في الأجناس والأنواع، ثم جعل في كل جنس ونوع غايةً وذروةً ونهايةً وفضيلةً لم يبلغ[١٠] غيره من جنسه ونوعه إليها، وجعل تلك الأجناس والأنواع إما أصلاً في الخلقة لا يستغني عالمُ البشر عنه[١١] ولا جسده يتم كونه وقوامه إلا به، وإما غذاءً له أو دواءً أو تجملاً[١٢] أو زينة[١٣] وآلة لا

---

[١] الأئمة: + سلام الله عليهم، ا، ث: + صلع، ب.

[٢] موازاة: مموازية، ت.

[٣] أفلاك: الافلاك، ا، ث.

[٤] ولكن: ولكنا، ت.

[٥] ليبحث: لبحث، ب.

[٦] ونقول: والتفاضل، ب.

[٧] والتفاضل: -، ب.

[٨] الدليل: الدلائل، ا، ث.

[٩] والأئمة عليهم السلام: - ا، ب.

[١٠] يبلغ: يبلع، ب.

[١١] عنه: منه، ا، ب، ت.

[١٢] أو تجملاً: وتجملاً، ا.

يستغني عنها، وجعل في كل شيء من ذلك منفعة لم تُجعل في غيره، وجعل لذلك الشيء عزاً وأحوج الخلق إلى ذلك اضطراراً وجبراً لا غناء لهم عن ذلك، ولا تنتظم[١] أمور جسدهم إلا به، وابتلاهم أبدًا في تحصيل ما يزيح علتهم في ذلك والسعي في طلبه واكتسابه، فإن لم يجده في موضعه أنفذ في طلبه أو سارع إلى موضع يجد ذلك فيه. وما دام هو في عالم[٢] جسده لا يستغني طرفة عين من التنسم[٣] والاستفادة من أصول عالمه ومن فروعه ومواليده ونباته وأغذيته، حكمة[٤] من اللّٰه جلّ جلاله وعدلاً منه ليكون ذلك شهوداً[٥] ومثالات جبريّات فانيات على ممثولاتٍ دينياتٍ باقياتٍ اختيارياتٍ،[٦] نَفْعُ كل واحد من الممثولات من الأصول والمواليد والأغذية والأدوية الدينية أجلّ وأفضل وأعزّ من المثالات الجبريات[٧] والاحتياج إليه أكثر من الاحتياج إلى الجبري الطبيعي لأن[٨] نفع الجبري[٩] راجع إلى الجسد ونفع ممثولاته راجع إلى

---

[١٣] أو زينة: وزينة، ا، ث.

[١] تنتظم: تنظم، ا، ب، ث.

[٢] عالم: علم، ت.

[٣] التنسم: +(حاشية) الالتماس، ا؛ النسيم، ث.

[٤] حكمة: حكمته، ب.

[٥] شهوداً: مشهوداً، ت.

[٦] إختياريات: اختيارات، ب، ت.

[٧] الجبريات: + فان الجبريات، ت.

[٨] لأن: فإن، ث.

[٩] نفع الجبري: نفعها، ا، ت: نفع الجبريات، ث.

الروح والنفس، فبمقدار زيادة فضل[١] الروح على الجسد يكون[٢] زيادة فضل الممثولات العقليات على المثالات الطبيعيات، وبمقدار زيادة فضل الباقي على الفاني يكون[٣] زيادة فضل الممثول على المثل، وبمقدار زيادة[٤] فضل[٥] كل واحد يكون الخلل بعدم كل شيء من ذلك. فإنّ مَن عدم شيئاً ممّا يحتاج إليه من الأشياء الجسدانيّة[٦] لا يكون هلاكه، وإن كان فيه هلاك[٧] فيكون[٨] هلاك جسده وهو لا شك[٩] يفنى ويهلك، وبعدم الممثول الديني يكون هلاك النفس ووقوعها في العذاب الأبدي. فلو[١٠] كان اجتهادهم[١١] في طلب ما يحتاج إليه النفس مثل اجتهادهم[١٢] وحرصهم في طلب ما يحتاج إليه الجسد لما وقع اثنان في شك وضلال[١٣] ولا تشبيه.

---

١ فضل: -، ب.

٢ يكون: -، ث.

٣ يكون: -، ث.

٤ زيادة: -، ا.

٥ فضل: -، ب.

٦ الجسدانية: الجسداني، ا.

٧ هلاك: هلاكه، ب، ت.

٨ وإن كان...فيكون: -، ث.

٩ شك: يشك، ث.

١٠ فلو: ولو، ا.

١١ اجتهادهم: + وحرصهم، ب.

١٢ اجتهادهم: اجتيادهم، ا.

١٣ وضلال: ولا ضلالة، ث.

[١٢] ونقول: إن جميع ما خلق اللّه تعالى على هذا[١] الترتيب في الخلقة وما أحوج الناس إليه كما ذكرنا تنبيهاً لهم على الممثول الديني ليكون[٢] شاهداً لمن يستشهد[٣] به ودلالة لمن يستدلّ[٤] به وتبصرة لمن يبصره ويعتبر وحجة على من أنكر الممثول الديني من الأئمة والحدود وعلومهم والاستفادة منهم كقبولهم استفادتهم[٥] من الأصول الطبيعية والكواكب والأفلاك.[٦] وإنما خلق اللّه تعالى هذه الأصول[٧] والأسباب والعلل الطبيعية جبراً[٨] لئلا يقدر أحدٌ أن ينكره[٩] أو يستشهد بها زوراً أو يغيرها أو يبدلها كما غيروا وبدلوا الشرع وكما غيروا ما أشهدهم عليه النبي صلوات اللّه وسلامه عليه في إثبات الإمامة والأئمة ووجوبها وموالاة الأئمة ووجوب الطاعة لهم والتوبيخ لمن عصاهم والوعد بالثواب لمن أطاعهم، وكما[١٠] غيّروا القرآن وحرّفوه.[١١] كما أخبر اللّه تعالى عنهم

---

[١] هذا: هذه، ت.

[٢] ليكون: وليكون، ب، ت.

[٣] يستشهد: استشهد، ا، ب، ت، ث.

[٤] يستدلّ: استدلّ، ث.

[٥] استفادتهم: واستفادتهم، ت.

[٦] والأفلاك: وأفلاك، ب.

[٧] الاصول: أصول، ث.

[٨] جبراً: جيراً، ث.

[٩] ينكره: ينكرها، ث.

[١٠] وكما: كما، ت.

[١١] حرّفوه: حرقوه، ا، ث.

بقوله: ﴿ يُحَرِّفُونَ ٱلْكَلِمَ عَن مَّوَاضِعِهِ وَنَسُوا۟ حَظًّا مِّمَّا ذُكِّرُوا۟ بِهِ ﴾[١] وكما قال تعالى ذكره:[٢] ﴿ إِنَّمَا ٱلنَّسِىٓءُ زِيَادَةٌ فِى ٱلْكُفْرِ ﴾[٣] ولم يكن ذلك نسياناً منهم، بل تناسوا تلك الشهادة كأن لم يسمعوها ولم يروها.

[١٣] وكما أن شهادة الآفاق والأنفس جبريّة ولا اختياريّة[٤] لا[٥] يمكن لأحد أن يغيّرها[٦] كذلك وضع الرسول صلى اللّٰه عليه وآله وسلم الشهادة جبراً لا اختيار[٧] للشاهد فيها بأن يغيّرها أو يبدّلها أو يكتمها، ومن غيّرها أو كتمها فقد أوعده[٨] بالعذاب الأليم، وأمر اللّٰه تعالى الحكم[٩] بشهادة شاهدين وذكر في قوله: ﴿ أَن تَضِلَّ إِحْدَاهُمَا فَتُذَكِّرَ إِحْدَاهُمَا ٱلْأُخْرَىٰ وَلَا يَأْبَ[١٠] ٱلشُّهَدَآءُ إِذَا مَا دُعُوا۟ ﴾[١١] يعنى أنّ[١٢] الحكم الحقيقي في الدين وإثبات الإمامة[١٣] والحدود بشاهدين[١٤] أحدهما وضعي شرعي والآخر

---

[١] سورة ٥ المائدة ١٣.

[٢] ذكره: -، ب، ت.

[٣] سورة ٩ التوبة ٣٧.

[٤] ولا اختيارية: والاختيارية، ت، ث.

[٥] لا: -، ث.

[٦] يغيرها: + او يبدلها، ا.

[٧] اختيار: اختياراً، ا، ب، ت.

[٨] أوعده: وعده، ت، ث.

[٩] الحكم: -، ا، ب، ث.

[١٠] يأب: يأبى، ا، ب، ث.

[١١] سورة ٢ البقرة ٢٨٢.

[١٢] أن: -، ت.

[١٣] وإثبات الامامة: واثبات الامام، ا، ث.

[١٤] بشاهدين: بشهادين، ت.

طبيعي جبري،[١] فإن أنكروا الشاهد[٢] الوضعي فالجبري الطبيعي[٣] الذي[٤] هو الآفاق والأنفس يُذكر ويقوي[٥] ويُصح[٦] شهادة الوضعي كما قال الله تعالى: ﴿ سَنُرِيهِمْ آيَاتِنَا فِي ٱلْآفَاقِ وَفِيٓ أَنفُسِهِمْ حَتَّىٰ يَتَبَيَّنَ لَهُمْ أَنَّهُ ٱلْحَقُّ ﴾[٧] وكما قال النبي صلى الله عليه وآله وسلم حيث[٨] قيل له: من يشهد على نبوّتك؟ قال: يشهد لي كل حجر ومدر،[٩] فأشار إلى شهادة الآفاق والأنفس.[١٠] وإذا شهد[١١] الشاهدان الشرعي والطبيعي،[١٢] ويكون العقل هو المزكي يزكّي الشهود من غير ميل ولا هوى، تبين[١٣] الحق سريعاً.[١٤]

[١٤] ونذكر الآن[١٥] التفاوت والتفاضل في كل أصل ومواليد،[١٦]

---

[١] طبيعي جبري: طبعي، ث.

[٢] الشاهد: الشهود، ا، ب، ت، ث.

[٣] الطبيعي: الطبعي، ث.

[٤] الذي: -، ب، ت؛ مكرر في ث.

[٥] ويقوي: وتقواى، ب.

[٦] ويصح: وتصح، ا؛ ويص، ب؛ تصحح، ث.

[٧] سورة ٤١ فُصِّلَتْ (حمَ السَّجدَة) ٥٣.

[٨] حيث: حين، ت.

[٩] ومدر: ومدى، ب.

[١٠] والأنفس: -، ب.

[١١] شهد: شاهد، اك أشهد، ت.

[١٢] الطبيعي: الطبعي، ث.

[١٣] تبين: يبين، ا؛ يتبين، ث.

[١٤] سريعاً: -، ب.

[١٥] الآن: لأن، ت؛ أن، ث.

ونستشهد من كل جنس ونوع بغايته[١] وذُروته على الإمام في كل عصر وزمان. وإن كان هذه الأجناس والأنواع[٢] تدل على الإمامة والأئمة[٣] على ترتيب آخر من جهة[٤] التسابيع مثل أن تشهد الكواكب السبعة على الأئمة السبعة[٥] وغير ذلك من التسابيع فلا يمنع أن يكون دليل[٦] من جهة الذروة[٧] والتمام من كل نوع وجنس على الإمام كما ذكرنا.[٨]

[١٥] ونقول: إنّ الحكماء من الفلاسفة ذكروا المقولات العشرة وقالوا: إنّه لا يقدر أحد أن[٩] يذكر[١٠] شيئاً أو يتكلم إلا من هذه العشرة، وهي الجوهر والكمّية والكيفيّة والإضافة والمكان والزمان والجِدة[١١] والنُّصْبة والفاعل والمفعول. فالغاية[١٢] من العشرة هو[١٣] الجوهر وبه يقوم

---

[١٦] سريعاً ونذكر ... ومواليد: -، ب.

[١] بغايته: بغاية، ث.

[٢] والأنواع: -، ا.

[٣] والأئمة: -، ث.

[٤] جهة: جملة، ت.

[٥] السبعة: -، بك السابعة، ت.

[٦] دليل: دليلاً، ب، ت، ث.

[٧] الذروة: الضرورة + (حاشية) الذروة ن، ث.

[٨] كما ذكرنا: كما نذكر، ا؛ يذكر، ث

[٩] أحد أن: احداً أن، ث.

[١٠] يذكر: أحداً، ث.

[١١] الجدة: الجلة، ت.

[١٢] فالغاية: والغاية، ث.

[١٣] هو: هي، ب.

الجميع وله الفضل على الجميع،[١] والتسعة قائمة به. فالجوهر الذي[٢] وصفوه دليل على الجوهر الحقيقي النوري العقلي الأبدي الذي منه[٣] تضيء جميع الأنفس، وبه يقوم جميع الأعراض الدينيّة التسعة، وهو المستغني عن جميع الخلق، لا يستفيد هو من أحد في[٤] العالم، والجميع يستفيدون منه ويحتاجون إليه، وهو الإمام عليه السلام،[٥] وسائر الحدود تحته مثل الأعراض[٦] التسعة.

[١٦] ونقول: إن العناصر الأربعة التي منها ركبت التراكيب: الأول منها[٧] اثنان فاعلان واثنان منفعلان، فالفاعلان[٨] هما الحرارة والبرودة، والمنفعلان هما اليبوسة والرطوبة، فإن[٩] غايتها وأشرفها الحرارة، ومنها الضياء والنور والحركة والعلو وبها قوام الثلاثة، ولها السبق في الأصل[١٠] والكون، ولا يتم أصل ولا مواليد إلا بها. كذلك الإمام ضياء الأنفس ومنه النّور العقلي والحركة والعلو ولا يتم من الأصول[١١] شيء إلا به ولا

---

[١] وله الفضل على الجميع: -، ث.

[٢] الذي: هو الذي، ت؛ هي الذي، ب.

[٣] منه: عنه، ا.

[٤] في: من، ب.

[٥] عليه السلام: سلام الله عليه، ب، ت، ث.

[٦] مثل الأعراض: مثلا لأعراض، ت.

[٧] منها: منهان، ت.

[٨] فالفاعلان: فان الفاعلان، ا.

[٩] فإن: وإن، ث.

[١٠] الأصل: الفضل، ث.

[١١] الأصول: الأصل، ا.

من المواليد الدينيّة. ثمّ الأفلاك[١] أجلّها وأعلاها فلك الأفلاك، والجميع يدور[٢] فيه، فكذلك هو في دينه فلك الأفلاك الديني للأفلاك[٣] الدينية، وجميع الكواكب والبروج الدينية تحت أمره يعملون.[٤] فإن قال قائل: إنّ هذا مثل على القائم، وكذلك[٥] أعلى[٦] أركان[٧] العالم[٨] دليل على العقل من الأصول الأربعة، قلنا: إنّ الإمام قائم[٩] وهو الناطق في وقته وزمانه،[١٠] فهو[١١] يقوم مقامه، والإمام مقامه مقام العقل الكلي في عالمه.

فصل[١٢]

[١٧] ونقول:[١٣] إن الأركان الأربعة أعلاها وأشرفها النار وهي الغاية والذروة التي لا[١٤] يبلغ إليها سائر[١٥] الأركان والطبائع، وكذلك[١٦] الإمام في

---

[١] الأفلاك: -، ا.

[٢] يدور: يدر، ا.

[٣] للأفلاك: الأفلاك، ت.

[٤] يعملون: يحملون، ب؛ ويعلمون، ت.

[٥] وكذلك: في كذلك، ا.

[٦] أعلى: على، ث.

[٧] أركان: اكان، ب.

[٨] العالم: العلم، ب.

[٩] قائم: + في وقته وزمانه، ا، ب، ت.

[١٠] وهو الناطق...وزمانه: -، ت.

[١١] فهو: وهو، ا، ب، ت.

[١٢] فصل: -، ث.

[١٣] ونقول: -، ث.

[١٤] لا: -، ا، ب، ت، ث.

[١٥] سائر: سرائر، ث.

وقته وزمانه أعلى أركان الدين وبه ضياء النفوس، ومن هذه[1] الجهة أمر إبراهيم عليه السلام بتعظيم النار، إن صحّ ذلك عنه، ومنعهم من إخمادها وإطفائها، وإنما الإشارة[2] كانت إلى تعظيم الإمامة وأن لا يطفئوها بظلم من يدعي منزلتها.[3] ووقع[4] عبدة[5] النيران في الشبهة ولم يعرفوا ممثولها،[6] وحكى الله تعالى عن الأضداد والغاصبين لموضع الإمامة[7] في قوله: ﴿ يُرِيدُونَ أَن يُطْفِئُواْ[8] نُورَ ٱللَّهِ بِأَفْوَٰهِهِمْ وَيَأْبَى ٱللَّهُ إِلَّآ أَن يُتِمَّ نُورَهُۥ وَلَوْ كَرِهَ ٱلْكَـٰفِرُونَ ﴾.[9]

[١٨] ونقول: إنّ الكواكب كثيرة وفيها[10] التفاوت والتفاضل، وغايتها وذروتها في الشرف والفضل هي الشمس، وبها تستضيء الأبصار الجسدانيّة وبها ينمو ويتم كل حيوان ونبات ومولود،[11] وكل نبات

---

[16] وكذلك: كذلك، ا.

[1] هذه: هذا، ب.

[2] الإشارة: الإشارات، ت.

[3] منزلتها: منزلتهم، ا، ب، ت، ث.

[4] وقع: وقعت، ا، ب، ت، ث.

[5] عبدة: عبده، ت.

[6] ممثولها: ممثولاها، ث.

[7] الإمامة: الإمام، ث.

[8] أَن يُطْفِئُواْ: ليطفوا،ا؛ ليطفؤوا، ب؛ ليطفيواه، ت؛ ان يطيفوا، ث.

[9] سورة ٩ التوبة ٣٢ .

[10] وفيها: فيها، ت.

[11] ومولود: ومواليد، ا، ب، ت، ث.

ومولود[١] لم يصل إليه تأثير الشمس لا ينمو.[٢] وكذلك الإمام هو شمس الدين، منه تستضيء البصائر وتضيء[٣] النفوس بنور الهداية والحكمة وتضيء قلوب أولياء الله.[٤] ومن هذه الجهة أشاروا إلى تعظيم الشمس ووقع[٥] عبدة الشمس في الشبهة، فإنّهم عرفوا المثل ولم يعرفوا الممثول، ومن هذه الجهة أشار النبي صلى الله عليه وآله وسلم إلى طلوع الشمس من المغرب إشارة إلى خروج الإمام سلام الله عليه من المغرب.[٦] فإنّ الشمس الجرمانيّة لو زالت عن ترتيب دورانها وطلوعها وغروبها عن[٧] مركزها طرفة عين لفسد العالم بأجمعه،[٨] وذلك ممتنع في العقول وفي الطبيعة. فلم يستقم قول النبي صلى الله عليه وآله وسلم إلا بالتأويل وقد صحّ تأويله بالعيان بحمد الله ومنّه.

[١٩] ونقول:[٩] إنّ البروج الاثني عشر أربعة منها أجل وأفضل، وواحد من الأربعة هو الغاية والذروة في الشرف، وكذلك[١٠] الواحد

---

[١] ومولود: ومواليد، ا، ب، ت، ث.

[٢] ينمو: ينمي، ب، ت.

[٣] وتضيء: وتستضي، ت.

[٤] أولياء الله: أولياءه، ا، ب؛ أوليائه، ث.

[٥] ووقع: ووقعت، ا، ب، ت، ث.

[٦] إشارة...المغرب: -، ب.

[٧] عن: من، ا، ث.

[٨] بأجمعه: باجمعها، ب.

[٩] ونقول: -، ث.

[١٠] وكذلك: كذلك، ا، ث.

الذي[١] تتحد[٢] به الإمامة من الاثني عشر هو أفضل الجميع وأشرفهم وأعلاهم.

فصل[٣]

[٢٠] والإقليم[٤] الرابع الذي هو بإزاء السماء الرابع وبإزاء[٥] الشمس هو أعدل الأقاليم وأفضلها وأشرفها، فكذلك[٦] الإمام هو أفضل الحدود السبعة وأجلّهم وغايتهم وذروتهم.

[٢١] ونقول: إنّ الجواهر المذابة من المعادن[٧] أفضلها الذهب، وهو الذي تجري عليه معاملات الناس وهو قيمة المقومات وهو الذي لا يؤثر فيه النار ولا الماء[٨] ولا يفسدانه.[٩] فكذلك الإمام عليه السلام هو أفضل الجواهر الدينية العقلية في وقته وزمانه وبه تتمّ معاملات الخلق وصلاحهم في الدين والدنيا.[١٠] وسائر الجواهر المذابة لكل منها غاية في التفاضل. ومن الجواهر الحجريّة غايتها الياقوت وغاية اليواقيت من الأبيض

---

[١] الذي: التي، ب.

[٢] تتحد: تحد، ث.

[٣] فصل: ونقول، ا.

[٤] والإقليم: والاقاليم، ث.

[٥] السماء الرابع وبإزاء: -، ث.

[٦] فكذلك: وكذلك، ت.

[٧] المعادن: المعدن، ت.

[٨] ولا الماء: والماء، ب.

[٩] يفسدانه: يفسدا، ا، ت؛ يفسده، ث.

[١٠] الدين والدنيا: الدنيا والدين، ب.

والأخضر والأصفر والأحمر[١] هو الياقوت الأحمر، وليس لغيره من الجواهر[٢] بقاء مثل بقائه،[٣] فإنّه يبقى[٤] بقاء عالمه لا يتغيّر بالنار والماء،[٥] وله صفاء ورونق ورزانة، وقد قبل[٦] من الآثار من أصله ما لم يقدر غيره على قبوله من الجواهر وسائر اليواقيت ولا الزمرّد ولا البَدَخْشي[٧] ولا[٨] البيجاد[٩] والعقيق والألماس والفيروزج،[١٠] وهو غاية الجواهر، يعني الياقوت الأحمر، كما أنّ الإمام غاية جميع الخلائق[١١] في وقته وزمانه، وقد تفرّد عن سائر الحدود الذين هم الحجج واللواحق والداعي والجناح والمأذون والمكلّب.[١٢] فالإمام هو الغاية الذي لا يبلغ في وقته وزمانه أحد إلى منزلته ومرتبته. وفي وجه آخر تكون السبعة من الجواهر دليلاً[١٣] على النطقاء السبعة والأئمة السبعة. وهذا الوجه الذي نستدل[١٤] به أقوى في

[١] والأحمر: -، ب.

[٢] الجواهر: اليواقيت، ث.

[٣] بقاء مثل بقائه: بقاء، ث.

[٤] يبقى: تبقى، ب.

[٥] بالنار والماء: بالماء والنار، ث.

[٦] قبل: قيل، ب، ث.

[٧] البدخشي: البن خسي، ا؛ البرخسي، ب؛ البرخس، ت، البرجيس، ث.

[٨] لا: -، ت، ث.

[٩] البيجاد: اليجاد، ب.

[١٠] والعقيق والألماس والفيروزج: - ب؛ ولا العقيق ولا الماس ولا الفيروزج، ا، ث.

[١١] الخلائق: الخلق، ا، ب

[١٢] والمكلب: المكلب، ب.

[١٣] دليلاً: دليل، ث.

[١٤] نستدل: يستدل، ا، ب، ت، ث.

موضعه، وذلك أنّ المثل[١] الطبيعيّ موجود في كل وقت وزمان، فينبغي أن يكون ممثوله موجوداً في كل وقت وزمان. فإنّ الأنجم والطبائع[٢] والمواليد والجواهر موجودة، فينبغي أن تكون الحدود أيضاً موجودة في كل وقت وزمان وتأثيراتهم في الأنفس موجودة.

[٢٢] ونقول: إنّ الحبوب التي تكون قوت الإنسان وغذاءه[٣] منها[٤] سبعة غايتها الحنطة، وهي أعدلها طبعاً وشرفاً وبها يقوم الجسد. كذلك الإمام هو الغاية والذروة ومنه تكون[٥] فوائد الأنفس وغذاؤها وبه قوامها وحياتها وبالعلوم التي[٦] تبلغ[٧] منه إليها.

فصل

[٢٣] وأمّا الأشجار المثمرة[٨] فغايتها وذروتها النخل، وهي[٩] مثل الإنسان منها ذكر وأنثى، تحتاج إلى[١٠] المزاوجة والفحل مثل الحيوان، ثمّ كلّ

---

[١] المثل: مثل، ت.

[٢] والطبائع: والصبايع، ب.

[٣] وغذاءه: وغذاء، ب.

[٤] منها: ومنها، ا.

[٥] تكون: يكون، ا، ب، ت.

[٦] وبالعلوم التي: وبالعلم الذي، ا، ب.

[٧] تبلغ: يبلغ، ا.

[٨] المثمرة: للمثمرة، ا؛ للثمرة، ب.

[٩] وهي: وهو، ث.

[١٠] إلى: -، ث.

شيء من النخل ينتفع به ولا يسقط منه شيء وتؤكل ثمارها[١] في كلّ وقت نيّاً ومطبوخاً. وفي النوم من رأى أنّه يجتني الرطب من النخل فتعبيره أنّه ينتفع من رجل مؤمن، والمؤمن في الحقيقة[٢] هو[٣] الإمام وهو رأس المؤمنين.

[٢٤] ونقول: إنّ من النبات ما يكون أدوية لطيفة يبلغ[٤] في اللطافة[٥] والفضل إلى أن يكون ترياقاً ينجو به من أشرف على الهلاك، ومنها ما يكون شفاءً من الداء المعضل، ومنها ما يكون دونها في الدرجة. فالغاية والذروة[٦] منها دليل[٧] على الإمام الذي يكون منه ومن كلامه ترياق الأنفس وشفاؤها[٨] وخلاصها من الهلاك والأمراض والشكوك والاختلاف. والذي يكون من الأدوية[٩] مثل السمّ القاتل والأشياء المضرّة مثلها[١٠] مثل الأضداد الغاصبين لمنزلة الأئمّة عليهم السلام، وهم السموم القاتلة الضّارة[١١] المهلكة لمن سمع منهم أو صحبهم أو مال إليهم إذا لم

---

[١] ثماره: ثمارها، ا، ب، ت، ث.

[٢] في الحقيقة: في هذا المكان ، ا، ب.

[٣] هو: وهو، ت.

[٤] يبلغ: تبلغ، ث.

[٥] اللطافة: للطافة، ا.

[٦] الذروة: الذزوة، ا.

[٧] دليل: دليلاً، ث.

[٨] شفاؤها: شفاءها، ا، ت.

[٩] الأدوية: الماليد، ت.

[١٠] مثلها: -، ث.

[١١] الضّارة: الضارية، ت، ث.

يلحقهم الإمام بالترياق الأعظم الذي يخلص[١] الأنفس من الهلاك. وهكذا[٢] الأحجار التي لا فائدة فيها ولا ينتفع بها فمثلها مثل[٣] الأضداد. ولذلك[٤] قال اللّه تعالى: ﴿ حَصَبُ جَهَنَّمَ أَنتُمْ لَهَا وَارِدُونَ ﴾،[٥] وقوله:[٦] ﴿ وَٱتَّقُواْ ٱلنَّارَ ٱلَّتِى[٧] وَقُودُهَا ٱلنَّاسُ وَٱلْحِجَارَةُ أُعِدَّتْ لِلْكَـٰفِرِينَ ﴾.[٨]

[٢٥] ونقول:[٩] إنّ الحيوان غايتها الفرس، ومن الطيور[١٠] النسر، ومن السباع الأسد. وتفاوُت[١١] أنواع الحيوان وتفاضلهم في القوّة والمنفعة وزيادة قبول الرياضة[١٢] وبلوغ كل نوع إلى غاية[١٣] وذروة دليل على أن[١٤] من يكون ذروة وغاية من جنس الحيوان ونوع البشر يكون غاية[١٥]

---

[١] يخلص: يخلض، ث.

[٢] وهكذا: هكذا، ا، ت، ث.

[٣] مثل: كمثل، ا، ت، ث.

[٤] لذلك: كذلك، ث.

[٥] سورة ٢١ الأنبياء ٩٨.

[٦] وقوله: + تعالى، ا.

[٧] واتقوا النار التي:-، ب.

[٨] سورة ٢ البقرة ٢٤.

[٩] ونقول: -، ث.

[١٠] الطيور: الطير، ث.

[١١] وتفاوت: تفاوة، ب.

[١٢] الرياضة: الرضة، ب.

[١٣] غاية: + من جنس الحيوان ونوع، ت.

[١٤] أن: -، ا، ب، ت، ث.

[١٥] وغاية: وعاية، ث.

الجميع، وهو الإمام سلام الله عليه.

[٢٦] ونقول: إنّ من النبات ما هو حلو طيّب لذيذ شهيّ ينتفع الناس به ومنها ما هو[١] مرّ ليس فيه فائدة ولا لذّة ومنها ما ليس له ثمر وهي ذات الشوكة ويتأذّى بها الناس.[٢] فالحلو[٣] الطيّب مثل على[٤] الأئمّة ومثل على كلامهم وعلومهم[٥] التي تشتهيها الأنفس وتلذّ الأعين، والمرّ المنتن وذات الشوكة مثل أئمّة أهل[٦] الظاهر. ولذلك قال اللّه تعالى: ﴿ أَلَمْ تَرَ كَيْفَ ضَرَبَ ٱللَّهُ[٧] مَثَلاً[٨] كَلِمَةً طَيِّبَةً كَشَجَرَةٍ طَيِّبَةٍ أَصْلُهَا ثَابِتٌ وَفَرْعُهَا فِي ٱلسَّمَاءِ تُؤْتِيٓ أُكُلَهَا كُلَّ حِينٍ بِإِذْنِ رَبِّهَا وَيَضْرِبُ ٱللَّهُ ٱلْأَمْثَالَ لِلنَّاسِ لَعَلَّهُمْ يَتَذَكَّرُون وَمَثَلُ كَلِمَةٍ خَبِيثَةٍ كَشَجَرَةٍ خَبِيثَةٍ ٱجْتُثَّتْ مِن فَوْقِ ٱلْأَرْضِ مَا لَهَا مِنْ قَرَارٍ ﴾.[٩]

[٢٧] ونقول: إن النبات منه ما يكون طيب الرائحة يستريح الناس بنسيمه[١٠] ورائحته ويشفيهم[١١] من كل داء وعلة، فغايتها في الطيب

---

[١] هو: يكون، ا.

[٢] بها الناس: به، ت.

[٣] فالحلو: فالحلول، ب.

[٤] على: -، ا، ث.

[٥] وعلومهم: وعلمهم، ت، ث.

[٦] أهل: -، ا.

[٧] أَلَمْ تَرَ كَيْفَ ضَرَبَ ٱللَّهُ: -، ا، ب، ت، ث.

[٨] مثلاً: ومثل، ا، ب، ت، ث.

[٩] سورة ١٤ إبراهيم ٢٤- ٢٦.

[١٠] بنسيمه: بشمه، ا.

والرائحة مثل على الإمام وكلامه الذى يستريح به النفوس،[١] والمنتن الكريه[٢] المؤذي دليل على أئمة الضلال وعلى كلامهم الذي تتأذى الأنفس به وربّما تهلك.

[٢٨] ونقول: إنّ الغزال الّذي يكون[٣] منه المسك والنحل الّذي يكون منه العسل فإنّ يعسوبهم دليل على الإمام، ولذلك قال النبيّ صلى اللّٰه عليه وآله وسلم لأمير المؤمنين عليّ عليه السلام: أنت[٤] يعسوب المؤمنين. وقال تعالى:[٥] ﴿ وَأَوْحَى رَبُّكَ إِلَى ٱلنَّحْلِ أَنِ ٱتَّخِذِى مِنَ ٱلْجِبَالِ بُيُوتاً وَمِنَ ٱلشَّجَرِ وَمِمَّا يَعْرِشُونَ ثُمَّ كُلِى مِنْ كُلِّ ٱلثَّمَرَاتِ فَٱسْلُكِى سُبُلَ رَبِّكِ ذُلُلاً يَخْرُجُ مِن بُطُونِهَا شَرَابٌ مُخْتَلِفٌ[٦] أَلْوَانُهُ فِيهِ شِفَاءٌ لِّلنَّاسِ ﴾.[٧]

[٢٩] ونقول:[٨] إنّ البشر غاية الحيوان والمواليد، ونفع جميع ما تقدّم على البشر من الأصول والفروع[٩] والمواليد راجع إلى البشر؛ وظهر فضائل

---

[١١] ويشفيهم: ويشفيه، ا، ب، ت.

[١] النفوس: -، ا، ب، ت، ث.

[٢] الكريه: الكرهية، ب.

[٣] يكون: تكون، ت.

[٤] علي أنت: أنت، ا؛ ياعلي أنت، ث.

[٥] وقال تعالى: و قال جلّ جلاله، ا، ث.

[٦] مختلف: مختلفة، ب.

[٧] سورة ١٦ النحل ٦٨-٦٩.

[٨] ونقول: -، ث.

[٩] والفروع: والفرع، ث.

العالم[١] وما فيه من الحيوان والنبات وغيرها ونفعها[٢] وعزّها وقيمتها وجودتها بالبشر. ولولا البشر لما ظهر فضل[٣] الأشياء ولا نظام العالم ولا تمّ شيء منه ولا من انتفاعه ولا من ادّخار شيء[٤] منه ولا من النبات والحيوان. فإنّ البشر هو الّذي يستعمل[٥] الماء وساقه إلى الأراضي وجعله تحت العقد العقلي وأنبطه[٦] من الأودية[٧] والأنهار والآبار،[٨] والبشر زرع[٩] الأراضي وغرس فيها وجعل منها[١٠] مساكن واستقى[١١] الماء للنبات والزرع وجعل الأرض تحت العقود العقليّة.

ثمّ البشر هو الّذي استعمل الرياح والهواء،[١٢] والبشر أخرج النار بالزناد من الطبائع وأظهر في الحيوان ما لم يكن بمزاوجة أحدهما[١٣] مع الآخر. ووصل الأشجار بعضها ببعض حتّى أظهر منها ثماراً لم تكن في العالم،

١ العالم: العلم، ا، ث.

٢ وغيرها ونفعها: وغيرهما ونفعهما، ث.

٣ فضل: فضائل، ب، ت، ث.

٤ من ادخار شيء: من الادخار بشيء، ا.

٥ يستعمل: استعمل، ا، ث، ج.

٦ وأنبطه: وأنبط، ا، ب، ت؛ وأنبطا، ث.

٧ الأودية: الأدوية، ت.

٨ الآبار: الأوبار، ت.

٩ زرع: ذرع، ب.

١٠ منها: فيها، ب، ت.

١١ واستقى: واسقى، ا، ت، ث.

١٢ هو الذي...والهواء: -، ب.

١٣ أحدهما: احداهما، ث.

وأخرج الجواهر من المعادن وجعل الأشجار والحبوب والثمار[١] الّتي فيها المنافع تحت الحكم والعقد، وحفظ صلاح الحيوان والنبات ونتاج الحيوان، وجعل الحيوان[٢] تحت حكمه وعقده. وكما أنّ غاية الحيوان والنبات والمعادن والمواليد كان البشر وبه تمّ[٣] صلاح الحيوان وما قبلها،[٤] وبه انتظمت أمورهم، كذلك كان الإمام غاية البشر وذروتهم وصفوتهم وكمالهم،[٥] وبالإمام انتظمت أمور البشر. وكما أنّ نفع جميع ما تقدّم على البشر راجع إلى البشر، كذلك نفع جميع البشر وصفوتهم راجع إلى الأئمّة سلام اللّه عليهم، ومنهم تعلّم البشر الفضائل والعلوم، ومنهم[٦] اقتبسوا العقول والدراية،[٧] وبهم كان صلاحهم في معاملة دينهم ودنياهم[٨] ومعادهم، وبهم اهتدوا إلى معرفة الصانع وعرفوا وجوب الشكر، للمنعم وكيفيّة أداء الشكر وبهم عرفوا الرسول وكيفيّة طاعتهم.

[٣٠] وكما أنّ نفع جميع الحيوان وما تقدمهم راجع إلى البشر وصار البشر بحكم ذلك سائسهم،[٩] كذلك رجع[١٠] نفع جميع البشر إلى

---

[١] والثمار: والنبات، ب.

[٢] وجعل الحيوان: -، ب، ث.

[٣] وبه تم: وبتم، ت.

[٤] قبلها: قبلهم، ا، ب.

[٥] وكمالهم: + نفع، ب.

[٦] ومنهم: -، ت.

[٧] الدراية: الرراية، ت.

[٨] دينهم ودنياهم: دنياهم ودينهم، ث.

[٩] سائسهم: سائسيهم، ت.

الأئمّة وصاروا سواس[١] البشر وآمريهم وناهيهم. ولولا الأئمّة وإرشادهم[٢] للبشر وهدايتهم وحفظ صلاحهم[٣] في معاشهم ومعادهم وحملهم[٤] على اقتناء الفضائل[٥] والاجتناب من الرذائل ومن العادات الحيوانيّة لما كان بين البهائم والبشر فرق، لا بل الحيوان كان أفضل لأنّ الإنسان إذا لم[٦] يقبل الرياضة ولم يحصل[٧] لنفسه الفضائل ولم يتعلّم من الأئمّة ولم يقتبس[٨] العقل منهم فهو شرّ من البهائم لأن البهائم لا تقدر[٩] على الفساد كما يقدر الإنسان، وفي البهائم منافع كثيرة، والبشر إذا لم[١٠] يكن له عقل ودين فهو كلّه شرّ وفساد. ومن أجل ذلك قال اللّه تعالى: ﴿ إِنَّ شَرَّ ٱلدَّوَآبِّ عِندَ ٱللَّهِ ٱلصُّمُّ ٱلْبُكْمُ[١١] ٱلَّذِينَ لَا يَعْقِلُونَ ﴾.[١٢] وقال

---

[١٠] رجع: راجع، ث.

[١] سواس: سوائس من، ث.

[٢] وإرشادهم: ورشدهم، ا، ت، ث.

[٣] صلاحهم: اصلاحهم، ب.

[٤] في معاشهم ومعادهم وحملهم: -، ب.

[٥] الفضائل: الفضل، ب.

[٦] إذا لم: إن لم، ث.

[٧] ولم يحصل: ويستحصل، ب، ت؛ ولم تحصل، ث.

[٨] يقتبس: يفتش، ت.

[٩] لا تقدر: لا يقدر، ا، ب، ت.

[١٠] إذا لم: ان لم، ث.

[١١] ٱلْبُكْمُ: والبكم، ت.

[١٢] سورة ٨ الأنفال ٢٢.

تعالى: ﴿ أُوْلَـٰئِكَ كَٱلْأَنْعَـٰمِ بَلْ هُمْ أَضَلُّ[١] أُوْلَـٰئِكَ هُمُ ٱلْغَـٰفِلُون ﴾.[٢]

وكما أنّه لو لم يكن البشر لما كان في خلقة الحيوان والنبات حكمة، وما كان ينتفع بها، فهكذا[٣] لولا الأئمة سلام اللّٰه عليهم لما كان في خلقة البشر حكمةٌ وما ظهرت فضيلته.[٤] فإنّ البشر[٥] خلقوا[٦] للدين وقبول الفضائل[٧] والعلم، فتعلموا العلم والدين من الأئمّة سلام اللّٰه عليهم[٨] وبهم يقوم الدين ويتم، ولو لم تظهر فضيلة البشر بالدين لما ظهرت فضيلة الحيوان والنبات وما كان في خلقة البشر والنبات والحيوان حكمة. ولو بطلت الحكمة في خلقهم لبطلت الحكمة في[٩] خلق العوالم[١٠] كلّها.

[٣١] فإذاً قد صح أنّ العوالم[١١] كلها خُلِقت للبشر والبشر خلقت[١٢]

[١] أضل: + سبيل، ب، ث.

[٢] سورة ٧ الأعراف ١٧٩.

[٣] فهكذا: هكذا، ا، ب، ت؛ كذلك، ث.

[٤] فضيلته: فضيله، ت.

[٥] البشر: -، ب.

[٦] خلقوا: خلق، ا، ت.

[٧] الفضائل: الفضل، ا.

[٨] سلام اللّٰه عليهم: -، ب.

[٩] خلقهم...في: -، ث.

[١٠] العوالم: العوام، ب.

[١١] أنّ العوالم: أنّ الخلائق و العوام، ب.

[١٢] خلقت: خلق، ث.

للأئمّة عليهم السلام[١] ولقبول الدين منهم وبهم تمّت وظهرت فضائلُه[٢] ونظامُه[٣] وقوامُه. فإذا خُلِقت[٤] العوالم والخلائق كلّها للأئمّة سلام اللّه عليهم وجميع منافع العوالم راجعة إليهم وسائر الخلق[٥] عيال لهم وكَلٌّ عليهم فما منوا[٦] به على الخلق فبفضلهم وكرمهم ورحمتهم، وما منعوا منهم فليس لأحد عليهم وجوب شيء أو منّة عليهم، ومن أخذ من الدنيا وما فيها شيئاً من غير إذنهم ورضاهم فذلك حرام عليهم وغصب. ومن أجل ذلك قال اللّه تعالى: ﴿ مَّآ أَفَآءَ ٱللَّهُ عَلَىٰ رَسُولِهِ مِنْ أَهْلِ ٱلْقُرَىٰ فَلِلَّهِ وَلِلرَّسُولِ ﴾ الآية،[٧] والفيء هو الرجوع، ولذلك[٨] سمّي الظل فيئاً[٩] لأنّه من ذلك الموضع خرج ورجع إليه، وجميع الدنيا من مال[١٠] الأئمّة خرج ومن ملكهم، وما رجع إلى ملكهم فهو فيء.

[٣٢] ونقول:[١١] إنّ النبات لمّا زاد[١٢] على الأرض بروح واحد وهو

[١] للأئمّة السلام اللّه عليهم: للأئمّة عليهم السلام، ت.

[٢] فضائله: فضيلته، ث.

[٣] نظامه: نظاه، ت.

[٤] خلقت: اختلقت، ث.

[٥] الخلق: الخلائق، ب.

[٦] فما منوا: فامنوا، ت.

[٧] سورة ٥٩ الحشر ٧.

[٨] ولذلك: وكذلك، ا.

[٩] فيئاً: الفيء، ا، ت.

[١٠] مال: -، ا، ب، ت.

[١١] ونقول:-، ث.

[١٢] زاد: زادت، ا.

روح النّماء صارت الأرض مسخّرة للنبات تحته،[١] ونبت عليها ونشف[٢] القوّة منها. ولما زاد الحيوان على النبات بروح واحد[٣] وعلى الأرض بروحين، روح النماء وروح الحسّ، سخّر الأرض[٤] ومشى عليها[٥] وسخّر النبات وأكل منه. ولمّا زاد[٦] الإنسان على الحيوان بزيادة روح النطق، سخّر الأرض[٧] وبنى[٨] عليها وزرعها وغرس فيها وجعلها تحت حكمه وعقده، فأكل[٩] النبات والثمار واستعمل منها ما شاء[١٠] وأحرق ما شاء وسخّر الحيوان وركب ما احتاج إليه منها وذبح وحلب وجزّ شعرها واستعملها فيما شاء جبراً منهم على كره الحيوان. فلمّا قام الإمام[١١] بزيادة أرواح وقوى وصفوة لم يكن للبشر مثل ذلك، فإنّ غاية صفوة الحيوان[١٢] البشرية[١٣] اتّحدت[١٤] بالإمام ولطافة[١٥] الطبيعة وغاية صفوتها وغاية الحيوان

---

[١] تحته: تحتها، ث.

[٢] نشف: نسق، ا؛ نشوء، ب؛ نشق، ث.

[٣] واحد: - ا، ب، ث.

[٤] الأرض: الارضين، ب.

[٥] عليها: على الأرض، ت.

[٦] ولمّا زاد: ولمّا ازداد، ت.

[٧] الأرض: الارضين، ب.

[٨] وبنى: وبين، ب؛ وبنا، ث.

[٩] فأكل: وأكل، ب.

[١٠] شاء: يشاء، ت.

[١١] الإمام + سلام اللّه عليه، ا، ث.

[١٢] الحيوان: للحيوان، ا.

[١٣] البشرية: البشر به، ا، ت، ث.

[١٤] اتحدت: اتحد، ا، ب، ت، ث.

الحسيّة وصفوتها وغاية سعادة الفلك واعتدال الطبيعة وغاية لطافة تأثير الأفلاك والكواكب[١] كلّها حتّى صار هو مخ العالم كله،[٢] ثم لطائف روح النطق والفكرة الصافية وكلية الروح العقلي اتحدت[٣] به، وكلية روح القدس التي[٤] لم يكن للبشر حظ قليل ولا كثير إلا من جهة الإمام ومنته على من اختاره ومنَّ عليه، واتَّحد به روح القدس[٥] الذي هو الروح السابع التام الذي أعدّه[٦] اللّٰه للبشر في عالم الجزاء، وهو روح الوحدة.[٧]

[٣٣] هذه بعض الفضائل الموهوبة له من اللّٰه تعالى، ثم المكتسب[٨] الذي لم يكن لأحدٍ مثله من الطهارة والأخلاق الرضية والجود والسَّخاء والحلم والشجاعة وغير ذلك مما لا يمكن[٩] لِأمثالنا تعديده، ثم البعد من كل دنسٍ وعيب ونقص. فلما جمع اللّٰه تعالى لهم[١٠] هذه القوى والفضائل والأرواح زيادة على البشر سخر لهم البشر بأجمعهم وملكهم جميع ما تقدم على البشر من الحيوان والنبات والأرض والمعادن، وسخر

---

[١٥] ولطافة: ولطافة تاثير الافلاك،ت.

[١] والكواكب: -، ث.

[٢] كله: كلها، ا، ب، ت.

[٣] اتحدت: اتحد، ا، ب، ت، ث.

[٤] التي: الذي، ا، ب، ت، ث.

[٥] القدس: + الإبداع، ت.

[٦] أعده: أعد، ث.

[٧] روح الوحدة: روح الواحد، ب، ت.

[٨] المكتسب: المكتب، ت.

[٩] مما لا يمكن: بما لا يمكن، ا؛ بما لم يكن، ث.

[١٠] جمع اللّٰه تعالى لهم: جمع الله تعالى، ب.

لهم جميع ذلك كما أن البشر سخر الحيوان وملكه بزيادة روح واحد ضعيف وكما أَن الحيوان سخر النبات بزيادة روح واحد ضعيف وكما أَن النبات سخر الأرض بزيادة روح واحدٍ ضعيف. وبزيادة مقدار أرواح الأئِمة سلام اللّٰه عليهم كان زيادة تمليكهم البشر وتسخيرهم وجواز الحكم عليهم بحسب ما[١] اقتضى القوى والأرواح فيما تقدم ذكرها[٢] من البشر جبراً، ليس لأحد من البشر أَن يخرج نفسه[٣] من حكم الإمام وملكه كما ليس للحيوان أَنْ يخرج من حكم البشر. وما يخرج من الحيوان من حكم البشر مثل السباع التي لا نفع فيها ولا فضيلة فقد حكم العقلُ والشرع بقتله وإتلافه وإهلاكه[٤] لِخروجه[٥] عن طاعة البشر ومن حكم ملكه.[٦]

وكذلك[٧] من خرج عن طاعة الإمام[٨] وتسبع فهو مثل السباع الضارية صار قتله مباحاً وإتلافه وإهلاكه بحكم خروجه عن ملك الإمام بالشرع والعقل والطبيعة والسياسة. ومَن أطاع الأئمة سلام اللّٰه عليهم[٩] وانقاد

---

[١] بحسب ما: بحسب، ت؛ بحساب، ث.

[٢] ذكرها: -، ب.

[٣] نفسه: مفسها، ب، ت، ث.

[٤] بقتله...وإهلاكه: بقتلهم...واهلاكهم، ا، ب، ت، ث.

[٥] لخروجه: لخروجهم، ا، ث؛ بخروجهم، ب، ت.

[٦] ملكه: ملكهم، ا، ث.

[٧] وكذلك: كذلك، ا.

[٨] الإمام: الامامة، ا.

[٩] الأئمة:+ سلام الله عليهم، ب.

لحكمهم في الدنيا[١] تخلص[٢] من السيف والعقوبة ويعيش في الأمن والصلاح والعدل، ويلزم على الإمام سلام اللّٰه عليه بحكم الملك والطبيعة والسياسة والشرع حفظ صلاحه، كما أن على البشر إذا ملك البهائم حفظ صلاحها وعلفها ورعايتها. ومن انقاد لحكمهم على الأرواح والأجساد يفيضون عليه من العلم والحكمة ما يحيى به،[٣] ويتنافس[٤] بين الخلق ويعيش في راحة العلم وطيبه، ويخرج من دار عمله[٥] إلى دار جزائه مستوي الصورة متهيئاً[٦] لقبول[٧] الجزاء والبقاء. ومن انقاد لحكمهم على الجسد ولا ينقاد لِحكمهم على الروح[٨] يقع في عقوبة الجهل والحيرة والشك والاختلاف والندامة ويصير إلى دار جزائه معوج الصورة غير متهيىء[٩] لقبول الجزاء ويبقى معاقباً.

[٣٤] ونقول:[١٠] إن البشر في كل وقت وأوان يحفظ صلاح الحيوان[١١] ويمنعه مما يضره ويسوقه إلى ما ينفعه ويحفظ مشربه[١٢] ومرعاه

---

[١] الدنيا: الدنياوي، ا.

[٢] تخلص: تخلص في الدنيا، ا، ب؛ ويتخلص في الدنيا، ت؛ وتخلص، ث.

[٣] ما يحيى به: ما يحيي، ب.

[٤] ويتنافس: يتنافس، ا، ت، ث.

[٥] عمله: علمه، ب، ت، ث.

[٦] متهيئاً: متهياء، ا، ب، ث؛ مهياء، ت.

[٧] لقبول: القبول، ت، ث.

[٨] الروح: الأرواح، ا.

[٩] متهيىء: مهياء، ا، ت؛ متهيأ، ب، ث.

[١٠] ونقول: -، ث.

[١١] الحيوان: -، ب.

ووقت نتاجه ونسله[١] ويمنعه عما يكون فيه هلاكه ومن مواضع ما يضر[٢] مأكوله ومشروبه، وربما تحرص البهائم على ذلك وهو يمنعه ويحفظ أنواع مصالحه جبرًا على كره الحيوان. وكذلك الإمام سلام الله عليه[٣] يحفظ عواقب أمور البشر ومصالحهم وجميع أحوالهم وأسبابهم ومعاملتهم وما تخفى[٤] مصالحه عليهم شفقة،[٥] ولولا الإمام لما[٦] كان للبشر نظام في دنياهم[٧] ولا أمن ولا خلاص من فساد[٨] مَن هو أقوى منه ولا نجاة من الاختلاف[٩] والعقوبة في المعاد. وكما أن البشر يحتمل من البهائم الأذى ويصبر على سوء آدابها[١٠] لما يلتمس من صلاحها ولِما يلزمه من حكم[١١] العلم، فلا يجوز لمن يعلم هلاك ذي روح وفساده وتلفه من غير موجب في الحكمة، بل يلزمه خلاصه من الهلاك. وهكذا حكم الأملاك يوجب في الحكمة حفظها ومنعها من التلف والخروج

---

[١٢] مشربه: مشرعه، ا، ب، ت، ج.

[١] ونسله: -، ب.

[٢] ما يضر: يضر، ث.

[٣] سلام الله عليه: -، ب، ت.

[٤] تخفى: يحفي، ث.

[٥] شفقة: + عليهم، ا.

[٦] لما : ما، ث.

[٧] دنياهم: دنياه، ا، ب، ت، ث.

[٨] فساد: فسادهم، ث.

[٩] الاختلاف: اختلاف، ث.

[١٠] آدابها: آدابهم، ا، ب، ت.

[١١] من حكم: وحكم، ث.

عن منافع الخلق،[1] فكذلك[2] الإمام سلام الله عليه يصبر على سوء آداب الخلق ويحتمل الأذى والمشقة منهم لما يوجب[3] حكم الملك وحكم العلم[4] إرشاد[5] الجاهل وحفظ صلاحه[6] ومنعه من الهلاك والتلف رجاء أن يرجع[7] في العاقبة إلى الصلاح والنجاة، ولا ينظر إلى سوء[8] آدابهم بجهلهم ولا[9] إلى قلة طاعتهم، بل ينظر إليهم بعين الرحمة.

[٣٥] ونقول:[10] إن البشر يحتمل من أولاده الصغار الأذى والمشقة ويترحم عليهم رجاء أن يبلغوا إلى حدّ الإنسانية ويكونوا مرشدين، فهكذا الإمام سلام الله عليه يحتمل من الخلق الأذى والتعب رحمة عليهم[11] وشفقة الآباء على الأولاد وينفق عليهم ديناً ودنيا رجاء أن يكون[12] منهم مرشدون ناجون.[13]

---

[1] الخلق: -، ث.

[2] فكذلك: وكذلك، ا، ب، ت.

[3] يوجب: + من، ب.

[4] العلم: العالم، ت.

[5] إرشاد: بارشاد، ا، ب؛ بارشاده، ث.

[6] صلاحه: + اهله، ب، ت، ث.

[7] يرجع: + يكونوا، ت.

[8] سوء: سواء، ا، ب، ت، ث.

[9] ولا: -، ا، ب، ت.

[10] ونقول: -، ث.

[11] عليهم: اليهم، ب.

[12] يكون: يكونوا، ا، ب، ت.

[13] مرشدون ناجون: مرشدين ناجين ا، ب، ت، ث.

[٣٦] ونقول:[١] إن المعلم يحتمل من الصبيان المشقة[٢] ويجبرهم[٣] على تعلم[٤] العلوم والآداب، والصبي يكره ذلك ويبغض المعلم ويختار[٥] اللعب والبطالة، والمؤدب يداريه[٦] ويحتمل منه علماً بأنه لو عَلِمَ ما فيه من الصلاح لما كرهه وأنه إذا بلغ إلى حد المعرفة يعلم نفع ذلك ويسره ويندم على تقصيره وترك طاعة المؤدب، فكذلك الإمام سلام الله عليه يحمل[٧] الخلق على صلاحهم ديناً ودنيا وهم يكرهون ذلك ويتعرضون لِما يعلمهم،[٨] وفي العواقب إذا ظهر[٩] لهم الصلاح في ذلك ندموا على ترك الطاعة.

[٣٧] ونقول:[١٠] إن الإنسان لما كان خلقته من الطبائع المختلفة المتضادة لم يخل[١١] من الأسقام والأمراض والعلل الطبيعية من تأثير المكان والزمان ومن تأثير الأفلاك والكواكب ومن[١٢] الغذاء والأشياء

---

[١] ونقول: نقول، ب؛ -، ث.

[٢] المشقة: المشفقة، ب

[٣] يجبرهم: يجبر، ث.

[٤] تعلم: تعليم، ا، ب، ت، ث.

[٥] يختار: يحتال، ب.

[٦] يداريه: يداوية، ب؛ بدرية،ت.

[٧] يحمل: يحتمل، ب، ت.

[٨] يعلمهم: يعالمهم، ت؛ يعاملهم، ا، ث.

[٩] ظهر: -، ب.

[١٠] ونقول: نقول، ب؛ -، ث.

[١١] يخل: يخلو، ا ،ب.

[١٢] ومن: من، ث.

المضادة[١] للطبع ومن كثرة[٢] الأكل وقلته ومن الإعياء والجماع وغير ذلك من أسباب العلل والأمراض، وكان[٣] الناس جاهلين بالطب، ولو كانوا[٤] ضائعين مهملين مع كثرة هذه الأمراض لفنى أكثر الناس وهلكوا وأدى ذلك إلى خراب العالم، ولكن الله تعالى خلق الأدوية[٥] بإزاء كل داء وأيّد الأنبياء والأئمة سلام الله عليهم حتى عرفوا منافع الأدوية[٦] وعرفوا السمائم[٧] وعرفوا الأمراض وعلّموا الخلق وفتحوا لهم طريق الطب حتى بنوا على ذلك الأساس وزادوا[٨] فيه[٩] بالتجربة والدربة[١٠] كما زادوا في سائر الحرف[١١] والصناعات[١٢] والعلوم مثل الهندسة والفلاحة والملاحة وغير ذلك حتى قام[١٣] في الخلق أطباء لمداواة الناس وجمعوا الأدوية من البلدان الشاسعة واجتهدوا في ذلك بعضه للنفع وبعضه لصلاح[١٤] الخلق،

---

[١] المضادة: المتضادة، ا، ب، ت، ث.

[٢] كثرة: كثر، ب.

[٣] وكان: فكان، ث.

[٤] كانوا: كان، ب.

[٥] الأدوية: كله اوديه، ب؛ ادويه، ت.

[٦] الأدوية: الاودية، ب.

[٧] السمائم: السمومات، ث.

[٨] وزادوا: وادوا، ث.

[٩] فيه:+ الطب، ب.

[١٠] والدربة: والدرية، ب، ث؛ والدرابة، ت.

[١١] الحرف: الحدق، ث.

[١٢] والصناعات: والصناعة، ا، ب، ت، ث.

[١٣] قام: قاموا، ا، ب، ت.

[١٤] لِصلاح: على صلاح، ت؛ للصلاح، ب.

يداوون الناس تارة بالأشياء الطيبة العذبة،[١] وتارة بالأشياء المُرة الحادة،[٢] ولعل المريض يكره ما يشفيه من الأشياء المرة[٣] المنتنة[٤] وهو يسقيه[٥] كرهاً أو اختياراً[٦] ويُبشّرهُ بصلاح العاقبة وينذره ويخوفه من الهلاك إن لم يشربه، أو يداريه[٧] ويحتمل منه المشقة، وربما منع المريض من الأكل والشرب وهو يشتهي[٨] ذلك، ويأمره بالاحتماء من الغذاء الذي كان يحبه ويوافقه في أوقات صحته، ويسقيه ما يشتد عليه ويؤثر فيه بالضعف ويكون على خطر الهلاك، وإن أعيا[٩] عن إصلاحه بالدواء يأمره[١٠] بالشق والبط والكي والقطع لبعض الأعضاء رجاء لِصلاح[١١] ما يبقى، والعاقل يحتمل ذلك لِما صح له ويعرف أنه أعلم منه بمصالحه وأنه مؤتمن أمين وأنه[١٢] يريد صلاحه وبرءه[١٣] في جميع ذلك. فإذا لم[١٤] يكن عاقلاً يكره

---

[١] الطيبة العذبة: الطبية العذب، ا؛ الطبيعية العذوبة، ب؛ الطبيعية الغذية، ت؛ الطبية العذبة، ث.

[٢] الحادة: الحارة، ا، ت، ث.

[٣] المرة :-، ت؛ المر، ب، ث.

[٤] المنتنة: والمنتن، ا، ب، ث،؛ المنتن، ت.

[٥] يسقيه: يشقيه، ب.

[٦] أو اختياراً: واختياراً، ا، ب، ث.

[٧] أو يداريه: ويداويه، ب، ت؛ ويداريه، ا، ث.

[٨] يشتهي: -، ب.

[٩] أعيا: اعياء، ب، ث.

[١٠] يامره: بامره، ت.

[١١] لصلاح: بصلاح، ث.

[١٢] أعلم...وأنه: -، ث.

[١٣] وبرءه: وبرؤه، ا، ب؛ -، ث.

[١٤] فاذا لم: وان لم، ا، ث؛ فان لم، ب؛ وان، ت.

الطبيب ويبغضه، والطبيب يترحم إذا رأى رجلاً مستوي الخلقة به علة إن لم يتداركه[١] هَلَكَ، فمن رحمته وتحننه[٢] عليه أن[٣] يشد المريض ويسقيه كرهاً، ولعل المريض يشتمه ويقصد ضربه ويجفوه،[٤] ويحتمل الطبيب ذلك منه رحمة عليه ومعرفة منه[٥] بأنه لو عرف وكان عاقلاً لما كره صلاحه، ولا يشتغل[٦] بمكافأته والإعراض عنه، بل يترحم عليه ويداويه حتى يعود إلى الصلاح.

[٣٨] فهكذا لَما كانت الأمراض الدينية كثيرة من اختلاف الناس وأهوائهم[٧] وميلهم إلى الراحة والإباحة والبدع والأهواء والمذاهب المختلفة والأقاويل المتناقضة والآراء المتشتتة والنفس الأمّارة[٨] بالسوء والليل مظلم والطريق مشتبه، والناس كانوا جاهلين بطب الأنفس ومداواتها وحفظ صحتها وبالمواضع المضرة والأشياء التي توجب[٩] الاحتماء عنها، وكانوا جاهلين بالطريق والمسالك الدينية، احتاج الخلق إلى دليلٍ وطبيب يداوي أمراضهم ويبين لهم رشدهم وينجي أرواحهم

---

[١] يتداركه: يتدارك، ا؛ يتداركها، ث.

[٢] وتحننه: تحنن، ب؛ وتحته، ت.

[٣] أن: -، ث.

[٤] يجفوه: يجفه، ب.

[٥] منه: -، ث.

[٦] ولا يشتغل: ولا شتغل، ث.

[٧] وأهوائهم: وأهواءهم، ا، ت.

[٨] الأمّارة: أمارة، ا، ب، ث.

[٩] توجب: يوجب، ب، ت.

بالرفق[١] والشَّفقة والنصيحة والتحنن والاحتمال والمداراة بأضعاف احتمال أطباء الجسد وشفقتهم، ولا يكون في معالجتهم[٢] طمع، ولا جر منفعة ولا دفع مضرة، ويكونون[٣] أمناء ثقات على الأنفس والأديان أكثر من أمانة[٤] أطباء الجسد وأكثر درية وتجربةً[٥] ومعرفةً.

[٣٩] فإن الغرر[٦] والخطر في مداواة[٧] النفس[٨] أكثر من الخطر في مداواة[٩] الجسد[١٠] والخطأ فيه أصعب، ووجوب ذلك[١١] اضطراري عقلي لا بد منه كما أن وجوب طبيب الجسد عقلي اضطراري[١٢] لا بد منه.[١٣] وهذا الطبيب[١٤] العالم الشفيق على الأنفس هو الإمام سلام الله عليه في كل وقت وزمان، ولولا رحمة الأئمة سلام الله عليهم وشفقتهم وتحننهم على الخلق لهلكوا ديناً ودنيا وآخرة وأولى، فإنهم سلام الله عليهم

١ أرواحهم بالرفق: بالرفق أرواحهم، ب.

٢ معالجتهم: مصالحهم، ا، ب، ت؛ مصلحتهم، ث.

٣ ويكونون: ويكونوا، ث.

٤ أمانة: -، ب، ث.

٥ تجربة: -، ب؛ وبتجربة، ث.

٦ فإن الغرر: فإن الغرد، ا، ب، ث؛ وان الغرور، ت.

٧ مداواة: مداوة، ب، ت، ث.

٨ النفس: النفوس، ب.

٩ مداواة: مداوة، ب، ت، ث.

١٠ وأكثر درية...الجسد: -، ث.

١١ ذلك: + انه، ا، ب.

١٢ اضطراري: -، ب.

١٣ لا بد منه: -، ت، ث.

١٤ الطبيب: طبيب، ب.

يداوون الخلق بالمداراة[١] والاحتمال والرفق ولا ينظرون إلى قلة طاعتهم[٢] وسوء آدابهم وأفعالهم. وإنما ينظرون إليهم بعين الرحمة ويجتهدون[٣] في حفظ صحتهم ومداواة أمراضهم تارةً بالغذاء المعتدل[٤] اللطيف لحفظ الصحة من العلوم اللطيفة المقوية للأنفس وتارة يقطعون عنهم الغذاء حتى لا يكون عليهم ثقلاً[٥] وتخمةً، وتارة يسقونهم[٦] الأدوية[٧] المرة المنتنه كرهاً لتخرج عنهم[٨] الكيموسات[٩] الفاسدة الردية، وتارةً يأمرونهم بالاحتماء حتى يضعفوا،[١٠] ويبشّرونهم وينذرونهم، كما يفعل أمير المؤمنين عليه السلام مع هؤلاء القوم وهم في جميع الأحوال يريدون فساداً، ولا يرى فيهم الصلاح ويصبر على أذاهم. نسأل اللّٰه أن يجعلنا ممن ينتفع[١١] بمداواة[١٢] إمام الزمان سلام اللّٰه عليه ولا يجعلنا ممن يحتاج إلى الكي والقطع بالإعراض عنا، ولولا[١٣] رحمة الأئمة[١٤] لما بقي على

---

١ بالمداراة: بالمدارة، ا، ب، ت، ث.

٢ طاعتهم: طاعة الخلق، ا، ث.

٣ ويجتهدون: ويجتهد، ت.

٤ المعتدل: -، ت.

٥ ثقلا: ثقل، ت.

٦ يسقونهم: يسقيهم، ا، ب، ت، ث.

٧ الأدوية: بالأدوية، ا، ت، ث.

٨ عنهم: منهم، ب، ث.

٩ الكيموسات: الكيموسادة، ث.

١٠ يضعفوا: يضعفون، ث.

١١ ينتفع: ننتفع، ث.

١٢ بمداواة: بمدوة، ا، ب، ت، ث.

١٣ عنا ولولا: عنه ولا، ا، ب؛ عنا ولا، ت.

ظهر الأرض أحدٌ كما قال الله تعالى: ﴿ وَلَوْ يُؤَاخِذُ ٱللَّهُ ٱلنَّاسَ بِمَا كَسَبُوا۟ مَا تَرَكَ عَلَىٰ ظَهْرِهَا مِن دَآبَّةٍ ﴾.[١]

[٤٠] ونقول:[٢] إن الحكماء وأهل البصائر بعمارة الدنيا المتبعين لأفعال الله تعالى[٣] في خلقته للعالم وعمارته وحفظ صلاح الخلق لما رأوا أرضاً طيبةً يعرفون أنها تقبل البذور[٤] وتنبت النبات ورأوا[٥] الماء منها[٦] بعيداً في أودية عميقة أو تحت[٧] الأرض اجتهدوا في إنباط المياه من تلك الأودية ومن تحت الأرض بحفر الأنهار والآبار وساقوا الماء إلى تلك الأرض[٨] ولم يروا في الحكمة ترك تلك[٩] الأرض الطيبة معطلة ضائعة وترك المياه من غير منفعة شفقة على الخلق وحفظاً[١٠] لصلاحهم[١١] وعمارة للدنيا. فكذلك الأئمة عليهم السلام[١٢] إذا رأوا الناس متهيئين[١٣]

---

[١٤] الأئمة: + الناس، ب.

[١] سورة ٣٥ فاطر ٤٥.

[٢] ونقول: -، ث.

[٣] تعالى: -، ب.

[٤] البذور: البذر، ب.

[٥] ورأوا: وروا، ث.

[٦] منها بعيدا: بعيدا منها، ب، ث.

[٧] او تحت: تحت، ب.

[٨] الأرض: لطيبته، ب، الطيبه، ت.

[٩] تلك: -، ث.

[١٠] حفظاً: حفضا، ت.

[١١] لصلاحهم: -، ب.

[١٢] عليهم السلام: سلام الله عليهم، ث.

[١٣] متهيئين: متهئين، ت، ث.

لقبول بذر الحكمة والعلم[١] وهم بعيدون من قبول ذلك يجتهدون،[٢] في حفر الأنهار برياضة متقدمة بأوقات كثيرة، وربما[٣] لا يعرفون سبب تلك[٤] الرياضة حتى إذا بلغت الحكمة إليهم يكونون متهيئين[٥] لذلك فيمكنهم[٦] قبولها، وربّما إذا أعيوا عن تبليغهم[٧] في الرياضة إلى تلك[٨] الدرجة يلقون الحكمة في مثالات كثيفة إما بالكلام أو بالفعل[٩] فيمكنهم[١٠] قبول تلك المثالات، ثم يتدرجون إلى معانيها ويرقونهم[١١] إليها.

[٤١] ومن هذه الجهة ينبغي أن يعتقد إمامة إمام الزمان ويعرف أنه رأس العالم وخليفة اللّٰه على خلقه وأن لا يعترض[١٢] على شيء من أوامر الإمام عليه السلام ونواهيه وأفعاله وأقواله ويعلم في الجملة أن كل ذلك حكمة وصلاح لِلخلق، وإن أشكل عليه وجه ذلك[١٣] في الوقت، ففي

---

[١] والعلم: -، ث.

[٢] بعيدون من قبول ذلك يجتهدون: من ذلك يجهدون، ث.

[٣] وربما: ربما، ا، ب، ث.

[٤] تلك: -، ث.

[٥] يكونون متهيئين: ويكونون متهيئين، ا، ب؛ ويكونون متهئين، ت؛ يكونون مهين، ث.

[٦] فيمكنهم: يمكنهم، ا، ب، ت، ث.

[٧] أعيوا عن تبليغهم: اعيا واعز تبليغهم، ا، ث؛ عيوا عن تبليغهم، ب؛ اعيلوا عن تبلغهم، ت.

[٨] تلك: -، ب.

[٩] أو بالفعل: وبالفعل، ب.

[١٠] فيمكنهم: يمكنهم، ا، ب، ت، ث.

[١١] ويرقونهم: يرتقون نهم، ت.

[١٢] يعترض: يتعرض، ث.

[١٣] ذلك: + حكمة، ت.

العاقبة يتبين له فوائده[١] كما ظهر وتبين في كثير مما لم يكن يعرف، وكما[٢] أنهم كثيراً مما[٣] يفعلون في الشريعة لم يكن عرفوا غرض واضعه ولا الحكمة[٤] فيه واستنكروا ذلك، ثم من رزقه الله معرفة معانيه عرف الحكمة فيه، وكما أنهم كثيراً مما يرون في العالم من الأشياء لا[٥] يعرفون الحكمة في خلقته[٦] ويظنون أنه لا[٧] فائدة فيه ولا في خلقته، فإذا علموا[٨] الحكمة فيه لا يستنكرونه، وكثيراً[٩] من الأشياء يرون أن خلقتها ضرر[١٠] وفساد، وأنه لا حكمة فيه ولا خير،[١١] فإذا عرفوا وجه الحكمة سكنوا من الاضطراب. ومن عرف الحكيم وأقر بأنه حكيم فينبغي أن يعرف ويقر أن جميع ما يفعله حكمة وأنه[١٢] لا يفعل شيئاً إلاَّ بالحكمة[١٣] ولا يأمر ولا ينهى ولا يقول شيئاً إلا لحكمة[١٤] وأنه لا يجوز من الحكيم العبث، ولو

---

[١] فوائده: فائده، ب.

[٢] وكما: فكما، ب.

[٣] مما: ما، ب.

[٤] الحكمة: لحكمة، ب.

[٥] لا: ولا، ت.

[٦] في خلقته: -، ب؛ في خلقه، ث.

[٧] لا: الا، ت.

[٨] علموا: -، ب؛ + أن، ا، ت، ث.

[٩] يستنكرونه وكثيراً: يستنكرون وكثيرا، ا؛ يستنكرونه كثيرا، ب، ت، ث.

[١٠] ضرر: ضرور، ب، ث.

[١١] فيه ولا خير: ولا خبر، ب.

[١٢] وأنه: فانه، ب.

[١٣] بالحكمة: لحكمة، ت.

[١٤] لحكمة: بالحكمة، ب، ت، ث.

جاز من الحكيم أن يفعل شيئاً[١] أو يقول أو يأمر أو ينهى وليس فيه حكمة لكان ذلك عبثاً، ولا يجوز العبث من الحكيم،[٢] ومن عمل[٣] شيئاً يكون فعله وغير فعله واحداً[٤] يكون سفيهاً خارجاً عن[٥] الحكمة.

[٤٢] وإذا لم يجز أن يكون من الحكيم فعل[٦] يكون وجوده وغير وجوده واحداً فكيف يجوز على الإمام سلام الله عليه أن يفعل فعلاً تكون[٧] الحكمة في غيره أو في خلافه أو الصّلاح[٨] في غيره وهو الحكيم المطلق والذي إذا منّ على أحد عبيده بحكمة يصير حكيماً؟ ومن[٩] يفعل فعلاً يجوز أن يكون الصّلاح والحكمة في غيره ففعله فساد وعبث، نعوذ بالله ممن يعتقد في إمام زمانه مثل ذلك، فإنه قد أخرجه عن الحكمة، وإذا أخرجه عن الحكمة[١٠] فقد خرج عن إمامته، وهذا هو الخروج من الدين، عصمنا الله وجميع المؤمنين عن مثل هذا الظن والخطرات والاعتقاد ورزقنا الرضى والتسليم.

---

[١] شيئاً: -، ب.

[٢] أن يفعل شيئاً...من الحكيم: -، ت.

[٣] عمل: يحمل، ب.

[٤] واحداً: واحد، ب.

[٥] عن: من، ت.

[٦] فعل: فعلا، ا، ب، ت.

[٧] تكون: يكون، ث.

[٨] أو الصلاح: والصلاح، ب، ث.

[٩] ومن: من، ب.

[١٠] وإذا أخرجه عن الحكمة: -، ب.

[٤٣] ونقول:[١] إن الأنعام السائمة التي فيها المنافع والفضيلة لا بد لها من راعٍ[٢] يرعاها ويحفظها ويختار مواضع علفها[٣] ومشربها ويحفظها من اللصوص والسباع، والتي لا يكون لها من يقوم بذلك تهلك ولا يمكنها القيام بأمور أنفسها[٤] ولا دفع[٥] السباع والقيام[٦] بصلاح أمورها. فكذلك الناس مثالهم مثل[٧] الأغنام إذا لم يكن لهم[٨] راعٍ[٩] يحفظ عليهم[١٠] يهلكون، والإمام هو راعيهم[١١] يحفظ عليهم أمور دينهم ودنياهم ويمنع عنهم أعداء الدين والدنيا. ولو كانوا مسيّبين لما بقي[١٢] اثنان منهم ولا نجا[١٣] واحدٌ منهم[١٤] من العذاب، ومن هذه الجهة يسمون أهل الممالك[١٥] رعية، فإنهم تحت رعاية راعيهم، والراعي في الحقيقة هو الإمام، وسائر

---

[١] ونقول: -، ث.

[٢] راع: راعي، ث.

[٣] مواضع علفها: من اصنع عقلها، ث.

[٤] أنفسها: نفسها، ث.

[٥] دفع: رفع، ث.

[٦] والقيام: ولا القيام، ت.

[٧] مثل: مثال، ث.

[٨] لهم: -، ث.

[٩] راع: راعي، ا، ب، ت، ث.

[١٠] عليهم: -، ا، ث.

[١١] هو راعيهم: راعيهم، ا، ث؛ راعيتهم، ت.

[١٢] بقي: يبقى، ا، ب، ت، ث.

[١٣] نجا: ينجى، ا، ب، ت، ث.

[١٤] منهم: -، ا.

[١٥] الممالك: المماليك، ث.

المدعين هم[١] ذئاب يفترسون الغنم.

[٤٤] ونقول:[٢] إن العالم مثله مثل الجسد، والجسد[٣] إذا لم يكن له رأس يكون جيفةً منتنةً بغير فائدة. كذلك العالم إذا لم يكن له رأس ورئيس وسائس يسوس أمور الدين والدنيا يكون مسبعة[٤] يفترس بعضهم بعضاً ولا يبقى العالم يوماً واحداً ولا يكون في خلقة العالم حكمة، والإمام[٥] هو رأس العالم وسائسه ومدبِّره.

[٤٥] ونقول: إن أعضاء البدن[٦] تتفاوت وتتفاضل، وأعلاها[٧] وأفضلها الرأس، وفيه الوجه الذي يعرف كل إنسان[٨] به ويميز بينه وبين[٩] غيره، ومن الأعضاء الباطنة[١٠] أفضلها الدماغ، وهو رئيس الجميع[١١] وهو معدن العقل. فكذلك الإمام[١٢] في العالم بمنزلة الرأس من الأعضاء وبمنزلة

---

[١] هم: -، ب.

[٢] ونقول: -، ث.

[٣] والجسد: -، ب.

[٤] مسبعة: السبعة، ث.

[٥] والإمام: فالامام، ا، ب، ت.

[٦] البدن: + الظاهرة، ب.

[٧] وأعلاها: أعلاها، ا، ب، ت.

[٨] إنسان: -، ت.

[٩] بين: -، ت.

[١٠] الباطنة: الباطن، ت.

[١١] الجميع: جميع، ب.

[١٢] الإمام: + سلام الله عليه، ث.

الدماغ، وعليه تدور[١] أمور[٢] الخلق كما أن على الدماغ يدور عمل البدن. ومن القوى التي[٣] في الإنسان ومن الأرواح أفضلها العقل، والإمام هو العقل[٤] الكلي في العالم، ومنه وبه يتحد إلى جميع أهل العالم.[٥]

[٤٦] ونقول:[٦] إن الرئاسة[٧] في الطبيعة موجودة في[٨] كل شيء[٩] كما ذكرنا، وهو موجود في الحيوان، والطيور مثل[١٠] الفحول تحفظ إناث جنسها وتؤدبها،[١١] فالديك[١٢] يحفظ[١٣] الدجاج ويؤدبها،[١٤] وكل جنس يحفظ صغار ولده[١٥] بمقدار طاقته ويمنع عن إناثه وعن ضعفاء[١٦] جنسه، والإناث والصغار بمنزلة المحتاج إلى الاستفادة والتعليم ممن هو[١٧] فوقه،

---

[١] تدور: يدور، ا، ب، ت.

[٢] أمور: -، ث.

[٣] التي: الذي، ا، ت، ث.

[٤] العقل: عقل، ب.

[٥] العالم: العلم، ب.

[٦] ونقول: -، ث.

[٧] الرئاسة: الرياسة، ا، ب، ت، ث.

[٨] في: وفي، ث.

[٩] شيء: + موجود، ت.

[١٠] مثل: مثال، ب.

[١١] وتؤدبها: ويؤدبها، ب.

[١٢] فالديك: والديك، ا، ب، ت.

[١٣] يحفظ: تحفظ، ت.

[١٤] ويؤدبها: ويؤدب، ت؛ ويؤدبه، ث.

[١٥] ولده: جنسه، ث.

[١٦] ضعفاء: صغار، ث.

[١٧] هو: -، ب، ت.

والكركي يطيع[١] لرئيسه والنحل يطيع ليعسوبه.

[٤٧] وإنما خلق الله تعالى العالم وجعل الخلق[٢] كما ذكرنا بعضه على هذا[٣] الترتيب والتفاوت والتفاضل[٤] وزيادة[٥] القوة والنقصان والشرف والضعة ليعرفوا أنه كما كان في كل نوع وجنس غاية وذروة ورأس في الشرف والفضل فالجميع[٦] أيضاً لا بد له من غاية وذروة في الشرف والفضل يكون رأس[٧] العالم وسائسه. فإذا قد[٨] تبين أن الرئاسة والسياسة واجبة في الطبع والخلقة والجبلة والفطرة ضرورية،[٩] ومن أنكر الشرع والدين فلا يمكنه أن ينكر السائس والرئيس[١٠] والمدبر للعالم لا في العقل ولا في العيان كما أنه واجب ضروري، فواجب أن يكون أفضل الجميع وأشرفهم وأتمهم وأعلمهم وأزكاهم بدليل ما ذكرناه من الخلقة[١١] والطبائع أن المقدم هو الإمام في كل شيء والرئيس والرأس، ولا يقع اسم الإمام

[١] والكركي يطيع: كالكركي يطع، ب.

[٢] الخلق: -، ث.

[٣] هذا: هذه، ت.

[٤] والتفاضل: -، ث.

[٥] وزيادة: زيادة، ث.

[٦] فالجميع: والجميع، ث.

[٧] رأس: رئيس، ب، ت، ث.

[٨] فإذا قد: فإذا فقد، ب؛ وإذا قد، ت.

[٩] ضرورية: ضروري، ا، ب، ت، ث.

[١٠] والرئيس: -، ث.

[١١] الخلقة: الخلق، ا، ت.

على المأموم ولا اسم[١] الفاضل على المفضول ولا اسم[٢] السابق على المسبوق. ومع ذلك فجميع[٣] أهل الملل والأديان والفلاسفة والدهرية والمعطلة أيضاً يقرون أن سائس العالم ينبغي أن يكون أفضلهم وأتم القوم فضيلةً وأعلمهم، ولا يوجد في العالم سائس[٤] بهذا الوصف إلا الأئمة سلام الله عليهم.

[٤٨] ونقول:[٥] إن الفلاسفة وضعوا السياسة على ثلاثة[٦] أقسام، سياسة الخاصة[٧] وسياسة الحامّة وسياسة العامة. فسياسة الخاصة سياسة الرجل نفسه،[٨] وسياسة الحامة سياسة الرجل أهل بيته[٩] وعياله، وسياسة العامة سياسة المدن[١٠] والكور.[١١] وسياسة الرجل نفسه ينبغي أن تكون[١٢] بحيث يمنعها عن جميع الرذائل والأخلاق السّيئة والعادات البهيمية[١٣]

[١] ولا اسم: واسم، ب.

[٢] ولا اسم: واسم، ب، ت، ث.

[٣] فجميع: لجميع، ب.

[٤] في العالم سائس: سائس في العالم، ت.

[٥] ونقول: -، ث.

[٦] ثلاثة: ثلثة، ا، ب، ت.

[٧] الخاصة: الخاص، ب.

[٨] نفسه: -، ب.

[٩] بيته: -، ب.

[١٠] المدن : -، ب.

[١١] والكور: الكور،ب؛ والكون، ث.

[١٢] تكون: يكون، ا، ب، ت، ث.

[١٣] البهيمية: البهيمة، ا.

والشهوات المذمومة ويسوس نفسه سياسة الرّجل الحازم[١] نفسه بنفسه[٢] فيعاقبها إذا أساءت[٣] بالذم والندامة ويثيبها إذا أحسنت بالمدح والسرور والحرص على مثله.[٤] وسياسة الحامة أن يسوس الرجل أهل بيته وعياله في حفظ صلاحهم وحملهم على اقتناء الفضائل[٥] والأخلاق الرضية ويعاقب من أساء منهم بالذم وغيره ويثيب من أحسن منهم بالمدح وغيره.

[٤٩] وسياسة العامة سياسة الرجل[٦] المدن يسوس المدن في حفظ صلاح معاشهم[٧] ويمنعهم من الأخلاق الذميمة والأفعال الردية ويحفظ على[٨] كل أحد منزلته ويعاقب من أساء منهم بالذم[٩] ويثيب من أحسن منهم بالمدح[١٠] ويحفظ ويسوس أمور دينهم ومعادهم. وهذا[١١] الذي وضعوا عليه اسم السياسة لا يوجد في العالم لا[١٢] في المدعين الإمامة ولا

---

[١] الحازم: +يعاقب، ت.

[٢] بنفسه: -، ث.

[٣] أساءت: ساءت، ا، ب، ث.

[٤] مثله: -، ب.

[٥] الفضائل: -، ب.

[٦] سياسة الرجل: -، ا، ب؛ سياسة، -، ث.

[٧] صلاح معاشهم: صلاحهم معائشهم، ث.

[٨] على: -، ث.

[٩] بالذم: -، ت، ث.

[١٠] بالمدح: -، ت.

[١١] وهذا: وهذه، ب.

[١٢] لا: ولا، ت.

في السلاطين ولا في علمائهم،[١] ولا توجد[٢] هذه الصفة إلا في الأئمة من آل محمد سلام اللّٰه عليهم، وليس[٣] في العالم من يشتغل دونهم. واجتمعت الفلاسفة على[٤] أن من لا يقوم بسياسة[٥] نفسه لا تكون له السياسة[٦] على حامته ومن لا يحسن سياسة[٧] الحامة لا يقع عليه[٨] اسم سياسة[٩] العامة بوجه من الوجوه. وأئمة أهل الظاهر[١٠] وسلاطينهم وعلماؤهم[١١] خالون[١٢] عن هذه الصفة، والذين قعدوا بمجالس[١٣] الأئمة وتسموا[١٤] بأسمائهم[١٥] لم يسوسوا أنفسهم ولا أهاليهم ولا الناس والذين نراهم اليوم مشتغلين باللهو والفسق والفساد. وهذه الصفة[١٦] التي[١٧] وصف

---

[١] علمائهم: علماءهم، ا، ب.

[٢] توجد: يوجد، ت.

[٣] وليس: + عليهم، ا.

[٤] على: -، ا، ب، ت، ث.

[٥] بسياسة: سياسة، ت.

[٦] لا تكون له السياسة: لا يكون سياسته، ب.

[٧] سياسة: سياسته، ت، ث.

[٨] عليه: -، ب.

[٩] سياسة: سياسته، ب، ت، ث.

[١٠] الظاهر: -، ب.

[١١] علماؤهم: علماءهم، ا، ث؛ علمائهم، ب، ت.

[١٢] خالون: خالين، ت.

[١٣] بمجالس: مجالس، ا، ب، ت، ث.

[١٤] تسموا: سموا، ب.

[١٥] بأسمائهم: باسماءهم، ا، ت.

[١٦] الصفة: الصفاة، ت.

[١٧] التي: الذي، ب.

الفلاسفة بها[١] السائس لم يقم أحد بها[٢] من سلاطينهم، ولعل واضع[٣] هذا الترتيب كان غرضه حث الناس على طاعة الإمام، فإنه وصف الإمام بصفة السائس حتى يطلبوا سائساً يكون على هذا[٤] الترتيب والوصف، وكل[٥] من لا يكون بهذه الصفة لا يقبلونه إلا[٦] أن يبلغوا إلى الإمام[٧] الحق.

[٥٠] ونقول:[٨] إنه لما كان الناس في وقت ولادتهم جاهلين لا علم لهم ولم[٩] يخرج العلم معهم من[١٠] الطبيعة ولا النطق احتاجوا إلى التعليم. والدليل على أن العلم لم يخرج من الطبيعة هو أنه لو خرج العلم من الطبيعة لكان الناس عالمين بالطبع ومتكلمين[١١] بالطبع،[١٢] كما أن نهيق[١٣] الحمار ونباح[١٤] الكلاب لما كان في الطبع ما احتاجوا فيه إلى التعليم،

---

[١] بها: به، ب، ت، ث.

[٢] بها: به، ب، ت، ث.

[٣] واضع: الواضع، ا، ب، ث.

[٤] هذا: هذه، ت.

[٥] وكل: كل، ت، ث.

[٦] إلا: الى، ا، ب.

[٧] الإمام: -، ب.

[٨] ونقول: -، ث.

[٩] ولم: ولا، ث.

[١٠] من: -، ب.

[١١] ومتكلمين: والمتكلمين، ب.

[١٢] بالطبع: + ما احتاجوا، ت.

[١٣] نهيق: نهق، ب.

[١٤] نباح: صياح، ا، ت، ث.

ولم يختلف نهيق الحمار ونباح[١] الكلاب[٢] بالهند والسند[٣] والروم والعرب، ولو كان النطق والعلم مطبوعاً لكان مثل ما ذكرنا لا يحتاج الناس فيه إلى التعليم ولكان[٤] الناس فيه متساوين لا يختلف أحدٌ من[٥] الآخر كما ذكرنا[٦] في نهيق الحمار أنه لا يختلف في موضع. فلما كان الناس محتاجين إلى التعليم وتعلم الواحد من الآخر إلى أن ينتهي إلى واحدٍ لم يتعلم من واحدٍ وإنما قِبلَهُ بالتأييد لا بالتعليم[٧] فنقصان الناس وحاجتهم إلى التعليم[٨] يوجب المعلِّم ويوجب لِلمعلمين نهاية[٩] وهو النبي والإمام عليهما السلام، وهذا من آكد الدليل على إثبات الإمامة والرسالة.[١٠]

[٥١] ونقول:[١١] إن اللّٰه تعالى خلق البشر مهيئين[١٢] لقبول العلم والحكمة ناقصين جاهلين، ولو تركهم سدى[١٣] لما كان عليهم تكليف[١٤]

---

[١] نباح: صيح، ا؛ صح، ت؛ ضج، ث.

[٢] لماكان في...ونباح الكلاب: مكرر في ب.

[٣] والسند: -، ا، ت، ث.

[٤] مثل...التعليم ولكان: -، ب.

[٥] من: مع، ا.

[٦] ذكرنا: ذكر، ت.

[٧] بالتعليم: + يوجب، ث.

[٨] فنقصان...التعليم: -، ب.

[٩] للمعلمين نهاية: للمتعلمين بنهاية، ب؛ للمتعلمين نهاية، ت.

[١٠] والرسالة: -، ب.

[١١] ونقول: -، ث.

[١٢] مهيئين: مهياء، ا، ت، ث؛ مهيأ، ب.

[١٣] سدى: سدا، ث.

[١٤] تكليف: تكاليف، ب.

ولا عمل ولا[١] ثواب ولا عقاب ولما كان في خلقتهم حكمة. فلما أَيَّدَ اللّٰه الأنبياء والأئمة وأعطاهم الحكمة والعلم أخبروا[٢] الخلق وبيّنوا[٣] لهم رشدهم وطريقهم إلى الحق وأَوْجَبوا[٤] عليهم التكليف[٥] والأمر والنهي، ولو لم يكن الأئمة لما صاروا مكلفين وما كان عليهم حجة. فالأئمة هم حُجج اللّٰه على خلقِهِ في كل وقتٍ في ابتداء تكليفهم وفي وقوعهم في الاختلاف. فلو وقع الخلق في اختلاف[٦] الفرق وكل[٧] واحد[٨] يحتج على الآخر[٩] بدليل آية[١٠] أو خبر أو قياس لا تقوم[١١] الحجة لواحد منهم على الآخر، ولو لم يكن في العالم إمام ينجيهم من الاختلاف والشبهة ويهديهم إلى الحق لما كان للّٰه على الخلق حجة بل[١٢] الحجة للخلق على اللّٰه، يقولون: ما وجدنا من يهدينا إلى الحق واشتبه علينا الحق من الباطل، فبالإمام تقوم[١٣] حجة اللّٰه على الخلق كما قال اللّٰه تعالى: ﴿ قُلْ[١٤]

---

[١] لا: -، ا.

[٢] أخبروا: وأخبروا، ب، ث.

[٣] وبيّنوا: بيّنوا، ب.

[٤] وأوجبوا: أوجبوا، ت.

[٥] التكليف: تكليف، ث.

[٦] اختلاف: الاختلاف، ث.

[٧] وكل: وبه كل، ا؛ به وكل، ب؛ فكان، ث.

[٨] واحد: -، ب.

[٩] الآخر: + منهم، ب.

[١٠] بدليل آية: بديل آية، ا؛ او اية، ب.

[١١] تقوم: يقوم، ا، ب، ت.

[١٢] بل: + يكون، ب.

[١٣] تقوم: يقوم، ا، ت، ث.

فَلِلَّهِ[1] ٱلْحُجَّةُ ٱلْبَٰلِغَةُ ﴾.[2]

[٥٢] ونقول:[3] إن الموضوعات التي تنسب إلى الحكماء فالحكماء في الحقيقة هم الأئمة سلام الله عليهم، ومنهم اقتبسوا أصل كل علم وحكمة مثل الحساب والهندسة، ولكل شيء من ذلك غاية ونهاية تدل على الإمام. وذلك أن الأشكال الهندسية[4] مثل المربّعات والمثلثات والمقوسات[5] وسائر الأشكال أتمها[6] وأفضلها الدائرة،[7] وهي أصل الجميع، ومنها يمكن أن يحمل[8] المربع والمثلث والمقوس. فإن المدوّر إذا ذُرِعَ[9] يخرج منها المربع وتبقى[10] المقوسات في الأطراف.[11] والمدور إذا أخذ قطره[12] وعموده[13] مستوى يكون أربع مثلثات، وسائر الأشكال

---

[14] قل: -، ا، ث.

[1] فَلِلَّهِ: ولله، ب.

[2] سورة ٦ الأنعام ١٤٩.

[3] ونقول: -، ث.

[4] الهندسية: الهندسة، ث.

[5] المقوسات: الموسات، ث.

[6] أتمها: -، ب.

[7] الدائرة: الزائرة، ا.

[8] يحمل: يجعل، ب.

[9] ذرع: رزع، ت؛ ادرع، ث.

[10] وتبقى: ويبقى، ا، ب، ت، ث.

[11] في الأطراف: -، ب.

[12] قطره: قطرة، ث.

[13] وعموده: وعمود، ا، ث.

كلها من[١] الدائرة اشتقت، وكل شكل داخل فيها، وهو التمام. ووضع الأشكال على مثل العالم والخلقة،[٢] والدائرة من الأشكال جعلت[٣] دليلاً وشاهداً على الإمام الذي هو دائرة[٤] الدين، وجميع الحدود داخلون[٥] تحت أمره ونهيه ومستفيدون منه. والدائرة مستغنية عن جميع الأشكال، وسائر الأشكال محتاج[٦] إليها كما أن الإمام مستغنى عن[٧] الحدود التي في وقته وزمانه، وجميع الحدود محتاجون إليه وهو محيط بالجميع.

[٥٣] ونقول:[٨] إن أصل الأعداد وعلتها هو الواحد وهو أتم الأعداد والمستغنى عن الاثنين فما فوقها إلى الألف، والألف وما دونه محتاج[٩] إلى الواحد، والإمام واحد في[١٠] عصره وزمانه، وجميع الحدود محتاجون إليه وهو مستغنى عنهم. فإن ظن بعض الناس أن الواحد يقع على بارئ[١١] البرايا فذلك ظنّ خطأ، فالواحد[١٢] علة الحساب وأصل الأعداد والاثنين

---

[١] من: في، ث.

[٢] والخلقة: والخليقة، ا.

[٣] جعلت: جعل، ا، ب، ت، ث.

[٤] دائرة: دائر، ا.

[٥] داخلون: داخل، ا، ب، ت، ث.

[٦] محتاج: محتاجة، ت.

[٧] عن: من، ب.

[٨] ونقول: -، ث.

[٩] محتاج: محتاجون، ث.

[١٠] في : -، ا، ب.

[١١] بارئ: باري، ا، ب، ث؛ الباري، ت.

[١٢] فالواحد: والواحد، ب.

واحد وواحد،[١] وكذلك[٢] الثلاثة.[٣] وإنما الواحد هو الإمام في حده ومنزلته فرد ولا[٤] يشاركه أحد من الخلق في عصره وزمانه.

[٥٤] ونقول:[٥] إن النقطة التي ذكرها أهل الحساب أنه لا جزء[٦] له وهو أصل الخط والسطح والجسم فذلك دليل على الإمام الذي لا يبلغ أحد إلى حده ومنزلته ولا يعرفه[٧] حق المعرفة ولا يقدر أن يصفه[٨] كنه صفته[٩] بل يقرّون[١٠] له بالعجز.

[٥٥] ونقول:[١١] إن الأيام سيّدها السبتُ، والشهور سيدُها شهر رمضان، وفي الساعات[١٢] ساعة واحدة مستجاب[١٣] فيها الدعاء. فلم يبق في العالم مخلوق ولا موضوع إلا ومن[١٤] جنسه ونوعِهِ غاية[١٥] وذروة في

[١] وواحد: واحد، ت.

[٢] وكذلك: كذلك، ا، ث.

[٣] الثلاثة: الثلثه، ا، ب، ت.

[٤] ولا: لا، ت، ث.

[٥] ونقول: -، ث.

[٦] جزء: جزاء، ا، ب، ث.

[٧] ولايعرفه: ويعرفه، ا،ت؛ ويعرف، ث.

[٨] يصفه: يصف، ب.

[٩] صفته: صفة، ب، ث.

[١٠] يقرون: يقترون، ب.

[١١] ونقول: -، ث.

[١٢] الساعات: الساعة، ب، ت.

[١٣] مستجاب: يستجاب، ا؛ مستجابة، ت.

[١٤] ومن: من، ب.

[١٥] غاية: عاية، ث.

الشرف والفضل لم يبلغ إليها غيره دالة على الإمام كما ذكرنا. ولو ذكرنا جميع ما يدخل في هذا الباب لخرجت الرسالة عن حدها، وفيما ذكرنا كفاية لمن تدبره،[١] ويمكنه[٢] أن يقيس[٣] على ما ذكرنا ما يريد من الأصول والفروع. والآن نذكر الاستشهاد من الفرائض وترتيبها نكتاً على الاختصار.

[٥٦] ونقول:[٤] إن في الصلاة[٥] وترتيبها وقيامها واستقبالها وقيام الإمام قدام[٦] الصفوف أقوى دليل على إثبات الإمامة، وذلك أن النبي صلى الله عليه وعلى آله أمر أولاً باستقبال القبلة، والقبلة مأخوذة[٧] من القبالة، وهي المحاذاة، والمتوجه إليها صوب وجهه وهو الأمام. ويقال:[٨] أمام الشيء، قبله وقدامه،[٩] وهو ضد الخلف والوراء والبعد، والإمام مشتق من معنى واحد[١٠] إنَّما[١١] سُمِّيَ إمام الصلاة[١٢] إماماً لهذا[١٣] المعنى لأنَّهُ مقدمهم.

---

[١] تدبره: تدبر، ا، ب، ت.

[٢] ويمكنه: يمكنه، ب؛ ويمكن، ت.

[٣] يقيس: يقس، ت؛ يقتبس، ث.

[٤] ونقول: -، ث.

[٥] الصلاة: الصلواة، ا.

[٦] قدام: قوام، ب.

[٧] مأخوذة: مأخوذ، ا، ب، ت، ث.

[٨] ويقال: يقال، ا.

[٩] وقدامه: -، ث.

[١٠] واحد: واحدة، ب.

[١١] إنما: وإنَّما، ث.

[١٢] الصلاة: الصلواة، ا.

والإشارة إلى القبلة هو الإشارة إلى الإمام وأمر الناس بالتوجه إليه والطاعة له في جميع العبادة والأخذ من جهته. وتوجه الرّجل إلى ما بين يديه في الصّلاة هو التوجه إلى القبلة من جهة الإمام في كل عبادته والطاعة له. ثم إذا كان صلاته[١] مع إمامه[٢] كما ذكره[٣] النبي صلى الله عليه وآله وسلم أن صلاة الجماعة سبع وعشرون صلاة من صلاة الفرد[٤] وفضيلتها بأن تكون مع الإمام وهو متوجه إليه متبوع له مقتدىً[٥] به نيَّةً وفعلاً، فهو دليل[٦] على أن جميع الطاعة ينبغي أن تكون خلف الإمام الأعظم مقتدىً به[٧] متبوعاً[٨] ومأموماً له حتى يكون لها فضلٌ. ثم أمر صلى الله عليه وآله وسلم أن يسوّوا الصفوف ولا يكون قيامهم مختلفين دليلاً على أنه لا يجوز أن تختلف[٩] قلوب المأمومين[١٠] المقتدين بالإمام ولا أفعالهم ولا أقوالهم.

---

[١٣] لهذا: هذا، ث.

[١] صلاته: صلواته، ث.

[٢] امامه: الامام، ث.

[٣] كما ذكره:؛ ما ذكره، ا، ب؛ ذكره، ت.

[٤] من صلاة الفرد: من صلوة الغد، ت؛ من صلوة الفذ، ا، ب.

[٥] مقتدى: مقتدٍ، ا؛ مقتد، ب؛ مقتدا مقتدا، ت.

[٦] فهو دليل: دليل، ا، ب، ث؛ دليلا، ت.

[٧] مقتدىً به: مقتدياً به، ا، ت، ث، ج؛ مقتدٍ به، ب.

[٨] متبوعاً: متبوعاً له، ب؛ -، ت.

[٩] تختلف: يختلف، ا، ب، ت، ث.

[١٠] المأمومين: المومنين، ب؛ المؤمنين، ث.

[٥٧] وأمرهم صلى الله عليه وآله وسلم بالإتباع لإمام الصلاة وإن طالت القراءة أو القيام[١] أو السجود،[٢] لا يخالفونه[٣] فعلاً ولا نية[٤] حتى أنه لو وافقه في فعله ولا يوافقه[٥] في نيته[٦] فلا تجزي[٧] صلاته، وإن سهى المأموم فالإمام يرفع عنه سهوه.[٨] فدلّ بهذا كله أن الإمام الجزئي[٩] الذي[١٠] ليس هو بإمام مطلق إذا وجبت طاعته وتزيد[١١] في ثواب تلك[١٢] العبادة أضعاف ذلك فكيف بطاعة[١٣] الإمام الأعظم الذي هو إمام[١٤] في جميع الشريعة والتأويل؟ وإذا[١٥] لم يجز أن يخالف الإمام[١٦] في شيء من أفعال الصلوة فكيف تجوز[١٧] مخالفة الإمام في أوامره ونواهيه في[١٨] حياة[١٩]

[١] أو القيام: والقيام، ت، ث.

[٢] أو السجود: والسجود، ت.

[٣] لا يخالفونه: ولا يخالفوه، ا؛ لا يخالفوه، ت، ث؛ ولا يخالفونه، ب.

[٤] ولا نية: ونية، ا، ث؛ ولا نيته، ب.

[٥] في فعله ولا يوافقه: -، ث.

[٦] نيته: نية، ا، ب.

[٧] تجزي: يجزي، ب.

[٨] سهوه: سهو، ب.

[٩] الجزئي: الجزي، ب، ت، ث.

[١٠] الذي: -، ث.

[١١] وتزيد: ويزيد، ا، ب، ت، ث.

[١٢] تلك: ذلك، ث.

[١٣] بطاعة: في طاعة، ا، ب، ت.

[١٤] إمام: الامام، ث.

[١٥] وإذا: إذا، ا، ت؛ وان، ث.

[١٦] يخالف الإمام: يخالفه، ا.

[١٧] تجوز: يجوز، ا، ث.

المؤمن؟ وكونه تحت الدعوة أبداً في الصَّلاة ما دام هو داخل[١] في ولاية الإمام، فإن خالفه بفعل أو بنيّة[٢] أو عزم فقد أبطل صلاته وخرج عن حكم المصلي. كما أنَّ المصلي إذا عزم على مخالفة الإمام[٣] فقد أبطل صلوته وركوعه وسجوده وقيامه وقعوده وحبط عمله[٤] وعليه أن يبتدئ[٥] بالصلاة فكيف بطاعة[٦] الإمام الأعظم الذي أوجب الله طاعته كلياً؟ وقال النبي صلى الله عليه وآله وسلم: الإمام ضامن، وليس المراد به إمام الصلاة، فإنه مفتقر إلى من يضمنه، وإنما الإشارة إلى الإمام سلام الله عليه يضمن تخليص المؤتم به من[٧] الشك والشبهة والحيرة والسهو ويضمن[٨] نجاته ما دام هو مقتدياً به تابعاً له. وأشار النبي[٩] صلى الله عليه وآله وسلم إلى مقام الإمام مقدَّماً على الجميع[١٠] وأمرهم صلى الله عليه وآله وسلم أن لا ينافسوا إمامهم في القراءة، وقال: إذا سجد فاسجدوا

---

[١٨] شيء من...ونواهيه في: -، ث.

[١٩] ونواهيه في حياة: ونهيه وحياة، ت.

[١] هو داخل: هو داخلا، ا؛ داخل، ب.

[٢] بنية: نية، ا، ب، ت.

[٣] على مخالفة الامام: -، ث.

[٤] عمله: -، ت.

[٥] يبتدئ: يبتدء، ب؛ يتبدئ، ت.

[٦] فكيف بطاعة: فكيف طاعة، ا؛ وكيف طاعة، ب، ت، ث.

[٧] من: -، ا.

[٨] ويضمن: ويضمنه، ث.

[٩] النبي: -، ا، ب، ت.

[١٠] الجميع: لجميع، ب.

وإذا ركع فاركعوا[١] وإذا قرأ[٢] فأنصتوا فإذا[٣] سلم فسلموا.

[٥٨] هذه كلها إشارة إلى طاعة الأئمة سلام اللّٰه عليهم وتعظيمهم في جميع أمورهم وثبات[٤] موضعهم في زمانهم ووجوب طاعتهم والتسليم[٥] إذا فرغ وسلم الأمر إلى[٦] من يسلمه إليه. فلو لم يكن في الشريعة من الدلالة[٧] على الإمام وطاعته إلا في الصلاة ففيها كفاية. ثم بيَّنَ أن الإمام يرفع عنهم السهو في الصلاة، أي أن الإمام يرفع عن القوم زلتهم ويستغفر لهم كما قال اللّٰه تعالى: ﴿ وَلَوْ أَنَّهُمْ إذ ظَّلَمُوٓاْ أَنفُسَهُمْ جَآءُوكَ فَٱسْتَغْفَرُواْ[٨] ٱللَّهَ وَٱسْتَغْفَرَ لَهُمُ ٱلرَّسُولُ لَوَجَدُواْ ٱللَّهَ تَوَّاباً رَّحِيماً ﴾.[٩] ولو رفع الإمام الغفران[١٠] وقبول التوبة عن هذه الأمة لهلكوا،[١١] وهم أكثر[١٢] احتياجاً إلى الغفران، لا بل كل ذلك باقٍ في كل وقت وزمان لمن أتى

[١] فاركعوا: فاذا ركعوا، ت.

[٢] وإذا قرأ: فإذا قرأ، ت؛ وإذا قري، ث.

[٣] فإذا: وإذا، ب، ت.

[٤] وثبات: وبيان، ث.

[٥] والتسليم: والتسلم، ا، ب.

[٦] إلى: -، ا.

[٧] الدلالة: الدلائل، ث.

[٨] فَٱسْتَغْفَرُواْ: فاستغفر، ا.

[٩] سورة ٤ النساء ٦٤.

[١٠] الإمام الغفران: الغفران، ا، ب؛ الإمام رفع الغفران، ت، ث.

[١١] لهلكوا: -، ت، ث.

[١٢] أكثر: أكثرهم، ث.

الإمام ويستغفر الإمام له، ويغفر اللّٰه كما كان لأولئك[١] القوم.

[٥٩] ونقول:[٢] إنَّ الجمعة[٣] لا تجوز إلا بالخطبة[٤] على المنابر[٥] والنَّاس يصلون خلف الإمام حتى يعرفوا أن طاعة الإمام لا تقوم عن[٦] الخلق في موضع. ثم الحج بأجمعه دليل على إثبات الإمامة، والحج هو القصد، والقصد يكون إلى أمر معلوم موجود[٧] حتى إذا ذكر[٨] القصد بالمعرفة يكون قصداً معروفاً لا يحتاج إلى البيان، وهو إشارة إلى القصد إلى الإمام. والكعبة دليل في بعض التأويل على الإمام، ثم وضعها في بادية ليس حولها عمارة لا يبلغون إليها إلا بشق الأنفس، وهي في[٩] موضع خال عن[١٠] الزرع[١١] والأشجار متنزه[١٢] عن المنفعة الدنياوية ليعرفوا أن ممثوله أيضاً لا يوصل اليه إلا بشق الأنفس والتعب والمضرة[١٣] من الأعداء وأنه لا ينبغي أن يكون القصد إلى الإمام والبلوغ إليه لسبب

[١] لأولئك: أولئك، ث.

[٢] ونقول: -، ث.

[٣] إنَّ الجمعة: إنَّ الحج الجمعة، ت.

[٤] بالخطبة: بخطبة، ا، ب، ت.

[٥] على المنابر: على المنبر، ث.

[٦] عن: على، ا، ب، ث.

[٧] موجود: موجوب، ا، ب، ت، ث.

[٨] ذكر: ذكرنا، ت.

[٩] وهي في: وهو، ت.

[١٠] عن: من، ب.

[١١] الزرع: الذرع، ا، ب.

[١٢] متنزه: المتنزه، ا، ب، ت، ث.

[١٣] والمضرة: والمقرة، ث.

دنياوي أو طمع أو مسرة[١] أو جاه دنياوي ولا يكون قصدُهُ إلى الإمام إلا للدين الخالص. فإذا استقبله[٢] شدة أو تعب أو قصد من العدو أو ملالة[٣] أو غير ذلك لا يضيق صدره ويصبر فيه، فقد عرفه ورآه في مثله الذي هو الحج. ثم طوافه واستلامه والإيماء[٤] به والسعي والرمي والإحرام[٥] والإمساك عن الطيب والجماع، وكل ذلك دليل على إثبات الإمامة والطاعة له في اختلاف أحوال[٦] المسترشدين وحفظ نفوسهم ورمي المذاهب المذمومة والعقائد الفاسدة.

[٦٠] ونقول:[٧] إن في إيجاب الزكاة وفروضها[٨] وحفظها وتفرقتها[٩] آكد دليل على وجوب الإمامة. وذلك أن الله تعالى أمر النبي صلى الله عليه وآله وسلم بأخذ[١٠] الصدقة منهم حيث قال: ﴿ خُذْ مِنْ أَمْوَالِهِمْ صَدَقَةً تُطَهِّرُهُمْ[١١] وَتُزَكِّيهِم بِهَا وَصَلِّ عَلَيْهِمْ إِنَّ صَلَوٰتَكَ سَكَنٌ لَّهُمْ ﴾.[١٢]

---

[١] مسرة: حسرة، ت.

[٢] فاذا استقبله: واذا استقبله، ا، ث؛ فاذاستقبله، ت.

[٣] ملالة: ملامة، ب، ت، ث.

[٤] والإيماء: والإيمان، ت، ث.

[٥] والإحرام: والحرم، ا؛ وللاحرام، ت.

[٦] أحوال: وأحوال، ت.

[٧] ونقول: -، ث.

[٨] وفروضها: وفرضها، ب، ت، ث.

[٩] تفرقتها: تفرقها، ا، ب، ت، ث.

[١٠] بأخذ: أن يأخذ، ب، ت.

[١١] تُطَهِّرُهُمْ: تطهر، ب.

[١٢] سورة ٩ التوبة ١٠٣.

فبيّن صلى اللّٰه عليه وآله وسلم فروض الزكاة ونصابها وكيفية أخذها، وأخذها بنفسه حتى عرفوا كيف تعطى وكيف تؤخذ.[١] وأخذ من جلس مجلس[٢] الأئمة وادعى أن الأخذ له واحتج على الأمة بهذه الآية وبفعل رسول اللّٰه صلى اللّٰه عليه وآله وسلم، وحارب بني حنيفة على ذلك وقتلهم، وأخذ من جلس بعده إلى[٣] أن انتهى[٤] إلى أئمتهم الذين أظهروا الفسق[٥] وآثروا بمال الزكاة وأنكروا أخذ[٦] الزكاة للإمام. وما أعجب حال هذه الأمة! أقروا[٧] بأن الآية ناسخة حكماً[٨] وقراءة وليست بمنسوخة، وأن سنة النبي صلى اللّٰه عليه وآله وسلم جرت في أخذها، كيف استجازوا تغيير[٩] حكم الآية وأمر اللّٰه تعالى وتغيير[١٠] السنة وسنة من ادعوا إمامتهم، ولم يكن لهم في تغيير[١١] ذلك قصد إلا الإنكار عن[١٢] مراتب الأئمة ووجوب الإمامة لأهل بيت النبي[١٣] صلى اللّٰه عليه وآله وسلم، وقد بين

---

[١] تؤخذ: يوخذ، ت.

[٢] مجلس: مجالس، ا، ب، ت، ث.

[٣] إلى: الا، ت.

[٤] انتهى: ينتهي، ب، ث.

[٥] الفسق: الفسوق، ت.

[٦] وأنكروا أخذ: أنكروا أخذ، ب، ت؛ وأنكروا وأخذوا، ث.

[٧] أقروا: وأقروا، ث.

[٨] حكماً: حكمها، ث.

[٩] تغيير: تغير، ا.

[١٠] تغيير: تغير، ا.

[١١] تغيير: -، ث.

[١٢] عن: من، ب، ت.

[١٣] النبي: رسول الله، ث.

الله تعالى في الزكاة وأخذها موقع الإمامة[١] والأئمة لما حرم الصدقة على النبي صلى الله عليه وآله وسلم حتى لا يتهموه في أخذها، وكذلك حرّمها على أهل بيته ليعرفوا أن الإمام منهم يقوم مقام النبي صلى الله عليه وآله وسلم في أخذها وهم مؤتمنون[٢] على ذلك.

[٦١] ولو كان الناسُ مؤتمنين[٣] على أداء الزكاة بأنفسهم وتفرقتها[٤] لأمرهُم الله تعالى بأداء ذلك كما أمرهم بالصلاة والصوم وغيرهما[٥] من الفرائض، ولم يأمرهم[٦] بتفرقه الصّدقة وأمر النبي صلى الله عليه وآله وسلم، ولو جاز ذلك لِلناس بأنفسهم لجاز[٧] في عهد النبي صلى الله عليه وآله وسلم، فإنهم[٨] كانوا أقوى ديناً ويقيناً وأكثر[٩] أمانة. أفبعدهم[١٠] صاروا أمناء على الزكاة؟ ولِمَ جاز عندهم الصلاة التي هي[١١] أفضل من الزكاة خلف أئمتهم وسائر الفرائض ولا يجوز إعطاء الزكاة لهم؟ ولِمَ هم كانوا[١٢]

---

١ الإمامة: الامة والايه، ث.

٢ مؤتمنون: موتمون، ت؛ مؤتمنين، ث.

٣ مؤتمنين: مؤتمين، ت.

٤ تفرقتها: تفرقها، ا، ب؛ تفريقها، ث.

٥ وغيرهما: غيرها، ب، ت.

٦ يأمرهم: يأمر تعالى لهم، ا.

٧ لجاز: مجاز، ت.

٨ فإنهم: وأنهم، ث.

٩ وأكثر: وكثر، ب.

١٠ أفبعدهم: وبعدهم، ا، ب، ت، ث.

١١ هي: -، ث.

١٢ هم كانوا: كانوا هم، ب، ت؛ كانوا، ث.

مؤتمنين[١] على الدماء والفروج عندهم وعلى[٢] الحكم على سائر وجوه الأموال وليسوا بثقات ولا بمؤتمنين[٣] في الزكاة؟ فإن كان القوم صادقين فيما يقولون في أئمتهم: إنهم ليسوا بمؤتمنين[٤] على الزكاة، فليسوا بأئمة[٥] بل هم خونة. وإذا[٦] كانوا خونة فلا[٧] يجوز الصلاة خلفهم ولا الجهاد ولا الحج[٨] ولا حكمهم على الفروج والدّماء والأموال. وإن كان القوم كاذبين فيما[٩] يقولون ويدعون[١٠] فعلماؤهم[١١] الذين يفتون بذلك هم الكاذبون وهم الذين يشهدون على إمامة هؤلاء، وشهادة الكاذبين لا تجوز.[١٢] وقد أمر الله تعالى النبي[١٣] صلى الله عليه وآله وسلم أن يزكيهم ويصلي[١٤] عليهم، فقال:[١٥] ﴿ وَتُزَكِّيهِمْ بِهَا[١٦] وَصَلِّ عَلَيْهِمْ إِنَّ صَلَوٰتَكَ

---

[١] مؤتمنين: بمؤمنين، ث.

[٢] وعلى: على، ت.

[٣] بمؤتمنين: بمؤمنين، ث.

[٤] بمؤتمنين: بمؤمنين، ث.

[٥] فليسوا بأئمة: فليسو بأئمتهم، ب.

[٦] وإذا: وان ، ث.

[٧] فلا: ولا، ت.

[٨] ولا الحج: والحج، ت.

[٩] فيما: فيها، ا، ب، ت.

[١٠] ويدعون: -، ا؛ يدعون، ب.

[١١] فعلماؤهم: فعلماءهم، ا، ب، ت، ث.

[١٢] تجوز: يجوز، ا.

[١٣] النبي: للنبي، ا، ب.

[١٤] ويصلي: ويصل، ث.

[١٥] فقال: وقال، ا، ب، ت.

[١٦] بها: -، ب.

سَكَنٌ لَّهُمْ ﴾.[١] فجعل التزكية لهم والصلاة عليهم والسكن والصلاة[٢] عوضاً لما أخذ منهم من الزكاة. ولو جعل لِأُولئك القرن[٣] الذين كانوا في عهد النبي صلى اللّٰه عليه وآله وسلم عوضاً[٤] من الزكاة ولم يجعل لمن بعدهم وهم أحوج إليه ممن كانوا في عهد النبي صلى اللّٰه عليه وآله وسلم[٥] فيكون ظلماً[٦] على من كان بعد أولئك القرن، واللّٰه تعالى منزه[٧] عن الظلم على العباد، وإنه[٨] تعالى ذكره لم يأمر بفريضة وجعل لها عوضاً في الدنيا والآخرة إلا[٩] وجعلها عاماً، بل التزكية[١٠] والصلاة والسكن باقية لمن أتى[١١] الإمام سلام اللّٰه عليه وأعطى زكاة ماله إليه ظاهراً وباطناً فيزكيه الإمام ويصلي عليه.[١٢] ولو لم يجب[١٣] الإمام إلا لهذا لكان[١٤]

---

[١] سورة ٩ التوبة ١٠٣.

[٢] والسكن والصلوة: والصلوة، ا، ب؛ والسكن، ت، ث.

[٣] القرن: -، ث.

[٤] عوضاً: عوض، ا.

[٥] عوض من...عهد النبي صلى اللّٰه عليه وآله وسلم:-، ث.

[٦] ظلماً: ظالماً، ا، ب.

[٧] منزه: متنزه، ا.

[٨] وإنه: انه، ب.

[٩] إلا: -، ا؛ -، ب.

[١٠] بل التزكية: بالتزكية، ث.

[١١] لمن أتى: الى أن أتى، ب، ث.

[١٢] عليه: عليهم ا؛ -، ب.

[١٣] يجب: يوجب، ا، ب، ث.

[١٤] لكان: لكانوا، ب.

كافياً. ثم تفريقه[١] الصدقات على أهلها لأنه[٢] يعرف من الذي يجب أداؤه[٣] إليه والذي لا يجوز، وإذا لم يوجد صنف من أهل الصدقات فإلى من يصرف نصيبه، والإمام هو الذي يحفظ بيت مال المسلمين ويصرف ماله[٤] فيما أوجب الوقت والدين.

[٦٢] ونقول:[٥] إن الجهاد أصل من أصول الدين ولا يجوز الجهاد إلا تحت راية الإمام ولا يقوم أمر الجهاد إلا بالإمام، وذلك أن الإمام أولاً يُحتاج إليه ليكون بيت مال المسلمين عنده مصوناً ويحفظ ثغور المسلمين والأسلحة، وينقذ أسارى المسلمين من أيدي الكفار ويفاديهم،[٦] ثم لا يجوز أن تخرج[٧] سرية إلا وعليهم أمير من جهة الإمام أو من جهة من أقامه الإمام. ثم الإمام أعرف بأوقات الصلح والهدنة وهو[٨] الذي يعقد ذلك. ثم إذا أخذ على الأسارى فهو يعرف من يجوز المن عليه أو الفداء أو القتل،[٩] وهو أعرف بصلاح أخذ الخراج والمال

[١] تفريقه: تفرق، ا؛ تفرقة، ب؛ يعرف؛ تفرقت، ث.

[٢] لأنه: + لا، ا، ت، ث.

[٣] أداؤه: اداءه، ا، ت، ث؛ اداه، ب.

[٤] ماله: مالها، ا، ب، ت، ث.

[٥] ونقول: -، ث.

[٦] الكفار ويفاديهم: -، ا.

[٧] تخرج: يخرج، ث.

[٨] وهو: -، ث.

[٩] أو الفداء أو القتل: والفداء والقتل، ث.

ليكون للمسلمين[١] رفاهية وجماماً.[٢] ثم الإمام[٣] يعرف الباغي وبه تصير الفئة فئة[٤] حق بكونها معه. والباغي هو الذي يخرج عن طاعة الإمام، وللإمام يجوز المحاربة معهم والقتال أو الصلح[٥] والهدنة. وقال الشافعي: لولا أمير المؤمنين علي بن أبي طالب سلام الله عليه لما عرفنا قتال أهل البغي ولا الباغي من المحق.[٦]

[٦٣] ثم الخمس الذي جعله الله تعالى مخصوصاً لأهل البيت سلام الله عليهم وللأئمة بدلاً عما حرم الله عليهم من الصدقات فجميع أعمال الصدقات والزكاة ووجوبها متعلقة بالإمام منوطة به. ثم الأعياد وشهر[٧] رمضان فالإمام يحفظ ويقبل شهادة الشاهد[٨] عندهم أيضاً، من قال الصوم[٩] بالرؤية والإفطار بالرؤية أو من أقامه الإمام. وصلاة العيدين وصلاة الجمعة لا تجوز جماعةً إلا بالخطبة، وهي موقوفة[١٠] على الإمام وحضوره أو من يكون من قبله. ورد[١١] الأربعة في الجماعة إلى[١٢] الاثنين

---

[١] للمسلمين: المسلمون، ا، ت، ث.

[٢] وجماما: -، ب.

[٣] الإمام: -، ت.

[٤] الفئة فئة: الفيئة فيئة، ت، ث.

[٥] أو الصلح: والصلح، ا، ب، ث.

[٦] الباغي من المحق: الباغين من المحق، ا؛ الباغ من المحق، ب؛ الباغي من الحق، ت.

[٧] وشهر: والشهر، ت.

[٨] الشاهد: + عنهم، ت.

[٩] الصوم: بالصوم، ت، ث.

[١٠] وهي موقوفة: -، ا، ب، ت، ث.

[١١] ورد: ودار، ت.

بالخطبة على الإمام.

[٦٤] ثم إقامة الحدود فإن الحدود[١] لا تجوز إقامتها إلا للإمام أو من أقامه الإمام،[٢] مثل القطع والضرب والرجم والحبس وأرش الجراحات والحكم فيها لا تجوز[٣] إلا بالإمام. ولو لم تكن دلالة على إثبات الإمامة لأهل بيت[٤] رسول الله إلا من جهة الحدود لكان كفاية.[٥] فإن المخالفين اتفقوا في ذلك أن[٦] من ليس له ولاية فلا[٧] يجوز حكمه في الحدود، فلو رأى رجل[٨] آخر يقتل رجلاً بغير حق فليس له أن يقتله، وإذا[٩] رأى أن يسرق[١٠] فليس له أن يقطع يده ولا الرجم ولا غير ذلك حتى أن عند أكثر الناس أن ليس لصاحب العبد أن يحد[١١] عبده المملوك وأن[١٢] يؤدبه، بل الإمام يؤدبه[١٣] ويحده، ولا يمكن رفع الحدود فلو رفع الحد[١٤] لهلك[١٥]

---

[١٢] إلى: على ، ب.

[١] فإن الحدود: -، ث.

[٢] الإمام: -، ب، ث.

[٣] لا تجوز: لا يجوز، ت، ث.

[٤] لأهل بيت: -، ا؛ لأهل البيت، ت.

[٥] الحدود لكان كفاية: الحدود لهلك الناس وخربت البلاد ولو اجيز لكان الكفاية، ت.

[٦] أن: -، ت، ث.

[٧] فلا: ولا، ت.

[٨] رجل: رجلا، ت، ث.

[٩] وإذا: وان، ث.

[١٠] أن يسرق: انه مسرق، ب؛ انه سرق، ت، ث.

[١١] يحد: يجد، ب.

[١٢] وأن: ولا ان، ا؛ ولا، ب، ت، ث.

[١٣] يؤدبه: -، ب.

الناس وخربت البلاد. ولو أجيز[١] للناس إقامة الحدود لقصد كل واحد منهم[٢] إلى قتل وضرب[٣] ثم ادعى أنه قتل رجلاً[٤] أو سرق مالاً فأقام عليه الحد،[٥] والذي يوجب عليه في كل يوم عشرين حداً فكيف[٦] يلي[٧] إقامة الحدود؟ وكيف يجوز أن يحد؟ ولو أجيز ذلك لجاز لكل متغلب أو خارجي فيكون في ذلك هلاك الناس.[٨] والفئة الباغية إذا أقاموا[٩] الحدود وأتلفوا النفوس إذا[١٠] قدر عليهم الإمام يغرم[١١] عليهم ما أتلفوا من الفئة المحقة[١٢] حتى يكون منعاً من بسط أيدي الظالمين إلى إهلاك[١٣] الناس وإتلاف[١٤] أموالهم. ثم يدعون أن ذلك كان[١٥] لحد موجب[١٦] عليهم، وقد

---

[١٤] فلو رفع الحد: -، ت؛ فلو رفع الحدود، ث.

[١٥] لهلك: + أكثر، ث.

[١] أجيز: أجير، ت؛ أخيز، ث.

[٢] منهم: -، ا، ب، ث.

[٣] وضرب: او ضرب، ب.

[٤] رجلاً: رجل، ت.

[٥] الحد: الحدود، ب، ت، ث.

[٦] فكيف: وكيف، ب، ث.

[٧] يلي: بلى، ا، ب، ت.

[٨] الناس: النفوس، ب.

[٩] إذا أقاموا: اذ قاموا، ت.

[١٠] إذا: إذ، ت.

[١١] يغرم: يعزم، ت.

[١٢] الفئة المحقة: الفئة الباغية المحقق، ت.

[١٣] اهلاك: هلاك، ب، ت.

[١٤] وإتلاف: واتلافهم، ا؛ والى اتلاف، ت، ث؛ والى اتلافو، ب.

[١٥] كان: -، ت.

بيّن الله تعالى في قوله: ﴿ أَتَأْمُرُونَ ٱلنَّاسَ بِٱلْبِرِّ وَتَنْسَوْنَ أَنْفُسَكُمْ ﴾،[١] فنبه الله تعالى أن من يحتاج إلى أن يؤمر[٢] بالمعروف وينهى عن المنكر فليس له أن يأمر بالبر[٣] وينهى عن المنكر،[٤] وبيّن في آية أخرى أن الأمر بالمعروف والنهي عن المنكر للأئمة[٥] سلام الله عليهم حيث قال: ﴿ كُنتُمْ خَيْرَ أُمَّةٍ أُخْرِجَتْ لِلنَّاسِ تَأْمُرُونَ بِٱلْمَعْرُوفِ وَتَنْهَوْنَ عَنِ ٱلْمُنكَرِ ﴾[٦] وهم الأئمة الوسط[٧] الذين هم الشهداء[٨] على الناس. وكيف يأمر بالمعروف من لا يفعله؟ وكيف ينهى عن المنكر من يحب المنكر ويأتي به في كل يوم مائة مرة؟ فكيف[٩] يجوز[١٠] لِأئمتهم ذلك وهم يعملون ما يوجب عليهم الحد في كل يوم وهو شهوتهم ومرادهم، ويقربون إلى أنفسهم من يحب ذلك ويفعله[١١] ويدخل[١٢] معهم في ذلك؟ وكيف ينكرون ذلك وهو عندهم الظرافة والفضل والمعاشرة والخفة

---

[١٦] موجب: يوجب، ب.

[١] سورة ٢ البقرة ٤٤.

[٢] يؤمر: يأمر، ث.

[٣] بالبر: بالمعروف، ث.

[٤] فليس له...المنكر: -، ب.

[٥] للأئمة: وهم الأئمة، ت.

[٦] سورة ٣ آل عمران ١١٠.

[٧] الوسط: الوسطي، ث.

[٨] الشهداء: شهداء، ت.

[٩] فكيف: وكيف، ت، ث.

[١٠] يجوز: تجوز، ب.

[١١] ويفعله: -، ث.

[١٢] ويدخل: ويدخله، ب.

والأدب، ومن[١] لا يدخل معهم في الشرب[٢] والفسق لا يقربونه ولا يستخدمونه وهو ثقيل عندهم؟ فهل يكون ذلك إلا تعليماً منهم لمأموميهم[٣] وحثاً لهم على الفساد[٤] والفسق[٥] ليكونوا[٦] مرضيين عندهم؟[٧]

[٦٥] ونقول:[٨] إن الحكم بين الناس في الدماء والفروج والأموال متفق عليه أنه لا يجوز إلا لمن يكون عارفاً بالحادثات وبالفتاوي[٩] فيها وبالأحكام والتنزيل والمعاني والناسخ[١٠] والمنسوخ والقياس عندهم ويقوم بشرائطه[١١] ويكون مأموناً على الدِّماء والأموال والفروج، وهل ممن ادعى الإمامة من المتغلبين من كان فيه هذه الشرائط؟ بل كلهم كانوا محتاجين إلى المتسمين[١٢] بالفقهاء والمنسوبين إلى العلم بغير حقيقة، ويعطونهم حطام الدنيا ويولونهم الأعمال ويجلسونهم في مجالسهم، فإذا

---

١ ومن: من، ا، ب، ت.

٢ الشرب: الشراب، ا.

٣ لمأموميهم: لمامومهم، ب.

٤ على الفساد: -، ا.

٥ والفسق: والفسوق، ت.

٦ ليكونوا: وليكونوا، ت.

٧ عندهم: -، ت.

٨ ونقول: -، ث.

٩ وبالفتاوي: والفتاوي، ت.

١٠ والناسخ: والتناسخ، ث.

١١ بشرائطه: بشرائط، ب.

١٢ المتسمين: المتمسكين، ت.

وقعت حادثة يقولون لهم: ماذا تقولون؟ فيقول أحدٌ[1] بقول أبي حنيفة: يجب عليه القتل، ويقول الآخر بقول الشافعي: لا يجب، ويقول الآخر بقول مالك:[2] طلقت امرأته، ويقول الآخر[3] بقول أحمد بن حنبل: لم يحرم[4] عليه المرأة،[5] وأعطوا رئاسة الدين لهم ليحكموا بما يريدون بأهوائهم وآرائهم حتى تركوا رئاسة الدنيا لهم ويشهدوا[6] لهم بالزورِ، فافتضحوا[7] واصطلحوا. فلا أدري ممن[8] أتعجب: ممن لا يستحيي أن يدعي الإمامة وهو لا يعرف من الدين شيئاً ولا من الأحكام حتى يحتاج إلى مثل هؤلاء العلماء؟ فإن كانوا هم العلماء، والأمر والحكم بقولهم، فهم الأئمة لا هذا الذي يدعي، وهو صنم منصوب ليس إليه من الأمر شيء ولا[9] ينفع ولا يضر، والعجب[10] ممَّن يقتدي بإمامته[11] ويكفيهم جهلهم وعارهم، فالإمام مثل المأموم والمأموم مثل الإمام.

---

[1] أحدٌ: احد منهم، ب؛ واحد، ت؛ -، ث.

[2] مالك: المالكي، ا، ب.

[3] الآخر: -، ث.

[4] يحرم: تحرم، ث.

[5] المرأة: امرأته، ث.

[6] ويشهدوا: ويشهدون، ا.

[7] فافتضحوا: وافتضحوا، ث.

[8] ممن: بمن، ا.

[9] ولا: لا، ب.

[10] والعجب: وأتعجب، ب؛ ولا العجب، ت.

[11] بإمامته: بامامتهم، ا، ب، ت، ث.

[٦٦] وإذا[١] كانت[٢] أئمتهم ليسوا من أهل الحكم والولاية لأنهم لا يعرفون العلم ولا يقومون بشرائطه وليس[٣] لهم عفة ولا صيانة، وعند أكثر[٤] من يقول بالاختيار أن الإمام إذا جار وفسق فقد انعزل عن الإمامة، ويعزل عند بعضهم، وكذلك القاضي عندهم إذا خان والوصي لا يكون له ولاية، وبعضهم يقولون: على الأمة[٥] أن يعزلوا[٦] الإمام إذا جار وفسق، وقال الشافعي ليس لفاسق ولاية حتى لو كان الرجل الفاسق له بنت فليس له ولاية عليها وليس له أن يزوجها من زوج، بل القاضي[٧] يزوجها، وليس له ولاية على ابنته،[٨] وعند الجميع لا تقبل[٩] شهادة الفاسق، فإذاً بالاتفاق والاجتماع[١٠] لم تكن أئمتهم من أهل الاجتهاد في الدين ولا ممن يجوز لهم[١١] تزويجهم لبناتهم ولا ممن تقبل[١٢] شهادتهم ولا ممن يجوز لهم إقامة الحدود، فإنهم[١٣] كانوا فساقاً وزناة وشراباً معروفين

---

[١] وإذا: وان، ث.

[٢] كانت: كان، ب؛ كانوا، ث.

[٣] وليس: ليس، ب.

[٤] أكثر: أكثرهم، ا، ت، ث.

[٥] الأمة: الامامة، ت.

[٦] يعزلوا: يعزل، ب.

[٧] القاضي: قاضي، ب.

[٨] ابنته: بنته، ت، ج.

[٩] لا تقبل: لا يقبل، ا، ب، ت.

[١٠] والاجتماع: والاجماع، ب، ث؛ ولاجماع، ت.

[١١] ممن يجوز لهم: يجوز لهم، ب؛ أئمتهم من...ممن يجوز لهم: -، ت.

[١٢] تقبل: يقبل، ا، ب، ت.

[١٣] فانهم: وانهم، ث.

مشهورين، ومن بقي منهم يجري[١] على سنتهم، ومن يكون بهذه الصفة كيف يكون أمير المؤمنين وخليفة رب العالمين وإماماً مفترض الطاعة؟ وإذا لم يكن[٢] لهم الولاية والحكم والشهادة فكيف يكون لمن يولونهم على الحكم ولاية وكيف[٣] يكون لمن يزكونهم شهادة؟ وكيف تجوز[٤] شهادتهم إذا قالوا: إن[٥] فلاناً يصلح للقضاء والشهادة والولاية؟ وهل[٦] في الدنيا أعجب من هؤلاء ومن مناقضات أحكامهم وأصول مذهبهم وأقوالهم وأفضح من إمامهم ومأمومهم؟

[٦٧] ولو ذكرنا جميع مناقضات أصولهم وفضائحهم لاحتجنا إلى التطويل وخرجنا عن الحدّ والمقصود، وفيما ذكرنا تبيين[٧] إبطال إمامتهم وتبيين[٨] أنّ جميع ما عملوا ويعملون باطل وظلمٌ وعدوانٌ، ويكفيهم ذلك عاراً وشناراً. فإذا بطلت[٩] إمامتهم كما ذكرنا وصح أن الإمامة من أصول الدين وهو ضروري لا بد منه وأن جميع الشرع والأحكام منوطة بالإمام

---

[١] يجري: -، ث.

[٢] لم يكن: لم تكن، ت.

[٣] وكيف: فكيف، ا.

[٤] وكيف تجوز: فكيف يجوز، ا، وكيف يجوز، ت.

[٥] إن: -، ب، ت.

[٦] وهل: -، ب.

[٧] تبيين: تبين، ب، ت.

[٨] وتبيين: وتبين، ب، ت.

[٩] بطلت: ابطلت، ث.

صح إمامة الأئمة الطاهرين من آل طه ويس[١] المعصومين من الفسق والطغيان والإفك والعدوان، والمطهرين[٢] من كل دنس وعيب،[٣] وفيما ذكرنا من الاستدلال من الشريعة كفاية. والآن نذكر من الأدوار الماضية وجوب الإمامة وأنه لم يخل وقت من الأوقات ولا زمان[٤] من إمام حق[٥] مفترض الطّاعة.

فصل

[٦٨] ونقول:[٦] إنه لو جاز أن يكون في الأرض خلائق ولا يكون فيها إمامٌ ولا خليفة لجاز في وقت آدم عليه السلام حيث كانوا ملائكة، فقال اللّه تعالى: ﴿ إِنِّي جَاعِلٌ فِي ٱلْأَرْضِ خَلِيفَةً قَالُوٓاْ أَتَجْعَلُ فِيهَا مَن يُفْسِدُ فِيهَا وَيَسْفِكُ ٱلدِّمَآءَ وَنَحْنُ نُسَبِّحُ[٧] بِحَمْدِكَ وَنُقَدِّسُ لَكَ قَالَ إِنِّي أَعْلَمُ مَا لَا تَعْلَمُونَ ﴾.[٨] وقد بيّن اللّه سبحانه[٩] في ذلك أنه لا تخلو[١٠] الأرض من

---

[١] ويس: ويسين، ب، ت.

[٢] والعدوان والمطهرين: والعدوان المطهرين، ا، ب، ت؛ والعدوان و، ث.

[٣] دنس وعيب: عيب ودنس، ب.

[٤] زمان: زمن، ا، ت.

[٥] حق: -، ب، ت، ث.

[٦] فصل ونقول: -، ا، ث؛ ونقول، ت.

[٧] نسبح: -، ب.

[٨] سورة ٢ البقرة ٣٠.

[٩] سبحانه: -، ب.

[١٠] تخلو: يخلو، ا، ب، ت، ث.

إمام وإن[١] كان القوم معصومين مقدسين، ليعرفوا أنهم إذا كانوا جهالاً وأكثرهم مفسدون[٢] كيف يستغنون عن الإمام؟ وبيّن[٣] اللّٰه تعالى في ذلك أنه لو جاز الإمام بالاختيار[٤] لكان الاختيار لِلملائكة[٥] ولا ردهم لأنهم كانوا معصومين عن الميل والهوى[٦] والظلم والرغبة[٧] في الدنيا والولاية، فلما لم يجز ذلك لهم لم يجز فيمن دونهم. وهذا المعنى مضمر في الآية لأن[٨] اللّٰه تعالى لما قال في حق الوالدين: ﴿ فَلَا تَقُل لَّهُمَآ أُفٍّ وَلَا تَنْهَرْهُمَا ﴾.[٩] فقد نهى عما هو أكثر من ذلك من الضرب والشتم، وإنما ذكر اللّٰه تعالى قصة[١٠] الأمم الماضية والأنبياء ليعرفوا[١١] أن في دور النبي صلى اللّٰه عليه آله وسلم يجب[١٢] ذلك ويكون[١٣] كما كان في سائر الأدوار، كما قال النبي صلى اللّٰه عليه وآله وسلم: كائن في أمتي ما كان في بني إسرائيل، وقال: لتسلكن سبل من كان قبلكم حذو النعل بالنعل

---

[١] وإن: ان، ت، ث.

[٢] مفسدون: مفسدين، ا، ب، ت، ث.

[٣] وبين: وقد بين، ث.

[٤] بالاختيار: باختيار، ب، ت.

[٥] لكان الاختيار لِلملائكة: لكان للملائكة الاختيار، ا؛ لكان الاختيار جاز لِلملائكة، ب.

[٦] والهوى: والهواء، ب.

[٧] والرغبة: والرعية، ث.

[٨] لأن: ان، ب، ت، ث.

[٩] سورة ١٧ الإسراء ٢٣.

[١٠] قصة: قصته، ث.

[١١] ليعرفوا: ليعلموا، ب.

[١٢] يجب: يوجب، ا، ب، ث؛ لوجب، ت.

[١٣] ويكون: وليكون، ب.

والقذة بالقذة حتى أنهم لو دخلوا جحر ضب لدخلتموه.

[٦٩] وفي قصة آدم دليل على أن الإمامة والخلافة لا تجوز بالاختيار ولا بالشورى، ولو كان ذلك جائزاً[١] لكان اختيار الملائكة أولى ومشورتهم أحرى لأنهم كانوا معصومين عن[٢] الحسد والبغي، وفيه دليل على أنه ليس للقوم أن يقولوا: فلان يصلح للإمامة أو لا[٣] يصلح، يحبون[٤] الواحد ولا يحبون[٥] الآخر. فإنهم لم[٦] يحبوا آدم، فأخبرهم اللّٰه[٧] تعالى عن خطأ قولهم، وعاتبهم[٨] ووبّخهم وأظهر بطلان قولهم، وذكره في القرآن ليعتبروا بذلك ولا يتكلموا في الإمامة وفيمن[٩] يختاره اللّٰه ورسوله للإمامة كما فعلوا، وفي إقامته ابنه للإمامة دليل على أن العالم لا يخلو من الإمام،[١٠] والناس كلهم مقّرون بأئمة دور آدم وينكرون أئمة دور محمد صلى اللّٰه عليه وآله وسلم، وقد بين اللّٰه عز وجل في قوله:[١١] ﴿ سُنَّةَ[١٢] مَن

---

[١] جائزاً: جائز، ت، ث.

[٢] عن: من، ب.

[٣] أو لا: ولا، ث.

[٤] يحبون: ويحبوا، ا؛ يحبوا، ت، ث.

[٥] يحبون: يحبوا، ا، ب، ت، ث

[٦] لم: لا، ث.

[٧] فأخبرهم اللّٰه: وأخبرهم، ت.

[٨] عاتبهم: عاقبهم، ب.

[٩] وفيمن: فيمن، ب؛ ولا فيمن، ت.

[١٠] الإمام: امام، ب.

[١١] عز وجل في قوله: تع، ب، ت، ث.

[١٢] سنة: + الله، ث.

قَدْ أَرْسَلْنَا قَبْلَكَ مِن رُّسُلِنَا وَلَا[١] تَجِدُ لِسُنَّتِنَا تَحْوِيلاً ﴾،[٢] وقال: ﴿ وَلَن تَجِدَ لِسُنَّةِ ٱللَّهِ[٣] تَبْدِيلاً ﴾،[٤] وهي سنة الإمامة، لا سنة الأعمال مثل الصلاة والصوم وغيرهِ، فإن النبي صلى اللّٰه عليه وآله وسلم غيّر سنن جميع[٥] الأنبياء في العبادات[٦] ولم يغيّر سنن[٧] الإمامة.

[٧٠] ونقول:[٨] إن نوحاً عليه السلام لما دعا الناس في السفينة شفقة عليهم وعلماً منه بهلاك من يتخلّف[٩] عنها باختياره وظنه أن صلاحهم في غير ذلك وما أدى إليه حالهم من الغرق، بيان[١٠] ذلك أن كل قوم يدعوهم نبيُّهم وإمامهم[١١] إلى أمرٍ وهم يمتنعون[١٢] عن ذلك فيكون هلاكهم في ذلك، ولم تكن السفينة إلا الإمام ودعوته[١٣] الناس إلى الإمام[١٤] كما قال النبي صلى اللّٰه عليه وآله وسلم مثل[١٥] أهل بيتي فيكم

---

[١] وَلَا: ولن، ب.

[٢] سورة ١٧ الإسراء ٧٧.

[٣] لِسُنَّةِ ٱللَّهِ: لسنتنا، ا، ب.

[٤] سورة ٣٣ الأحزاب ٦٢؛ -، ب.

[٥] فإن النبي صلع غير سنن جميع: فالنبي ص غير سنن، ب؛ فإن النبي صلع غيرجميع؛ سنن، ت، ث.

[٦] العبادات: العبادة، ا، ب، ت.

[٧] سنن: سنة، ت.

[٨] ونقول: -، ث.

[٩] يتخلف: تخلف، ب.

[١٠] بيان: وبيان، ا.

[١١] وإمامهم: او لماهم، ب؛ او امامهم، ث.

[١٢] يمتنعون: يمنعون، ث.

[١٣] دعوته: دعوة، ث.

[١٤] الإمام: -، ب.

كمثل سفينة[١] نوح عليه السلام، من ركبها نجا ومن تخلف عنها غرق". وأقام نوح ابنه سام للوصاية[٢] والإمامة، ثم بعده واحداً بعد[٣] واحد بالنصّ والتوقيف[٤] إلى إبراهيم عليه السلام، وهم مقرون بأئمة دور نوح عليه السلام وينكرون أئمة آل محمد صلى الله عليه وآله وسلم، والسنة ما غيرت ولا بدلت ولا الناس استغنوا عن الإمام.

[٧١] ثم[٥] لما قام إبراهيم عليه السلام أمر بتعظيم النيران،[٦] فإن صح ذلك عنه فهو إشارة إلى تعظيم نور الإمامة. وقد ذكرنا ذلك فيما تقدم، ثم بنى إبراهيم وإسماعيل عليهما السلام البيت وأمر[٧] الناس بتعظيمه إشارة إلى أن الإمامة في بيته وفي أولاده، وحث[٨] الناس على تعظيم الإمامة وتعظيم أهل البيت وطاعتهم.[٩]

[٧٢] فلما قام موسى عليه السلام أمرهم بالتوجه إلى بيت المقدس ولم يكن لموسى أولاد وبيت تكون الإمامة فيهم، فأشار إلى بيت

---

[١٥] مثل: -، ث.

[١] كمثل سفينة: كسفينة، ب، ت، ث.

[٢] للوصاية: للوصية، ث.

[٣] بعد: -، ب.

[٤] والتوقيف: والتوفيق، ب.

[٥] ثم: -، ث.

[٦] النيران، النار، ت.

[٧] وأمر: وامروا، ث.

[٨] وحث: وحظ، ث.

[٩] وطاعتهم: -، ب.

المقدس[١] وقال: كل من يتحد[٢] به روح القدس من بني إسرائيل فهو إمامكم وقبلتكم. وقام عيسى عليه السلام ولم يكن له بيت ولا ولدٌ وأمر القوم بالتوجّه إلى المشرق كما يحكى[٣] عنه، فإن[٤] صح ذلك فإن أمره بالتوجه إلى المشرق[٥] هو التوجه إلى موضع شروق نور[٦] الإمامة، أي أن من يشرق ذلك النور منه فهو إمامكم وقبلتكم.

ولما قام النبي صلى الله عليه وآله وسلم[٧] خاتم النبيين أمر الناس بصرف وجوههم عن بيت المقدس إلى الكعبة وجعل الكعبة قبلة المسلمين، والكعبة هي التي[٨] بناها إبراهيم عليه السلام وإسماعيل إشارة إلى[٩] أن القبلة رجعت إلى بيت إبراهيم الذي هو[١٠] بيت إسماعيل، أي أن الإمامة رجعت إلى أولاد إسماعيل الذين هم أولاد النبي صلى الله عليه وآله وسلم. وأمر الناس بتعظيم البيت والحج إليه[١١] ما لم يأمر به أحد من

---

١ ولم يكن...إلى بيت المقدس: -، ب.

٢ يتحد: يتخذ، ث.

٣ يحكى: حكى، ث.

٤ فإن: وان، ث.

٥ كما يحكى...المشرق: -، ب.

٦ نور: -، ث.

٧ وعلى آله: -، ا ، ب، ت.

٨ هي التي: الذي هو، ا ، ب، ت.

٩ إلى: -، ث.

١٠ الذي هو: التي هي، ث.

١١ اليه: عليه، ب.

الأنبياء تنبيهاً على فضل[١] أئمة آل محمدٍ صلى الله عليه وآله وسلم على سائر[٢] الأئمة في الأدوار الماضية. وهل في الدنيا أعظم ظلماً من هذه الأمة يقرون بأئمة كل دورٍ من أدوار الأنبياء ويقرون أن العالم لا يخلو من إمام[٣] ولم يكن قط في الأدوار الماضية إمام[٤] بالاختيار، وينكرون إمامة آل محمد صلى الله عليه وآله وسلم وينكرون[٥] النصّ ويدعون الاختيار؟[٦] وقال الله تعالى: ﴿ وَرَبُّكَ يَخْلُقُ مَا يَشَاءُ وَيَخْتَارُ مَا كَانَ لَهُمْ الْخِيَرَةُ[٧] ﴾ ولو كانت الإمامة بالاختيار[٨] لاختار كل قوم من أحبَّ.[٩] وقد ذكر الشيوخ حديث النصّ والاختيار، ونحن[١٠] شرطنا أن نذكر ما لم يذكره الشيوخ في كتب إثبات الإمامة، وفيما ذكرنا كفاية، ونثبت أن الإمام يكون الأفضل والأعلم والأشرف.

[٧٣] ونقول:[١١] إن الفضائل التي ذكرها الله تعالى وفضل بها بعض الناس على بعض في ثلاثة أشياء في العلم والجهاد والتقوى، كما قال

---

[١] فضل: افضل، ب.

[٢] أئمة ...سائر: -، ب.

[٣] امام: الامام، ا، ب، ث.

[٤] امام: اماماً، ث.

[٥] إمامة آل...وينكرون: -، ب.

[٦] الاختيار: لاختيار، ا.

[٧] الخيرة: الخبرة، ا.

[٨] بالاختيار: في الاختيار، ب، ث.

[٩] أحب: احبوا، ت، ث.

[١٠] ونحن: نحن، ت.

[١١] ونقول: -، ث.

الله تعالى: ﴿ فَضَّلَ ٱللَّهُ ٱلْمُجَٰهِدِينَ عَلَى ٱلْقَٰعِدِينَ أَجْرًا عَظِيمًا دَرَجَٰتٍ[١] ﴾[٢] وقوله: ﴿ هَلْ يَسْتَوِى ٱلَّذِينَ يَعْلَمُونَ وَٱلَّذِينَ لَا يَعْلَمُونَ ﴾[٣] وقوله: ﴿ وَٱلَّذِينَ أُوتُوا۟ ٱلْعِلْمَ دَرَجَٰتٍ ﴾[٤] وقوله: ﴿ إِنَّ أَكْرَمَكُمْ عِندَ ٱللَّهِ أَتْقَىٰكُمْ ﴾[٥] ولا يمكن[٦] لأحدٍ أن[٧] يقول: إن أبا بكر كان أعلم الناس، فإنه لم يكن يعلم من القرآن إلا ثلاث عشر سورة، وإذا لم يعرف القرآن فكيف كان يعرف تأويله ومعانيه وأحكامه وناسخه ومنسوخه ومحكمه ومتشابهه؟ وهل يقدر أحد أن يروي عنه حكمةً أو علماً[٨] أو أحكاماً[٩] في حادثة؟ ولا من عمر[١٠] ولا من غيره، ومن يدعي ذلك فليأت به.

وأما الجهاد فالخاص والعام يعرفون[١١] أنهم لم يجاهدوا يوماً من الأيام بأيديهم، وحروب أمير المؤمنين معروفة مشهورة، ولو لم يكن من المثالب[١٢] في الجهاد إلا فرارهم يوم حنين وترك عمر أمرَ النبي صلى الله

---

[١] دَرَجَٰتٍ: + منه، ب، ث.

[٢] سورة ٤ النساء ٩٥.

[٣] سورة ٣٩ الزمر ٩.

[٤] سورة ٥٨ المجادلة ١١.

[٥] سورة ٤٩ الحجرات ١٣.

[٦] ولا يمكن: ولم يكن، ث.

[٧] أن: -، ث.

[٨] حكمة أو علماً: علماً أو حكمة، ت، ث.

[٩] أحكاماً:+ اما، ث.

[١٠] ولا من عمر: ولاعمر من، ت.

[١١] يعرفون: يعرفوا، ث.

[١٢] المثالب: المثالث، ت.

عليه وآله وسلم ووصيته في حفظ الجبل ودخوله[١] في ذم المسلمين، والنبي صلى اللّٰه عليه وآله وسلم وأمير المؤمنين علي عليه السلام يحاربان ويقتلان من العدو حتى انهزم العدو.

وأما التقوى فأي تقوى كان لهم وقد غصبوا حقَّ أمير المؤمنين وحق أهل البيت؟ وإذا لم يكن علم فلا يكون هناك تقوى، وإنما التقوى يكون بالعلم، يعرف ما يكون له وعليه. ويحكى عن محمد بن الحسن[٢] صاحب أبي حنيفة أنه سأله بعض المحتسبين[٣] أن يصنّف كتاباً في الزهد فصنّف[٤] كتاب البيوع، فقيل له في ذلك، فقال: من لا يحسن الفقه والبيع والشرى[٥] كيف يأكل الحلال؟ ومن لا يأكل الحلال[٦] فلا زهد له، فإذاً قد صح بما ذكرنا من الآيات أن الإمامة كانت لأمير المؤمنين سلام اللّٰه عليه لأنه[٧] كان السابق في الفضائل وكان أعلمهم وأتقاهم وأكثرهم جهاداً.

[٧٤] ونقول: إن هؤلاء لم يدعوا الفضل ولا العلم ولا التقوى

---

[١] الجبل ودخوله: الخيل والدخول، ت.

[٢] الحسن: حسن، ت، ث.

[٣] المحتسبين: المستجيبين، ت، ث.

[٤] فصنف: وصنف، ا.

[٥] والشرى: والشرا، ث.

[٦] ومن لا يأكل الحلال: -، ث.

[٧] لأنه: انه، ا؛ اذا، ث.

لأنفسهم كما يدعي[١] أصحابهم لهم، وذلك أن أبا بكرٍ أول من صعد المنبر، فقال: وليتموني[٢] ولستُ بخيركم. فإن كان صادقاً فيما قال فالمدعون له كاذبون، وإن كان هو[٣] كاذباً في قوله فالكاذب لا يكون إماماً. فإن قالوا: إن ذلك للتواضع،[٤] قلنا: إن للتواضع[٥] موضعاً، فإن النبي صلى الله عليه وآله وسلم كان يذكر نفسه بما خصه الله تعالى به[٦] من المنزلة والرتبة[٧] ولم يذم نفسه ولم يدخل ذلك في الكبر، وقال: أنا سيدُ العرب ولا فخر، وأنا سيد ولد آدم ولا فخر، وأنا أفصح[٨] العرب[٩] ولا فخر. وقال أمير المؤمنين علي بن أبي طالب[١٠] عليه السلام: سلوني قبل أن تفقدوني، وقال: لو[١١] ثنيت لي وسادة وجلست عليها لحكمت لأهل التوراة بالتوراة ولأهل الإنجيل بالإنجيل ولأهل الفرقان بالفرقان،[١٢] فأمثال[١٣] ذلك مما[١٤] يكثر ذكره ولم يدخل ذلك في الكبر[١٥] ولا في ترك

---

[١] يدعي: يدعون، ا، ت، ث.

[٢] وليتموني: وليتكم، ث.

[٣] هو: -، ت.

[٤] ذلك للتواضع: ذلك هو تواضعا، ث.

[٥] وقد ذكر الشيوخ في حديث...إن للتواضع: -، ب.

[٦] به: -، ث.

[٧] الرتبة: المرتبة، ب، ت، ث.

[٨] وأنا أفصح: انا افصح، ا، ث.

[٩] أنا سيد العرب...وأنا أفصح العرب أنا سيد ولد آدم ولولا فخر: وقال أنا سيد العرب، ب.

[١٠] بن أبي طالب: -، ا.

[١١] لو: لي، ث.

[١٢] الفرقان بالفرقان: القرآن بالقرآن، ب، ت.

[١٣] فأمثال: وأمثال، ث.

التواضع، وفي قول أبي بكر: وليتموني[١] ولستُ بخيركم، دليل من[٢] قوله أنه لم يقدمه اللّٰه ورسوله[٣] ولا أشار إليه[٤] في أمر الصلاة ولا غير ذلك. وقال أبو بكر: إنَّ لي شيطاناً[٥] يعتريني، فإذا أحسنتُ فأطيعوني وإن أسأت فقوموني، وهذا أولاً قد شهد على نفسه بالجنون لأن من يعتريه الشيطان فهو مجنون،[٦] وقد ذكر أنه يأتي بالكبائر[٧] فيجب عليهم أن يمنعوهُ ويقوموه،[٨] والمجنون ومن[٩] يعتريه الشيطان لا يجوز أن يكون إماماً بالاتفاق لأنه يأمر المأمومين بما يؤديه الشيطان، وقد أقر على نفسه أنه يسيء[١٠] والإساءة هي[١١] المعصية يدخل فيها[١٢] الارتداد والزنى والقتل. وكل شيء داخل في هذا. والشيطان يأمر بذلك[١٣] كله ويحسنه في عينه

---

[١٤] مما: ما، ث.

[١٥] في الكبر: في اكبر، ت؛ بالكبر، ث.

[١] وليتموني: وليكم، ث.

[٢] دليل: -، ث.

[٣] اللّٰه ورسوله: الله ع ل ولا رسوله صلع، ا؛ الله ولا رسوله، ث.

[٤] إليه: -، ت.

[٥] شيطانا: شيطانان، ت.

[٦] مجنون: بجنون، ب.

[٧] بالكبائر: الكبائر، ث.

[٨] ويقوموه: ويقومه، ا؛ فيقوموه، ب.

[٩] ومن: من، ب.

[١٠] يسيء: سيء، ب، ث.

[١١] هي: هو، ا.

[١٢] فيها: فيه، ا، ب.

[١٣] بذلك: في ذلك، ا.

كما قال الله تعالى: ﴿ ٱلشَّيْطَانُ يَعِدُكُمُ ٱلْفَقْرَ وَيَأْمُرُكُم بِٱلْفَحْشَآءِ ﴾[١] وقد أخبر عن نفسه أن كل[٢] ذلك متوقع عنه[٣] فقوله:[٤] فقوموني،[٥] فالتقويم إنما[٦] يحتاج إليه[٧] في العظائم والكبائر، فإن الصغائر تسقط بالاستغفار، وأخبر عن نفسه أنه تُرفع[٨] عن الخلق طاعته وليس عليهم أن يطيعوه، وشهد على نفسه أنه قرين الشيطان كما قال الله سبحانه:[٩] ﴿ وَمَن يَعْشُ عَن ذِكْرِ ٱلرَّحْمَٰنِ نُقَيِّضْ لَهُ شَيْطَاناً فَهُوَ لَهُ قَرِينٌ[١٠] ﴾.[١١] وذكر الرحمن هو أمير المؤمنين عليه السلام وبإعراضه عنه قيض الله له شيطاناً يعتريه فهو[١٢] له قرين. وشهد[١٣] على نفسه أنه يحتاج إلى تقويم الناس له،[١٤] والذي يقوّمه فهو الإمام وهو فوقه، وشهد على نفسه أنه معوج، والمعوج[١٥] لا

---

[١] سورة ٢ البقرة ٢٦٨.

[٢] أن كل: ان لك، ت.

[٣] عنه: منه، ب، ث.

[٤] فقوله: وقوله، ث.

[٥] فقوموني: قوموني، ث.

[٦] إنما: ايما، ت.

[٧] إليه: -، ا، ب، ت، ث.

[٨] ترفع: يرفع، ث.

[٩] سبحانه: تعالى، ب، ت، ث.

[١٠] فَهُوَ لَهُ قَرِينٌ: وهو له قرين، ب؛ فهو له قرينا، ت.

[١١] سورة ٤٣ الزخرف ٣٦.

[١٢] فهو: وهو، ت.

[١٣] وشهد: ويشهد، ب.

[١٤] له: -، ث.

[١٥] والمعوج: فالمعوج، ب.

يكون إماماً. فإنه في وقت اعوجاجه واعترائه[١] الشيطان يأمر الناس بالاعوجاج وبما يكون طاعةً للشيطان[٢] وعصياناً للرحمن،[٣] وربما يأمره[٤] الشيطان بالكفر والردة وهو يأمر الناس بما يختار لنفسه، والشيطان عدو الله، فمن كان قرين عدوّ الله[٥] فهو عدوّ الله.[٦] وهل في الدنيا أعجب[٧] من هؤلاء القوم؟ فلو قام منادٍ[٨] في السوق وينادي[٩] على نفسه أن له شيطاناً[١٠] يعتريه، إذا أساء فقوموه، وامنعوه[١١] إذا أراد أن يفسد[١٢] ثياب الناس أو يحرقها[١٣] أو يلوثها، ففي ذلك قوموه وامنعوه،[١٤] لما دفع إليه أحد ثوباً يبيعه مخافة أن يفسده، ولو قال عدل عند القاضي: إن له شيطاناً يعتريه فإذا أساء في الشهادة فقوموه، لما قبل القاضي شهادته بعد

---

١ اعترائه: اعتريه، ب.

٢ طاعة للشيطان: طاعة الشيطان، ث.

٣ وعصياناً للرحمن: وعصيان الرحمن، ب.

٤ يأمره: يأمر، ث.

٥ قرين عدوّ الله: قرينه، ب.

٦ الله: لله، ا.

٧ أعجب: عجب، ث.

٨ منادٍ: منادي، ب، ت، ث.

٩ وينادي: ينادي، ث.

١٠ شيطانا: شيطان، ب.

١١ وامنعوه: منعوه، ب.

١٢ أن يفسد: يفسد ان، ب.

١٣ يحرقها: يخرقها، ب.

١٤ و امنعوه: او منعوه، ت.

ذلك فيما قيمته عشرة دراهم.[١] ثم يدّعون إمامته[٢] ويعتقدونها وله أخبار كثيرة كلها حجة عليه.

[٧٥] وأما عمر فإنه أول من[٣] صعد المنبر بعد أبي بكر فقال: إن بيعة أبي بكر كانت فلتة فوقى اللّٰه شرها، فمن عاد إلى مثلها فاقتلوه. فبيَّن في هذا[٤] بطلانَ ما ادعى[٥] أهل الظاهر من إقامة[٦] أبي بكر للصلاة وأنه أوجب الإمامة، وأنه كان إشارة[٧] إليه بالإمامة، وفيه إبطال[٨] لما يدعون من الأخبار مثل قولهم: اقتدوا باللذين من بعدي[٩] أبي بكر وعُمر، وجميع ما يروى في إمامة أبي بكر وعمر وعثمان،[١٠] فإن ذلك كله كذب وزور وضعوه[١١] بعدهم، وذلك أن عمر قال: كانت بيعة أبي بكرٍ فلتة، والفلتة هو الذي عن غير تدبير وتفكر ومقدمة قبله. فجميع ما يروون[١٢]

---

[١] دراهم: درهم، ب.

[٢] إمامته: امامتهم، ب.

[٣] فإنه أول من: فأول من، ا؛ فانه أول ما، ب؛ فانه لما، ت؛ فانه، ث.

[٤] هذا: هذه، ث.

[٥] ما ادعى: ما ادعوا، ا، ت، ث؛ ما ادعوه، ب.

[٦] إقامة: امامة، ا، ب، ث.

[٧] إشارة: اشار، ب، ث.

[٨] وفيه إبطال: وإبطالا، ا، ت؛ وإبطال، ب، ث.

[٩] بعدي: بعد، ب.

[١٠] وعمر...وعمر وعثمان: -، ث.

[١١] وضعوه: وضعوها، ا، ب، ت، ث.

[١٢] يروون: يرون، ت.

مثل[١] ذلك فهو باطل بقول[٢] عمر، فإنه أصدق قولاً[٣] عندهم[٤] منهم، وشهد أن ذلك كان شراً ولم يكن خيراً، والفعل الذي يكون شراً[٥] ليس[٦] هو من الدين والإمامة بشيء. وأما ما قال: إنه وقى الله شرها، فلم يق الله تعالى شر ذلك، فكل[٧] ضلالة وخلاف وبدعة وظلم وغشم وقتل بغير حقٍ وغصب[٨] وأخذ[٩] مال وإباحة فرج[١٠] ودم وتغيير دين من وقت النبي صلى الله عليه وعلى آله إلى يوم القيامة كان من شر تلك البيعة وعليهم وزرها[١١] كما قال النبي صلى الله عليه وآله وسلم: من سنّ سنة حسنة فله أجرها وأجر من عمل بها إلى يوم القيامة ومن سنَّ سنة سيئة فعليه وزرها ووزر من عَمِلَ بها[١٢] إلى يوم القيامة. وكل بدعة ضلالة وكل ضلالة[١٣] سبيلها إلى النار، والبيعة في الإمامة بدعة، والفلتة تكون بدعةً ولا تكون سنةً.[١٤]

---

[١] مثل: قبل، ا، ت، ث؛ -، ب.

[٢] بقول: لقول، ث.

[٣] قولاً: -، ا، ت، ث؛ قول، ب.

[٤] فانه أصدق قولا عندهم: فان الصدق، ث.

[٥] ولم يكن خيرا...شراً: -، ث.

[٦] ليس: اليس، ث.

[٧] فكل: وكل، ت.

[٨] وغصب: وغضب، ث.

[٩] وأخذ: -، ب.

[١٠] فرج: فروج، ا.

[١١] وزرها: ردّها، ث.

[١٢] بها: -، ث.

[١٣] وكل ضلالة: كل ضلال، ت.

[١٤] سنةً: -، ب.

وقد شهد أن جلوس أبي بكر لم يكن بفضلٍ[١] ولا نسب ولا علم ولا جهاد ولا تقوى ولا ورعٍ، وإنما[٢] كانت بيعتُه فلتةً وكانت شراً، وبإقراره[٣] أنهم كانوا أشراراً والأشرار هم أهل النار، ويجب قتل الأشرار بقوله:[٤] من عاد إلى مثلها فاقتلوه، وكل فعل يوجب القتل في ثاني[٥] الفعل يوجب في الأول، كما أنه إذا أوجب في الثاني[٦] الردة أوجب[٧] في الأول وكقتل[٨] النفس إذا أوجب[٩] في الفعل الثاني أوجب[١٠] في الأول، وما لم يوجب في الأول لا يوجب[١١] في الثاني. وهل[١٢] قال ذلك إلا خوفاً من أنهم إذا أجازوا[١٣] مثل هذا المنكر وتغيير أمر الإمامة وإنكارهم فعل النبي صلى اللّٰه عليه آله وسلم وفعل اللّٰه تعالى والقرآن والأخبار وفضيلة أمير المؤمنين[١٤]

---

[١] بفضل: بفضيلة، ت.

[٢] وإنما: إنما، ث.

[٣] بإقراره: باقرارهم، ث.

[٤] بقوله: وبقوله، ب، ت، ث.

[٥] ثاني: الثاني، ت.

[٦] أوجب في الثاني: وجب في ثاني، ث.

[٧] أوجب: يوجب، ا، ب، ت، ث.

[٨] وكقتل: كقتل، ا، ث؛ كقتله، ب.

[٩] أوجب: وجبه، ب.

[١٠] أوجب: اوجبه، ب، ت.

[١١] لا يوجب: لم يوجب، ث.

[١٢] وهل: فهل، ث.

[١٣] اذا أجازوا: اذا جاوز، ت؛ أجازوا، ث.

[١٤] المؤمنين: + مولانا، ت.

علي بن أبي[١] طالب صلوات اللّٰه عليه[٢] وإشهار النبي صلى اللّٰه عليه وآله وسلم نصّ يوم غدير خمٍ وسائر الأخبار ونبذوا[٣] جميع[٤] ذلك وراء ظهورهم وبنوا[٥] أساساً لم يكن له أصل[٦] ولا حجة ولا برهان إلا البيعة بعضها بالاختيار وبعضها بالكره، فلغيره أن يأخذ البيعة من قوم[٧] آخرين ويقوم ويدعي الإمامة وليس بأيديهم حجة يمنعونه[٨] إلا البيعة، وليس هو أولى وأحق به[٩] من غيره. فأراد أن يحسم[١٠] ذلك الأمر من تلك الجهة فأتى بمثل هذا القول، وإنما أجرى اللّٰه تعالى ذلك على لسانه ليظهر عوارهم ونفاقهم وكذبهم على لسانهم.

[٧٦] وأما قوله للمرأة حين خطب وقال: لا تغالوا في صدقات النساء،[١١] إلى آخر الخبر، فقيام[١٢] المرأةِ وردّها عليه وقوله لمن حوله: كل

---

[١] أبي: -، ا.
[٢] علي بن ابي طالب صلوات اللّٰه عليه: -، ب.
[٣] ونبذوا: نبذوا، ت.
[٤] جميع: -، ب.
[٥] وبنوا: وبنوه، ا، ب، ت، ث.
[٦] أصل: اصلا، ب.
[٧] قوم: قوام، ت.
[٨] يمنعونه: يمنعوه، ت.
[٩] به: -، ا، ب، ث.
[١٠] يحسم: يحشم، ت.
[١١] صدقات النساء: صدقاتهن، ب، ت، ث.
[١٢] فقيام: وقيام، ا، ب، ت، ث.

الناس[١] أعلم من عمر، تسمعون مثل هذا ولا تردونه عليّ حتى ترده[٢] عليّ امرأة من آخر القوم ليست[٣] هي بأعلم[٤] الناس[٥] دليل على أنه لم يكن يعرف[٦] القرآن ولا الأحكام[٧] ولا السنة[٨] ولا كان يحفظ ما جرى[٩] طول أيام النبي صلى الله عليه وآله وسلم ولا بعده من الأحكام حتى غلط في مثل هذا.[١٠] ولو سئل هذا[١١] من صبي لما أشكل[١٢] عليه، وليست هذه بمسألة مشكلة، وقد رد بهذا[١٣] على الله وعلى رسوله وقد شهد على نفسه بالحق حيث قال: كل الناس أعلم من عمر، وأنصف[١٤] من نفسه ولكن الشنآن[١٥] في من كانوا يرون ويسمعون مثل هذه الفضائح ثم يطيعونه،[١٦] وهم كما قال الله تعالى: ﴿ فَٱسْتَخَفَّ قَوْمَهُۥ فَأَطَاعُوهُ ﴾.[١٧]

---

[١] الناس: -، ث.

[٢] ترده: ترد، ب.

[٣] ليست: ليس، ت.

[٤] بأعلم: من اعلم، ب.

[٥] الناس: النساء، ب.

[٦] يعرف: -، ب.

[٧] ولا الأحكام: والأحكام، ب، ت، ث.

[٨] لا السنة: -، ب؛ السنة، ت.

[٩] يحفظ ما جرى: يحفظها، ب؛ يحفظ ما اجري، ا.

[١٠] هذا: -، ب.

[١١] هذا: هذه، ب.

[١٢] أشكل: شكل، ت.

[١٣] بهذا: بها، ت.

[١٤] أنصف: انفق، ب.

[١٥] الشنآن: الثنان، ا، ت؛ الشبنأن، ب؛ الثنأ، ث.

[١٦] يطيعونه: يطيعونهم، ا، ب، ت، ث.

فإن كان عمر[١] صادقاً فيما قال فكل الناس أعلم منه، ولا يمكنهم أن يحملوا هذا على التواضع، بل هو خجل[٢] وعجز، والحال والحكم يشهدان[٣] على تصديق قوله وهو عيان. وفي قوله دليل على أنه كان يأتي في سائر الأوقات ما كان يحتاج أن يرد عليه، وفي قوله: "لولا علي لَهلك عمر"،[٤] دليل على أنه أتى بما هلك ديناً، وإن لم يهلك بالجسد، وبين فيه أنه ما كان يعرف من الأحكام شيئاً ولم[٥] يحكم بشيء دون حضرة أمير المؤمنين سلام الله عليه[٦] إلا وتحير[٧] فيه وافتضح.

[٧٧] وفي[٨] قوله حين جعل الشورى بين ستة نفر: إن استخلفت[٩] عليكم فقد اقتديت بمن هو خير مني،[١٠] يعني أبا بكر، وإن لم أستخلف[١١] عليكم فقد اقتديت[١٢] بمن هو خير مني،[١٣] يعني النبي صلى

---

[١٧] سورة ٤٣ الزخرف ٥٤.

[١] عمر: عمرا، ت.

[٢] بل هو: -، ب.

[٣] يشهدان: يشهد، ا، ب، ت، ث.

[٤] دليل على انه...لهلك عمر: -، ت.

[٥] ولم: لم، ت.

[٦] عليه: مكرر في ت.

[٧] إلا وتحير: الا تحير، ت، وتحير، ث.

[٨] وفي: في، ب.

[٩] استخلفت: استخلف، ث.

[١٠] مني:- ب.

[١١] وان لم أستخلف: وان استحلفت، ب.

[١٢] اقتديت: اقتدت، ث.

[١٣] مني: + منه، ا.

اللّٰه عليه وآله وسلم، فشهد أن النبي لم يستخلف أبا بكر ولا أشار إليه ولا فوض الإمامة إلى الخلق ولا أمر أبا بكر[١] بالصلاة إشارة إلى الإمامة وأنه لم يكن خليفة[٢] رسول اللّٰه صلى اللّٰه عليه وآله وسلم، فإن كان الأمر كما قال فلم لم[٣] يدع أبو بكر الأمر[٤] كما كان من غير خليفة؟ وإن كان الواجب اختيار الناس[٥] وبيعتهم وبذلك تنعقد[٦] الإمامة فلِمَ لم[٧] يدعهم يجتمعون ويختارون[٨] من يريدون ولِمَ افتات[٩] على الخلق بما كان مفوضاً إليهم وعمل ببدعة؟ وإن كان الواجب ما عمله[١٠] أبو بكر فلم لم يقتد[١١] به عمر بل جعل الأمر شورى بين ستة نفر[١٢]؟ ثم أفعاله من وضع الخراج والدَّواوين[١٣] والأرزاق وغيرها مما يطول ذكرها.

[٧٨] ثم عثمان[١٤] عمل ما عمل من الخيانة في بيت مالِ المسلمين

---

١ ولا أشار اليه...أبا بكر: -، ت.

٢ خليفة: بخليفة، ا، ث.

٣ لم: -، ث.

٤ أبو بكر الأمر:ابو بكر، ا؛ ابا بكر، ت.

٥ الناس: للناس، ث.

٦ تنعقد: تقعد، ب.

٧ لم: -، ب.

٨ يجتمعون ويختارون: يجتمعوا ويختاروا، ا، ب، ت، ث.

٩ ولم افتات: ولم -، ب؛ ولم يفتات، ت؛ ولم يفت، ث.

١٠ عمله: علمه، ث.

١١ قتد: يقتدي، ث.

١٢ نفر:- ب، ت، ث.

١٣ الدَّواوين: الدواوي ، ت.

١٤ ثم عثمان: ان تقول، ب.

وطرد[١] أبا ذر عن[٢] المدينة وضرب[٣] ابن مسعود ورد مروان بن الحكم[٤] واستوزره. وما عمل من حديث محمد بن أبي بكر حتى خرج عليه بعض المهاجرين والأنصار فحاربوه، وسائر المهاجرين والأنصار ينظرون ويرونه أهلاً لذلك ولا يعينونه.[٥] ثم لما قتل تركوه ثلاثة أيام ولم يدفنوه غيظاً[٦] من أفعاله وسيرته، ولم يدعوه يدفن عند قبر النبي صلى اللّٰه عليه وآله وسلم ونفوه من[٧] مقبرة المسلمين. ثم بعد ذلك طلبوا دمه وحاربوا أمير المؤمنين. ولو ذكرنا فضائحهم والحجج[٨] عليهم والرد على مقالتهم وأفعالهم لطال الكتاب، وفيما ذكرنا[٩] كفاية لمن أنصف ولم ينكر العيان.

[٧٩] والآن نذكر بعض فضائل ولي العصر[١٠] والزمان أمير المؤمنين عليه السلام وإن كان مثلي لا يبلغ إلى تلك الدرجة التي تمكنه[١١] أن يذكر فضائله على كنهها، كما قال اللّٰه تعالى: ﴿ وَمَا قَدَرُواْ[١٢] ٱللَّهَ حَقَّ

---

[١] وطرد: فطرد، ب.

[٢] عن: من، ب، ث.

[٣] وضرب: وخرب، ا؛ وحرب، ت.

[٤] الحكم: حكم، ت.

[٥] أهلاً لذلك ولا يعينونه: اهل ذلك ولا يعينوه، ب.

[٦] غيظا: غيظٌ، ث.

[٧] من: عن، ت.

[٨] والحجج: والحجة، ب.

[٩] ذكرنا:+ فيها، ب.

[١٠] العصر: -، ا.

[١١] تمكنه: يمكنه، ا، ب، ت، ث.

[١٢] قَدَرُواْ: قدر، ب، ث.

قَدْرِهِ ﴾.[١] ولكني[٢] أقول على مقدار علمي وطاقتي، وأمير المؤمنين أولى من يقبل عذرعبيده كما أن اللّٰه تعالى مع كثرة نعمه[٣] على عبيده لما طالبهم بالشكر على النعم[٤] وعجزوا عن إقامة[٥] الشكر بإزاء النعم سامحهم واقتصر منهم بقول:[٦] ﴿ ٱلْحَمْدُ لِلَّهِ رَبِّ ٱلْعَـٰلَمِينَ ﴾[٧] تأديباً لخلقه حتى إذا وجب شكر المنعم عليهم وعجزوا عن[٨] إقامة الشكر بإزاء النعمة[٩] يأتوا[١٠] بمقدار طاقتهم ولا يدعوا الشكر أصلاً لعجزهم عن أدائه[١١] بحسب واجبه.

ونقول:[١٢] إن اللّٰه تعالى أشرق الأرض بنوره كما وعد وأخبر بقوله: ﴿ وَأَشْرَقَتِ ٱلْأَرْضُ بِنُورِ رَبِّهَا ﴾[١٣] أرض الظاهر بعدل أمير المؤمنين وأرض الباطن بالعلم والبيان.

---

[١] سورة ٦ الأنعام ٩١.

[٢] ولكني: ولكن، ب.

[٣] نعمه: نعمته، ب، ت.

[٤] النعم: المنعم ، ا، ب، ت.

[٥] إقامة: -، ب.

[٦] بقول: بقوله، ب، ث.

[٧] سورة ١ الفاتحة ١.

[٨] عن: عنه، ب.

[٩] سامحهم...بإزاء النعمة: -، ت.

[١٠] يأتوا: وباتوا، ت؛ باتوا، ث.

[١١] أدائه: آداءه، ا؛ اداءهم، ب.

[١٢] ونقول: -، ث.

[١٣] سورة ٣٩ الزمر ٦٩.

[٨٠] ونقول:[١] إنه لما كان في كل نوعٍ وجنسٍ وأصلٍ وفرعٍ وشرعٍ غايةٌ وذروةٌ في الشرف والفضل والرتبة[٢] والدرجة والمنزلة لم يبلغ غيره إلى ذلك هكذا وجب[٣] أن يكون للأئمة سلام اللّٰه عليهم غاية وذروة ونهايةٌ لم يبلغ ممن مضى إلى[٤] تلك الدرجة والنهاية إليها، وتلك الغاية والنهاية أمير[٥] المؤمنين وهو غاية الغايات[٦] والنهايات[٧] التي لم يكن فوقها[٨] غاية ونهاية.[٩] وكما أن بقيام البشر ظهرت حكمة العالم وما كان فيه من الحيوان والنبات وتم صلاحهم[١٠] بالبشر ورجع نفع الجميع إلى البشر، وبالأئمة[١١] عليهم السلام تم فضائل البشر وظهرت الحكمة في خلقتهم[١٢] ورجع نفع جميع البشر إلى الأئمة. فكذلك[١٣] بأمير[١٤] المؤمنين تم[١٥] أمور

---

[١] ونقول: -، ث.

[٢] والرتبة: والمرتبة ، ا.

[٣] وجب: اوجب، ب، ث.

[٤] إلى: -، ب.

[٥] أمير: وامير، ب.

[٦] وهو غاية الغايات: فهو غاية غايات، ب.

[٧] والنهايات: والنهاية: ا، ث؛ ونهاية النهايات، ت.

[٨] فوقها: فوقه، ا، ب، ت.

[٩] غاية ونهاية: نهاية، ا، ب، ت، ث.

[١٠] صلاحهم: صلاحه، ب، ث.

[١١] وبالأئمة: والأئمة، ب.

[١٢] خلقتهم: خلقهم، ب

[١٣] فكذلك: وكذلك، ا، ب، ت، ث.

[١٤] بأمير: وبأمير، ب.

[١٥] تم: ثم، ت، ث.

الأنبياء والأوصياء[١] والأئمة، وانتظم أمرهم[٢] وظهر تمام الحكمة في موضوعاتهم[٣] وشرائعهم وتأويلاتهم، وهو سلام الله عليه مثل الرأس وهم مثل الجسد، وهم كالبدن وأمير المؤمنين كالروح، ولا يتم الجسد إلا بالروح،[٤] وأمير المؤمنين مثل القلب وسائر من مضى كالأعضاء، وباتحاد[٥] الروح والحياة إلى القلب تقبل[٦] جميع الأعضاء[٧] الحياة والجزاء[٨] وكل ظفر وشعر وطرفٍ يأخذ حظه من الجزاء[٩] بواسطة القلب، وهو العلم[١٠] الحسي الذي هو جزاء العمل[١١] الذي[١٢] حصل من الجنين في دار عمله طول[١٣] مدته في الأحوال الستة من السلالة إلى الخلق[١٤] الآخر.

---

[١] والأوصياء:- ب، ث؛ والاسس، ت.

[٢] أمرهم: -، ب؛ امورهم، ث.

[٣] موضوعاتهم: مصنوعاتهم، ث.

[٤] ولا يتم الجسد الا بالروح: وبالروح يتم الجسد، ت؛ بالروح يتم الجسد، ث؛ وهم كالبدن ...إلا بالروح:-، ب.

[٥] وباتحاد: وباتخاذ، ب.

[٦] تقبل: يقبل، ا، ب، ت.

[٧] وباتحاد...الأعضاء: -، ث.

[٨] والجزاء: والاجزاء، ث.

[٩] حظه من الجزاء: حصنه من الاجزاء، ث.

[١٠] العلم: الحلم، ا.

[١١] العمل: + الحسي، ب، ت.

[١٢] الذي: لا العلم الذي هو جزاء، ا؛+ العلم، ت.

[١٣] طول: طوله، ت.

[١٤] الخلق: كلف، ث.

وكذلك[١] بأمير المؤمنين يبلغون إلى الجزاء وقبول الحياة في الحال[٢] السابعة وهو سلام الله عليه الذي تمنى[٣] كل واحد[٤] أن يكون هو، وهو الذي وعد الله الخلق[٥] بإيفاء[٦] الأجر به[٧] وفي يومه حيث قال: ﴿ إِنَّمَا تُوَفَّوْنَ أُجُورَكُمْ يَوْمَ ٱلْقِيَـٰمَةِ فَمَن زُحْزِحَ عَنِ ٱلنَّارِ وَأُدْخِلَ ٱلْجَنَّةَ فَقَدْ فَازَ[٨] ﴾[٩] وهو الذي أمر جميع الخلق بالإيمان به وبيومه في قوله: ﴿ يُؤْمِنُونَ بِٱللَّهِ وَٱلْيَوْمِ[١٠] ٱلْأَخِرِ ﴾.[١١]

[٨١] وكما أن[١٢] تمامية البشر كانت[١٣] لأنه آخر مواليد[١٤] العالم وأنه قبل جميع ما كان لسائر المواليد وزاد عليه بأشياء لم يكن للمواليد[١٥]

---

[١] وكذلك: فكذلك، ت.

[٢] الحال: الحالة، ث.

[٣] تمنى: يتمنى، ث.

[٤] واحد: احد، ب، ت، ث.

[٥] الخلق: عباده، ث.

[٦] بإيفاء: ايفاء، ا، ب، ث.

[٧] الأجر به: الاجرية، ب؛ الاجرية به، ت.

[٨] فاز: + وما الحيوة الدنيا الا متاع الغرور، ب.

[٩] سورة ٣ آل عمران ١٨٥.

[١٠] وَٱلْيَوْمِ: وباليوم، ت.

[١١] سورة ٣ آل عمران ١١٤.

[١٢] أن: كان ان، ا؛ كان، ب، ت، ث.

[١٣] كانت: كان، ا، ب، ت؛ -، ث.

[١٤] مواليد: المواليد، ب.

[١٥] وزاد عليه ...المواليد: -، ث.

منها[١] حظ وكما أن الأئمة حصل لهم جميع ما كان للبشر من الفضائل[٢] وكانوا في البشرية غايتهم وذروتهم وصفوتهم، ثم أمكنهم قبول ما لم يكن في قوة البشر وكان نفع جميع من تقدم[٣] راجع إليهم فكذلك[٤] أمير المؤمنين سلام الله عليه جمع فضائل[٥] من تقدَّمه[٦] ورجع نفعهم وعلمهم إليه وزاد على ذلك أضعاف ذلك. وكما[٧] أن قوة النبي وفضله كان لأنه جمع[٨] فضائل من مضى[٩] في الأدوار[١٠] وجميع[١١] علومهم وزاد على ذلك كذلك أمير المؤمنين عليه السلام جمع فضائل كل[١٢] من مضى في الأدوار من الأنبياء والأتماء والحكماء[١٣] وزاد[١٤] على ذلك بأشياء عجزوا عنها،[١٥] ولولا قيامه بهذه المنزلة[١٦] لما كان في[١٧] قيامهم سلام الله عليهم

---

[١] منها: منه، ا، ب، ت، ث.

[٢] الفضائل: الفضل، ث.

[٣] تقدم:+ اليه، ب.

[٤] فكذلك: وكذلك، ب، ت.

[٥] فضائل: فضل، ب.

[٦] تقدمه: تقدم، ث.

[٧] وكما: فكما، ب.

[٨] جمع:+ من، ت.

[٩] لأنه جمع فضائل من مضى: مكرر في ب.

[١٠] في الأدوار: -، ا، ب، ث.

[١١] وجميع: وجمع، ت، ث.

[١٢] جمع فضائل كل: جمع فضائل، ب؛ -، ت.

[١٣] والحكماء: + والاوصياء، ب.

[١٤] وزاد: والزاد، ت.

[١٥] عنها: عنه، ا، ب، ت، ث.

[١٦] بهذه المنزلة: بهذا المنزلة، ا، ت.

تَمام الحكمة،[١] فمحصول جميع العوالم اليوم من الروحاني والجسماني والوضعي هو أمير المؤمنين عليه السلام ولأجله خلقت،[٢] والجميع[٣] كانوا عماله ودعاة إليه وإلى[٤] يومه، وهو الذي قام في العالم بتمام الخلافة لبارئ البرايا في خلقه. وإنما قلنا: إنه المتم[٥] لجميع من مضى، ولعل قائلاً[٦] يقول: إن هذه صفة[٧] القائم الأخير[٨] وأمير المؤمنين عليه السلام ليس هو الأخير، قلنا: إن أمير المؤمنين عليه السلام[٩] هو قائم[١٠] وقته وزمانه وقائم من مضى ومتمهم،[١١] وهو السادس الذي يكون تمام أمر السابع به وهو يفرغ مما يحتاج إليه السابع، كما أن النبي صلى اللّٰه عليه وآله وسلم وضع جميع ما احتاج إليه القائم، ويكون تمام أمره فيما وضع النبي صلى اللّٰه عليه وآله وسلم ورتبه، وهو سلام اللّٰه عليه هو التاسع من

---

[١٧] في: من، ث.

[١] الحكمة: حكمته، ب.

[٢] خلقت: خلقة، ت.

[٣] والجميع: الجميع، ب.

[٤] وإلى: إلى، ت.

[٥] المتم: المتمم، ب.

[٦] قائلاً: قائل، ث.

[٧] صفة: الصفة، ت.

[٨] الأخير: الاخر، ب.

[٩] ليس...عليه السلام: -، ث.

[١٠] قائم: + في، ت.

[١١] ومتمهم: ومتممهم، ب، ت؛ وممتهم، ث.

حساب آخر، وأمر السابع الذي[١] مضى إنما[٢] يتم بالتاسع كما أن[٣] تَمامية الأعضاء السبعة ونظامها وعملها تظهر[٤] بالتسعة بأربع طبائع[٥] وخمس حواس، وتمام الخلقة يكون بتسعة أشهر، والحساب وضع على التسعة، وحيوان دار البقاء يقوم بأربع طبائع روحانية وخمس حواس روحانية، كما قال الله تعالى: ﴿ وَإِنَّ ٱلدَّارَ ٱلْأَخِرَةَ لَهِيَ ٱلْحَيَوَانُ لَوْ كَانُواْ يَعْلَمُونَ ﴾.[٦]

[٨٢] وأمير المؤمنين هو[٧] الثاني من حساب آخر، وابتداء كل دور أحكم[٨] أمره بالثاني، وهو السادس[٩] الذي يفتح الله بسيفه جميع العالم كما فتح بالنبي صلى الله عليه وآله وسلم السادس من آدم، وهو سلام الله عليه قام في العالم بتمام الخلافة لبارئ البرايا في خلقه يعامل الخلق في جميع أحواله مثل معاملة الله تعالى في خلقه وفي خلقتهم[١٠] وأرزاقهم وسعة الرحمة عليهم. وكل من قام قبله قام بجزء قليل وقام أمير المؤمنين عليه السلام بالكل، والخليفة هو الذي يقوم[١١] فيمن استخلف عليهم

---

[١] الذي: اليه، ت

[٢] إنما: وانما، ث.

[٣] أن: انه، ا، ب، ت.

[٤] تظهر: يظهر، ا، ب، ت، ث.

[٥] طبائع: طابع، ت.

[٦] سورة ٢٩ العنكبوت ٦٤.

[٧] هو: هي، ت.

[٨] كل دور أحكم: كل دور حكم، ب؛ كل دور الحكم، ت.

[٩] السادس: + من، ث.

[١٠] خلقتهم: خلقهم، ث.

[١١] يقوم: + بالكل، ب.

بجميع ما قام المستخلف. وإنما سمي آدم وسائر[١] الخلفاء خليفة لأنه كان ابتداء لمن يقوم بالخلافة، والذين قاموا بعده قاموا ببعض شرائط الخلافة، فسموا بذلك الاسم، ومن يقوم ببعض[٢] الشيء سمي باسمه، وقام أمير المؤمنين عليه السلام بحقيقة الخلافة[٣] ديناً ودنيا. وقال النبي صلى اللّٰه عليه وآله وسلم: السلطان ظل[٤] اللّٰه في الأرض، وإنما أراد به[٥] أمير المؤمنين، فإن ظل الشيء الذي[٦] يحاكي الذي أظل[٧] بجميع ما[٨] فيه، ولم يقم[٩] من يفعل مع الخلق مثل[١٠] فعل اللّٰه تعالى إلا أمير[١١] المؤمنين. وقال أيضاً النبي صلى اللّٰه عليه وآله وسلم: إن اللّٰه تعالى نزع بالسلطان أكثر مما نزع بالقرآن، وأمير[١٢] المؤمنين عليه السلام هو الذي نزع اللّٰه به ما لم ينزع بالقرآن.

---

[١] آدم وسائر: سائر، ا.

[٢] شرائط...ببعض: -، ث.

[٣] الخلافة: + فسئموا بذلك الاسم ، ث.

[٤] ظل: ضل، ث.

[٥] به: + إلا، ب.

[٦] ظل الشيء الذي: ظل الشيء، ب، ت؛ ضل الشيء، ث.

[٧] أظل: اضل، ث.

[٨] ما :+ كان، ت.

[٩] يقم: يكن يقيم، ا؛ يكن يقم، ب، ت، ث.

[١٠] مثل: + ما، ث.

[١١] إلا أمير: لأمير، ث.

[١٢] وأمير: فأمير، ب.

[٨٣] وقالت[١] الفلاسفة: إن الفلسفة هي التشبه[٢] بالبارئ سبحانه على حسب طاقة البشر، وإنما التشبه[٣] بالبارئ سبحانه هو أن يفعل مع خلقه مثل فعله تعالى ذكره ويعاملهم ويعامل نفسه مثل فعل اللّٰه تعالى معه ومع الخلق وعلى[٤] مثال الخلقة. وهذا الكلام سرقه[٥] الفلاسفة من أهل الحقيقة، وإلا فلم يقم من الفلاسفة وغيرهم بحقيقة هذا القول إلا أمير المؤمنين عليه السلام. فإن جميع معاملته مع الخلق مثل[٦] معاملة اللّٰه تعالى مع[٧] خلقه في خلقة العالم والرزق وغيره. ونذكر الآن من ذلك شيئاً يسيراً مما يليق بهذا الوقت الذي نحن فيه.

[٨٤] ونبتدىء أولاً ونقول:[٨] إن شفقة أمير المؤمنين عليه السلام[٩] ورحمته وإحسانه وعفوه واحتماله من سوء آداب[١٠] هؤلاء القوم من قلة طاعتهم بحيث لا يمكن لمثلي صفة[١١] كل ذلك اقتداء بأفعال اللّٰه تعالى

---

[١] وقالت: وقال، ت.

[٢] هي التشبه: هو التشبيه، ا، ت؛ -، ب.

[٣] التشبه: التشبيه، ا،ب، ت.

[٤] وعلى: على، ث.

[٥] سرقه: سرقوه، ا، ب، ت، ث.

[٦] معاملته مع الخلق مثل: -، ث.

[٧] مع: من، ت.

[٨] ونبتدأ أولا ونقول: -، ث.

[٩] السلام: + فإن جميع، ث.

[١٠] آداب: ادب، ت.

[١١] صفة: وصفه، ت.

في خلقه واتباعاً لأمر اللّٰه تعالى[١] وتادياً بآدابه تعالى.[٢] فإن اللّٰه[٣] منَّ على خلقه بإحسانه إلى البر والفاجر والمؤمن والكافر، ولو أعطى الدنيا للمؤمن[٤] ومنعها من الكافر[٥] لكان إيمان الخلق للدنيا لا للّٰه ولا لدينه،[٦] ولو منع[٧] عن جميع المؤمنين وأعطى الكافرين[٨] لرجع أكثر الناس عن إيمانهم[٩] ودخلوا[١٠] في الكفر. فأعطى الكافر ومنع الكافر وأعطى المؤمن ومنع المؤمن وأعطى كل واحد منهما في وقت ومنعهما في وقت، كذلك أعطى[١١] أمير المؤمنين[١٢] عليه السلام الدنيا للمسلم والكافر ومنع المسلم ومنع الكافر. وكذلك أعطى المؤمن والمنافق ومنع المؤمن والمنافق،[١٣] وأعطى كل واحد منهما في وقت ومنعهما في وقت، ولو أعطى كله للمؤمن[١٤] لكان إيمان الناس أكثره[١٥] للدنيا، ولو منع عن جميع

---

[١] لأمر اللّٰه تعالى: لأمره، ب، ت، ث.

[٢] تعالى: + ذكره، ب.

[٣] فإن اللّٰه: -، ا، ت، ث.

[٤] للمؤمن: للمؤمنين، ب.

[٥] الكافر: الكافرين، ب.

[٦] لدينه: للدين، ب.

[٧] منع: -، ت

[٨] الكافرين: الكافر، ت، ث.

[٩] إيمانهم: ايمانه، ا، ب، ت، ث.

[١٠] ودخلوا: ودخول، ث.

[١١] أعطى: يعطي، ا، ب، ت؛ -، ث.

[١٢] المؤمنين: + أعطى، ث.

[١٣] ومنع المؤمن والمنافق: -، ب؛ ومنع المؤمن ومنع المنافق، ث.

[١٤] للمؤمن: للمؤمنين، ب، ث.

المؤمنين في جميع الأوقات ليئسوا[١] وفترت نياتهم. وأعطى[٢] سلام الله عليه زماناً للمؤمنين من النعيم[٣] ما لم يعطه أحد[٤] ومنعهم زماناً صلاحاً لهم حتى[٥] لا يكونوا من جملة من حكى الله تعالى عنه:[٦] ﴿ كَلَّآ إِنَّ ٱلْإِنسَٰنَ لَيَطْغَىٰٓ أَن رَّءَاهُ ٱسْتَغْنَىٰٓ ﴾.[٧]

وإن الله تعالى أعطى الدنيا[٨] للبر والفاجر حتى لا يكون فعل البر بسبب الدنيا[٩] والإمساك عن الفجور بسبب الدنيا[١٠] والإمساك[١١] عن العصيان بسبب[١٢] الدنيا فيذهب عنهم حظ الآخرة،[١٣] بل يكون خالصاً لله ودينه،[١٤] وكذلك[١٥] أمير المؤمنين عليه السلام يعطي للبر والفاجر. وإن

---

[١٥] أكثره: أكثر، ا، ت.

[١] ليئسوا: لياءسوا، ا؛ ليائسوا، ب، ت، ث.

[٢] وأعطى: او اعطى، ب.

[٣] من النعيم: من النعم، ب، ت.

[٤] أحد: احدا، ا، ب، ت،ث.

[٥] حتى: -، ث.

[٦] عنه: -، ا، ب، ت،؛ عنهم، ث.

[٧] سورة ٩٦ العلق ٦-٧.

[٨] الدنيا: الديني، ا.

[٩] الدنيا: + فيذهب لهم أجر الآخرة، ت.

[١٠] للبر...الدنيا: -، ث. الدنيا: الديني، ا.

[١١] عن الفجور بسبب الدنيا والإمساك: -، ب.

[١٢] بسبب: -، ا، ب؛ بسببه، ث.

[١٣] الدنيا فيذهب عنهم حظ الآخرة: -، ا، ب، ث.

[١٤] ودينه: بدينه، ب.

[١٥] وكذلك: فكذلك، ب، ث.

الله تعالى أعطى الدنيا[١] لمن يطيعه ولمن يعصيه حكمة منه لأن لا تكون[٢] الطاعة بسبب الدنيا والإمساك عن العصيان بسببه، بل تكون[٣] خالصاً لله، وكذلك يعطي أمير المؤمنين عليه السلام[٤] العاصي[٥] والمطيع اقتداء بفعل الله تعالى، ولأن لا تكون[٦] طاعة الخلق له[٧] من جهة الدنيا، فيذهب عنهم حظ الآخرة.

[٨٥] وإن الله تعالى أعطى الدنيا للعابد وغير العابد لأن لا تكون[٨] عبادة الخلق للدنيا،[٩] فكذلك أمير المؤمنين يعمل مع خلقه، لا ينظر إلى فسادهم وعصيانهم بل ينظر إليهم[١٠] بعين الرحمة. والله تعالى أعطى الدنيا للأحمق[١١] والجاهل وأعطى للعالم والعاقل ومنع عنهما، كذلك أمير المؤمنين يعطي للأحمق والجاهل[١٢] والعالم والعاقل حكمة منه وفضلاً.

---

[١] الدنيا: الديني، ا،ج.

[٢] تكون: يكون، ب، ت.

[٣] تكون: .يكون، ا، ت، ث.

[٤] وكذلك يعطي أميرالمؤمنين عليه السلام: فكذلك امير المؤمنين يعطي، ب؛ فكذلك امير المؤمنين عليه السلام يعطي، ت، ث.

[٥] العاصي: للعاصي، ث.

[٦] تكون: يكون، ا، ب، ت، ث.

[٧] له: -، ب.

[٨] تكون: يكون، ا، ب، ت، ث.

[٩] للدنيا: للديني، ا، ج.

[١٠] إليهم: -، ت.

[١١] أعطى الدنيا للأحمق: يعطي الاحمق، ب.

[١٢] وأعطى...والجاهل: -، ث.

فلو أعطى العالم[١] والعاقل ومنع غيرهم[٢] لكان تعلُّم الناس العلم للدنيا، واستعمالهم العقل[٣] واقتناؤهم[٤] الفضائل[٥] كان للدنيا ويئس[٦] الجاهل[٧] والأحمق. واللّٰه أعطى الدنيا للأحمق والجاهل وأعطى الدنيا[٨] للظالم والعادل[٩] والسخي والبخيل والشريف والدني والوضيع ولصاحب[١٠] كل فضيلة ولمن عدم تلك الفضيلة ساوى بينهم في إعطاء الدنيا حكمة منه ورحمة وفضلاً، كذلك أمير المؤمنين سلام اللّٰه عليه ساوى بين الجميع[١١] اقتداءً بأفعال اللّٰه تعالى ورحمة[١٢] على خلقه ليصل كل أحد بقسطه من إحسان أمير المؤمنين وبره.

[٨٦] وإن اللّٰه تعالى ستر أمور[١٣] الدنيا ونيل الخلق منها[١٤] والسبيل

---

[١] والعالم والعاقل...فلو أعطى العالم: وأعطي للعالم، ا؛ -، ت، ث.

[٢] غيرهم: غيرهما، ا.

[٣] العقل: -، ب.

[٤] واقتناؤهم: واقتناءهم، ا، ب، ت، ث.

[٥] الفضائل: الفضل، ب، ت.

[٦] ويئس: وائس، ا؛ وبئسوا، ت.

[٧] الجاهل: والجاهل، ت.

[٨] للأحمق والجاهل وأعطى الدنيا: -، ب.

[٩] والعادل: والعارف، ا، ت، ث.

[١٠] والدني والوضيع ولصاحب: والدين والوضيع وصاحب، ت.

[١١] الجميع: جميع، ت.

[١٢] ورحمة: رحمته، ب.

[١٣] أمور: امر، ا.

[١٤] منها: منه، ا، ب، ت، ث.

إليها[١] في جميع الوجوه وستر وجوه المكاسب والأفعال على الخلق حتى أن الواحد يستغني والآخر لا يجد الخبز،[٢] والواحد[٣] يستغني[٤] من[٥] تجارة والآخر يذهب رأس ماله، والواحد[٦] يستغني عن[٧] الزرع والآخر يذهب بذره، والواحد يستغني عن[٨] الصيد والآخر[٩] محروم،[١٠] كل ذلك لحكمة[١١] بالغة لئلا يوجد إلى سبب الدنيا وصولاً، فتبطل[١٢] سائر الأسباب ويدخل في الخلق الخلل ويخرب العالم، فكذلك[١٣] أمير المؤمنين عليه السلام معاملته مع خلق[١٤] اللّه على ذلك في الدنيا،[١٥] ستر[١٦] عنهم سبب[١٧] ذلك

---

[١] إليها: إليه، ا، ب، ت، ث.

[٢] الخبز: الخير، ت.

[٣] والواحد: والآخر، ث.

[٤] والآخر...يستغني: -، ت.

[٥] من: عن، ب.

[٦] والواحد: والآخر، ث.

[٧] عن: من، ث.

[٨] الزرع والآخر ...يستغني عن: -، ت؛ عن: من، ث.

[٩] والآخر: + يكون، ب؛ الآخر يذهب، ث.

[١٠] محروم: محروما، ب.

[١١] لحكمة: حكمة، ب.

[١٢] فتبطل: ونقول فتبطل، ت.

[١٣] فكذلك: وكذلك، ث.

[١٤] خلق: خلقة، ب.

[١٥] على ذلك في الدنيا: في الدنيا على ذلك، ب، ت، ث.

[١٦] ستر: + عليهم، ث.

[١٧] سبب: تسبب، ا، ب.

حتى أن الواحد يتسبب إليه بسبب فيعطيه، والآخر يتسبب[١] بذلك السبب فيمنعه، فلو عرفوا سبباً واحداً[٢] يصلون من عند أمير المؤمنين عليه السلام إلى الدنيا به لبطلت[٣] سائر الأسباب وكل من عجز عن ذلك يئس[٤] من رحمته وصار محروماً، ولم يكن ذلك فضلاً.

[٨٧] وكذلك معاملته سلام الله عليه في تقريبه[٥] للناس وتبعيدهم،[٦] فلو[٧] كان سلام الله عليه[٨] في جميع الأوقات يبعد المنافق ويقرب المؤمن لصار الناس مؤمنين لتقريبه لا للدين، وكذلك لو أبعد جميع المؤمنين في جميع الأوقات لتنافروا ووقع في قلوبهم الفزع من غضب أمير المؤمنين عليه السلام أو من زلة[٩] جرت منهم[١٠] أوجب ذلك، فلا يزال يعاملهم[١١] على ما يوجب الوقت والحال ترغيباً وترهيباً وتبعيداً وتقريباً وإعطاءً ومنعاً وعقوبةً وعفواً، كل ذلك اقتداءً لأفعال[١٢] الله تعالى وآدابه ليكون الناس

---

[١] يتسبب: + اليه، ت.

[٢] واحداً: واحد، ت.

[٣] لبطلت: ليطلب، ت.

[٤] يئس: ائس، ا، ب، ت.

[٥] في تقريبه: وتقريبه، ب.

[٦] وتبعيدهم: وتبينهم، ت.

[٧] فلو: ولو، ت.

[٨] عليه: + تقريبه للناس، ا، ب.

[٩] زلة: زلت، ث.

[١٠] منهم: عنهم، ا، ب، ت، ث.

[١١] يعاملهم: + سلام الله عليه، ث.

[١٢] لأفعال: بافعال، ت، ث.

أبداً بين الخوف والرجاء لا يأمنون[١] فيجترئون ولا ييأسون[٢] ويقنطون أخذاً[٣] في جميع ذلك بآداب الله تعالى مع خلقه، وكما أن الله سبحانه أعطى من غير حساب وأعطى من لا يخاف الفقر ونفاد الأموال[٤] كذلك أمير المؤمنين سلام الله عليه أعطى من لا يخاف الفقر ونفاد الأموال خارجاً عن إعطاء البشر.[٥]

[٨٨] ومن نظر بعين الحقيقة إلى أفعال أمير المؤمنين عليه السلام في الدين والدنيا يجد[٦] كل ما يفعل مع الخلق من الأمر والنهي والإعطاء والمنع موازياً لأفعال الله تعالى. وإنما تحيّر[٧] الخلق في ذلك لأنهم ينظرون[٨] إلى أفعاله عليه السلام من أفعال البشر ومما سمعوا ويقيسون فعل أمير المؤمنين عليه السلام على أفعال سائر الخلق وأفعال سائر الملوك وما سمعوا ورأوا أو عقلوا،[٩] فيرون ذلك بخلاف ما اعتادوا وتحابوا،[١٠] فوقعوا[١١] في التحير والاضطراب والتفكر. ولو نظروا[١٢] إلى ذلك

[١] لايأمنون: لايؤمنون، ث.
[٢] فيجترئون ولاييأسون: فيجترون ولا يأسون، ا، ث؛ فيخبرون ولا يأسون، ت.
[٣] أخذاً: احدا، ث.
[٤] ونفاد الأموال: والنفاذ، ا، ث.
[٥] البشر: البشرية، ا، ت، ث.
[٦] يجد: -، ت.
[٧] تحير: يختبر، ث.
[٨] ينظرون: لا ينظرون، ث.
[٩] أو عقلوا: وعقلوا، ث.
[١٠] وتحابوا: وتحبوا، ت، ث.
[١١] فوقعوا: فرفعوا، ث.

من أفعال الله تعالى مع خلقه لكان ذلك هيناً[١] عليهم، وإنما صعب ذلك عليهم لأنه لم يقم بذلك من لدن آدم عليه السلام إلى يومنا هذا أحد. وإن قام في وقت فبجزء قليل من مثل ذلك، كما يحكى من فعل العالم مع موسى عليه السلام ولم يصبر على ذلك لما نظر إلى فعله من فعل[٢] نفسه ومن[٣] علم نفسه وعقله، ولو نظر إلى ذلك من أفعال الله تعالى لكان على خلاف ما ذهب إليه، وما يحكى من حكم داود عليه السلام وأمر الله تعالى بما تحير فيه ودهش من حديث[٤] صاحب الكرم وصاحب الثور، وكما أخبر الله تعالى في قوله: ﴿ يَوْمَ يَدْعُ ٱلدَّاعِ إِلَىٰ شَيْءٍ نُّكُرٍ خُشَّعاً أَبْصَٰرُهُمْ ﴾.[٥] وقال: ﴿ وَقَدْ كَانُواْ يُدْعَوْنَ إِلَى ٱلسُّجُودِ وَهُمْ سَٰلِمُونَ ﴾.[٦] والعجب من هؤلاء لا يطيقون من هذه الأفعال الدنياوية، فكيف يطيقون الابتلاء[٧] بالأفعال[٨] الدينية والابتلاء بأشياء أصعب من ذلك؟ فإن كل ما يوجد في الطرفين يكون معدوماً في الوسط وما كان في الوسط يكون معدوماً في الطرفين، والقوم يقيسون الأمور على ما رأوا

---

[١٢] نظروا: نظر، ث.

[١] هيناً: هنياً، ا.

[٢] فعل: + الى، ت.

[٣] ومن: من، ا، ت، ث.

[٤] حديث: -، ث.

[٥] سورة ٥٤ القمر ٦-٧.

[٦] سورة ٦٨ القلم ٤٣.

[٧] الابتلاء: الابتداء، ت.

[٨] بالأفعال: -، ا، ت، ث.

في الوسط وهم في الطرف، ولأجل ذلك[١] تحيروا ولا يقدرون على حمل ذلك ولا يصبرون عليه.[٢]

[٨٩] ونقول:[٣] إن الناس لما رأوا عطايا الملوك[٤] تكون إما لموجب خدمة أو قربة[٥] أو حقٍ واجب أو محبة[٦] أو حاجة أو جر منفعة أو دفع مضرة أو سبب داعية أوجب[٧] ذلك مما يخافون شرَّه أو يرجون خيره أو يخافون لسانه[٨] أو طلب[٩] مدح أو ثناء[١٠] ومباهاة[١١] أو لطلب[١٢] شكر أو منة[١٣] أو أجرة لعامل ورزق[١٤] ويكون[١٥] ذلك بتقدير وحساب وعطايا أمير المؤمنين عليه السلام خارجة من ذلك[١٦] كله لأن الإعطاء لهذه الأسباب

---

[١] ولأجل ذلك: الأجل لذلك، ث.

[٢] عليه: -، ت.

[٣] ونقول: -، ث.

[٤] الملوك: المملوك، ب، ت.

[٥] وللناس وتبعيدهم...خدمة أو قربة: -، ب؛ قربة: قرابة، ث.

[٦] محبة: صحبة، ث.

[٧] أوجب: وأوجب، ب.

[٨] يخافون لسانه: يخافونه لشأنه، ب.

[٩] طلب: لطلب، ب.

[١٠] أو ثناء: وثناء، ت.

[١١] ومباهاة: أو مباهات، ب؛ أو مباهاة، ث.

[١٢] لطلب: طلب، ث.

[١٣] أو منة: ومنة، ت، ث.

[١٤] ورزق: او رزق، ب.

[١٥] ويكون: فيكون، ا.

[١٦] ذلك: -، ث.

لا يسمى[١] كرماً ولا فضلاً[٢] ولا جوداً، وإنما هو إما لقضاء[٣] واجب[٤] لما مضى أو إعطاء سلَف[٥] لمستقبل،[٦] ومنع الواجبات[٧] وقضاء الحقوق يكون لؤماً وبخلاً، وكذلك من أسلف مالاً لغرض مستقبل لا يعد فعله جوداً[٨] ولا كرماً ولا فضلاً، وكذلك ما[٩] يكون مع[١٠] الامتنان لا يعد جوداً ولا كرماً ولا فضلاً.[١١] وإعطاء اللّٰه[١٢] سبحانه خارج عن جميع ذلك،[١٣] فليس لأحدٍ على اللّٰه إيجاب شيء[١٤] ولا يطلب اللّٰه من الخلق عوضاً، فكذلك أمير المؤمنين لا يعطي لأحد[١٥] لهذه الأسباب ولا[١٦] يطلب عوضاً من ذلك، كما قال اللّٰه تعالى حكاية عن أمير المؤمنين علي بن أبي[١٧] طالب

---

١ يسمى: + ذلك، ب.

٢ ولا فضلاً: و فضلا، ت.

٣ هو إما لقضاء: هو مالقضاء، ث.

٤ واجب: الواجب.

٥ سلف: وسكن، ب.

٦ لمستقبل: لمستقيل، ت.

٧ الواجبات: الواجب، ث.

٨ فعله جوداً: جودا، ا، ب، ت؛ جواد، ث.

٩ ما: كلما، ب.

١٠ مع: من، ث.

١١ ولا فضلاً: -، ت، ث.

١٢ وإعطاء اللّٰه: وعطاء الله، ت؛ وعطا الله، ث.

١٣ ذلك: + ما ذكرناه، ب.

١٤ شيء: بشيء، ث.

١٥ لأحد: حدا، ب.

١٦ ولا: والا، ب.

١٧ أبي: -، ا، ب، ت، ث.

عليه السلام: ﴿ لَا نُرِيدُ[١] مِنكُمْ جَزَآءً وَلَا شُكُوراً ﴾،[٢] بل يعطيهم ابتداء[٣] وجوداً وكرماً[٤] وفضلاً اقتداءً بأفعال اللّٰه تعالى مع خلقه. ولو نظروا إلى أفعال أمير المؤمنين عليه السلام بهذه[٥] العين لما وقعوا في التحير، لكن[٦] بعضهم ينظرون إليه[٧] بعين التقصير والقياس على أفعال سائر الخلق، وبعضهم ينظرون إليه بعين الغلوّ يدعون له الإلهيّة. وفعله سلام اللّٰه عليه خارج عن كلا[٨] الوجهين، بل هو الخليفة الكلي للّٰه تعالى على عباده.

[٩٠] وكما أن[٩] اللّٰه تعالى ستر أسباب الدنيا عن الخلق وبين أسباب الدين والوصول إليه وبين أسباب رضائه تعالى وشرحه على لسان نبيّه[١٠] وأعطى العلم والحكمة لأهله ومنعهما[١١] من غير أهله وجعل ﴿ مِن[١٢] بَيْنِ أَيْدِيهِمْ سَدّاً وَمِنْ خَلْفِهِمْ سَدّاً ﴾[١٣] ونصب[١٤] أعلام الهدى والداعي

---

[١] نُرِيدُ: نزيد، ب.

[٢] سورة ٧٦ الإنسان ٩.

[٣] ابتداء: ابتلاء، ث.

[٤] وجوداً وكرماً: وكرماً وجوداً، ث.

[٥] بهذه: بهذا، ا، ب، ت.

[٦] لكن: لكنهم، ت.

[٧] إليه: -، ا، ث.

[٨] كلا: كل، ا، ب، ت؛ كلي، ث.

[٩] وكما أن: كان، ب؛ كما أن، ت، ث.

[١٠] نبيه: رسوله، ب.

[١١] منعهما: منعها، ت.

[١٢] مِن: -، ا.

[١٣] سورة ٣٦ يسٓ ٩.

[١٤] نصب: نصب لهم، ب.

والدليل والهادي إلى نعيم الآخرة وأظهر أسبابها وفتح[١] أبوابها ليصل إليها مستحقها وينحسر عنها غير مستحقها حكمة بالغة، كذلك أمير المؤمنين[٢] ستر أسباب الدنيا والوصول إليها[٣] من جهته وأعطاها لمستحقها[٤] وغير مستحقها[٥] وبين أسباب الدين والعلم والحكمة[٦] وأعطاها لأهلها ومستحقها من غير منع ولا بخل، وأنعم على الخلق وأفاض عليهم ما لم يفض به أحد في سائر الأوقات والأزمان، ومنع ذلك من غير أهله وميز أهل[٧] الحق من أهل الباطل اقتداء بفعل اللّٰه عزّ وجلّ وآدابه[٨] في سياسة الدين والدنيا[٩] وعمارة الآخرة والأولى.

[٩١] نسأل اللّٰه أن يوزعنا[١٠] شكر ما أنعم علينا قولاً وفعلاً ونية[١١] ويوفقنا[١٢] للقيام بطاعة ولي العصر والزمان سلام اللّٰه عليه ويرزقنا الجهاد بين يديه باليد واللسان والقلب، وأن يفتح له مشارق الأرض ومغاربها،

---

[١] وفتح: -، ب، ت، ث.

[٢] المؤمنين: + علي، ب.

[٣] إليها: اليه، ا، ب، ت، ث.

[٤] لمستحقها: لمستحقه، ا، ب، ت، ث.

[٥] وغير مستحقها: -، ب؛ وغير مستحقه، ا، ت، ث.

[٦] والعلم والحكمة: والحكمة والعلم، ا.

[٧] وميز: + بين، ب.

[٨] آدابه: من ادابه، ث.

[٩] الدين والدنيا: الدنيا والدين، ا.

[١٠] نسأل...يوزعنا: ونسأل...يورعنا، ت.

[١١] ونية: ونيتا، ا.

[١٢] ويوفقنا: وتوفيقا، ب.

ويطهر[١] بسيفه الأرض من الكفر والشرك والنفاق[٢] بمنه وطوله. ويسأل العبد ويرغب في إنعام أمير المؤمنين سلام الله عليه ويلتمس الأمر العالي[٣] بالنظر فيما[٤] جمعه العبد[٥] وألفه والإجازة[٦] له على الصحيح والصواب منه،[٧] والتنبيه على الخطأ إن كان فيه ليشكر[٨] العبد ويزيد له في البصيرة واليقين، ويكون ذلك هداية ودليلاً للمسترشدين[٩] وحجة على الجاحدين،[١٠] والحمد لله[١١] حمد الشاكرين الذاكرين القانتين والصلاة على رسوله سيدنا محمد وآله أجمعين.[١٢]

---

[١] ويطهر: ويظهر، ب، ت. [٢] والنفاق: والنفاك، ت. [٣] العالي: العلي، ت.
[٤] فيما: فيها، ا. [٥] جمعه العبد: اجمعه العيد، ب. [٦] والإجازة: واجازة، ب، ث. [٧] منه: منها، ا، ب، ت. [٨] فيه ليشكر: فيها ليشكر، ا، ب، ت؛ فيه يشكر، ث. [٩] للمسترشدين: للمرشدين، ا، ت، ث. [١٠] الجاحدين: الجاهدين، ب. [١١] لله: + رب العالمين، ب، ت، ث.
[١٢] الشاكرين...أجمعين: الشاكرين العارفين والصلاة على رسوله سيدنا محمد النبي وآله الأئمة الطاهرين الهادين وحسبنا الله ونعم الوكيل ونعم المولى ونعم النصير ولا حول ولا قوة إلا بالله العلي العظيم، ب، ث؛ +، وكان الفراغ من تحريره، ث.

تمت الكتاب بعون الله وحمده ومادة وليه سلام الله عليه وقت العصر يوم الجمعة وهو اليوم السابع والعشرين من شهر ربيع الآخر سنة ١١٣٤ في سنة الف ومائة وأربع وثلاثين من الهجرة من مكة حرسها الله تعالى تمت كتاب إثبات الإمام بحمد الله الملك المنان بعون أولياءه ذي العلم والبيان مالك خانبهاي طهفوجي ساكن بهانبوري وإن من ادعاه فهو كاذب، ا؛

تمت تم الكتاب في درس سيدنا زين الدين طول الله عمره سنة ١٢٠٤ كاتبه مالك عبد العلي ملا شيخ بهائي من بهانبوري، ب؛

تمت تمام قد تمت هذا الكتاب في ليلة السادس عشر من شهر شعبان الكريم سنة ١٢٥٩ بخط عبد مولانا نجم الدين طول الله عمره اسماعيل بن ملا خان بهاري ديوان بفرمائش ملا غلام حسين جي بن ميان خان عامل اندور سلمه الله كتبه على يدي سيدي ومولاي ميا صاحب عبد المحسين حرس الله مهجته بحق سيدنا محمد وعترته صلوات الله عليه، ت.

الفهرس العام

فهرس الآيات القرآنية

(٣٩) سُورَةُ الزمر

(٤١) سُورَةُ فُصِّلَتْ

(٤٣) سُورَةُ الزخرف

(٤٩) سُورَةُ الحُجُرَات

(٥٤) سُورَةُ القمر

(٥٨) سُورَةُ المجادلة

(٥٩) سُورَةُ الحَشْر

Aḥmad b. Ibrāhīm al-Naysābūrī

Kitāb ithbāt al-imāma

Arabic Text